P9-DHZ-685

WITHDRAWN

REDWOOD

LIBRARY
NEWPORT
R.I.

Gift of
Theodore Holcomb

Napoleon's Family

By the same author

The First Bourbon
The Monks of War
Prince of the Renaissance
The Bourbon Kings of France
Eleanor of Aquitaine
The Hundred Years War
Monks and Wine
Marie Antoinette
Richard III
Naples
Italy's Knights of St. George

Desmond Seward

NAPOLEON'S FAMILY

VIKING

For Peter and Barbara Drummond-Murray of Mastrick

VIKING
Viking Penguin Inc.
40 West 23rd Street,
New York, New York 10010, U.S.A.

First American edition
Published in 1986

Copyright © Desmond Seward, 1986
All rights reserved

Photo credits appear on page viii.

LIBRARY OF CONGRESS CATALOGING IN PUBLICATION DATA
Seward, Desmond, 1935–
Napoleon's family.
Bibliography: p.
Includes index.
1. Bonaparte, Napoleon, 1769–1821—Family.
2. Bonaparte family.   3. France—History—Consulate and
Empire, 1799–1815—Biography.   I. Title.
DC216.S49   1986   944.05′092′24   [B]   85-29584
ISBN 0-670-81146-7

Printed in the United States of America by
The Book Press, Brattleboro, Vermont
Set in Plantin

1 2 / 6 / 6

Dc
216
.S49
1986

OCT 17 2001

Contents

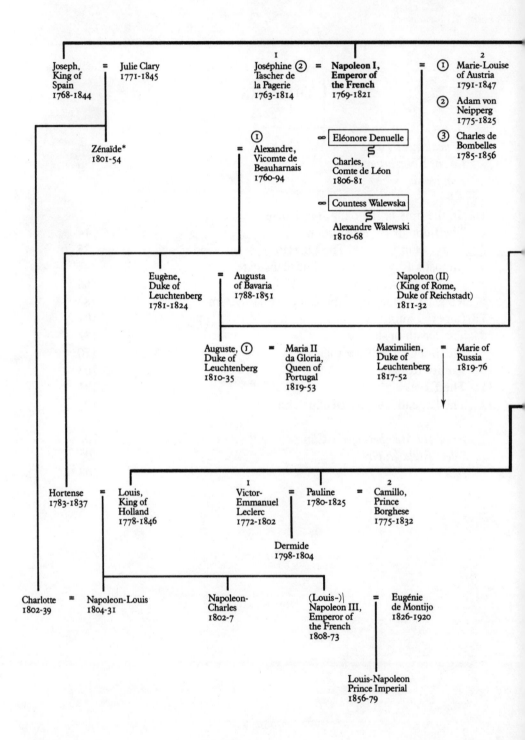

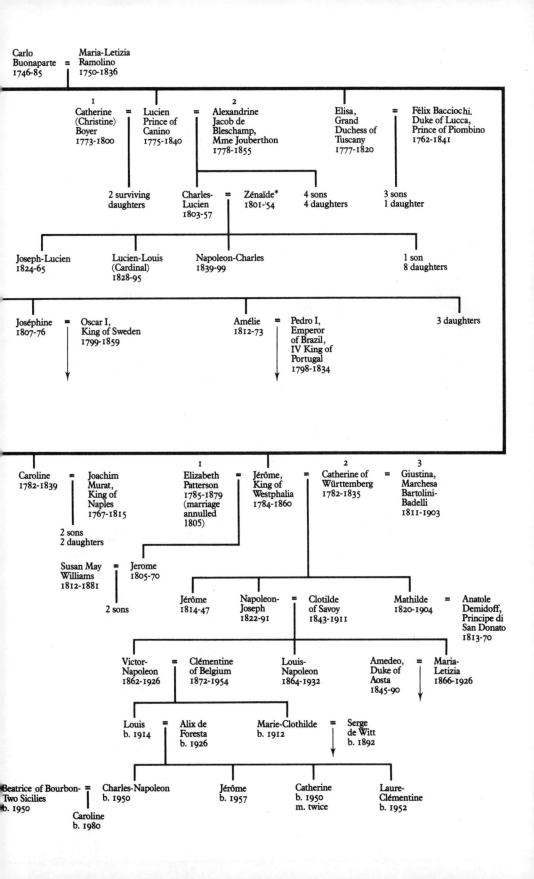

Carlo Buonaparte 1746-85 = Maria-Letizia Ramolino 1750-1836

1
Catherine (Christine) Boyer 1773-1800 = Lucien Prince of Canino 1775-1840 = 2 Alexandrine Jacob de Bleschamp, Mme Jouberthon 1778-1855

Elisa, Grand Duchess of Tuscany 1777-1820 = Félix Bacciochi, Duke of Lucca, Prince of Piombino 1762-1841

2 surviving daughters

Charles-Lucien 1803-57 = Zénaïde* 1801-'54

4 sons 4 daughters

3 sons 1 daughter

Joseph-Lucien 1824-65

Lucien-Louis (Cardinal) 1828-95

Napoleon-Charles 1839-99

1 son 8 daughters

Joséphine 1807-76 = Oscar I, King of Sweden 1799-1859

Amélie 1812-73 = Pedro I, Emperor of Brazil, IV King of Portugal 1798-1834

3 daughters

Caroline 1782-1839 = Joachim Murat, King of Naples 1767-1815

1
Elizabeth Patterson 1785-1879 (marriage annulled 1805) = Jérôme, King of Westphalia 1784-1860 = 2 Catherine of Württemberg 1782-1835 = 3 Giustina, Marchesa Bartolini-Badelli 1811-1903

2 sons 2 daughters

Susan May Williams 1812-1881 = Jerome 1805-70

2 sons

Jérôme 1814-47

Napoleon-Joseph 1822-91 = Clotilde of Savoy 1843-1911

Mathilde 1820-1904 = Anatole Demidoff, Principe di San Donato 1813-70

Victor-Napoleon 1862-1926 = Clémentine of Belgium 1872-1954

Louis-Napoleon 1864-1932

Amedeo, Duke of Aosta 1845-90 = Maria-Letizia 1866-1926

Louis b. 1914 = Alix de Foresta b. 1926

Marie-Clothilde b. 1912 = Serge de Witt b. 1892

Beatrice of Bourbon-Two Sicilies b. 1950 = Charles-Napoleon b. 1950

Jérôme b. 1957

Catherine b. 1950 m. twice

Laure-Clémentine b. 1952

Caroline b. 1980

Illustrations
(*following page 88.*)

Foreword

'Joseph! If our father could see us!'

NAPOLEON ON THE MORNING OF HIS CORONATION

'My brothers are nothing without me; they are great men only
because I have made them great. Everything that the French
have heard about them has been heard from me. There are
thousands of people in France who have done the state better
service.'

NAPOLEON

One cold December night 400 men of the Imperial Guard bivouacked
outside Paris in readiness to provide Napoleon with an escort. They wore
the uniforms in which they had marched as conquerors into nearly
every European capital. But the uniforms were faded and patched, the
bearskins moth-eaten and many of the wearers grizzled old men. For this
was 1840.

In a bid for popularity King Louis Philippe had dispatched his son the
Prince de Joinville to bring the Emperor's body back to France from St
Helena in the South Atlantic, where he had died in 1821 as a prisoner of
the British. The British garrison on the island had escorted the coffin
down to the French warship sent to fetch it, with full military honours
and playing the Dead March from *Saul*. A million people assembled to
greet its arrival in Paris, drums beating to arms in the streets from half
past six in the morning, the crowds singing over and over again, *'Vive
mon grand Napoléon.'* The huge funeral car, drawn by sixteen black
horses with white plumes sweeping down to their haunches, was of gilt
with a pall of purple velvet. Four battered veterans, among them Marshal
Oudinot, rode by its side holding the cords of the pall. Behind marched
the Old Guard. When the car reached the Invalides, where the remains
were to lie beneath the golden dome, a chamberlain announced, 'The
Emperor!' Then the Prince de Joinville stepped forward and said to the
King, 'Sire, I present the body of the Emperor Napoleon.' The King
replied, 'I receive it in the name of France.' Bonaparte had won his last,
posthumous, campaign.

The return to his former capital was the final climax to the career of a
man who had begun as the son of a Corsican squireen, whose modest

1

origins had subjected him to a 'cascade of disdain' in his youth. Everyone knows and marvels at his story. What is less well known is how the Emperor took his family with him in his meteoric ascent. No family ever received such amazing promotion. Its members sat on the thrones of France, Spain, Naples, Tuscany, Rome, Holland and Westphalia. Their true fascination is as social mountaineers who beat the class system of their day. Their elevation horrified the old ruling families throughout Europe, but was an inspiration to countless talented men and women of humble background. The 'big people' of Ajaccio had been utterly insignificant in pre-1789 France, whose rigid society formed an all but geological barrier to their rising in the world and was unimpressed by rustic little nobles with foreign accents. Yet the Bonapartes did not so much oust the *ancien régime* as try to join it.

Napoleon's career – and his family's elevation – was made possible by the French Revolution. This began with the calling of the Estates General by Louis XVI in 1789 to discuss the nation's finances, but at once became a popular movement for radical reform which quickly grew more and more extreme. By 1792 a constitutional monarchy no longer satisfied the French who deposed Louis and set up a republic in his place. So anxious were the Jacobins – the extreme revolutionaries who at first directed the republic – to break with the past that not only was Christianity outlawed but a new calendar was introduced, with such strange months as *Vendémiaire* and *Brumaire*. Titles and feudal privilege had been abolished very early on and now it was made a crime even to be an aristocrat. The Bonapartes, who had renounced their nobility from the start, became enthusiastic Jacobins from motives of the purest opportunism. As soon as the Revolution faltered and Napoleon's star began to ascend, they hastened to acquire wealth and position, and did not rest until they had obtained thrones for themselves.

Privately the Emperor came to have no illusions about his brothers and sisters. On at least one occasion during the days of his glory he reproached them bitterly. 'I don't think that anyone has ever been more unfortunate in his relations,' he told them one quiet evening at the Tuileries. 'If we sum up, Lucien is an ingrate, Joseph a Sardanapalus, Louis a paralytic and Jérôme a rake.' Then he lowered his eyes and drew a circle in the air. 'And you, ladies, you know perfectly well what you are.' On St Helena when fabricating the Napoleonic legend, that masterpiece of propaganda by a ruined and defeated man, he took pains to disguise the failings of his 'dynasty'. What he told his secretary Las Cases about them – who recorded it in his best seller, *The Memorial of St Helena* – was a travesty of his true opinion.

Joseph would have ornamented society anywhere, Lucien adorned any political assembly. Jérôme would have governed well when mature. Louis would have charmed and attracted wherever he went. My sister Elisa had the mind and strength of a man – she had to be unusually stoical in adversity. Caroline is very clever and capable. Pauline, probably the most beautiful woman of her time, has been and will be to the end of her life the best creature in the world. As for my mother, she deserves to be revered. What large family could make a finer-looking group? Political differences aside, we genuinely loved one another. I never lost my feelings as a brother. I loved them all and I think they all loved me.

This book will show that Napoleon's real view of the Bonapartes was nearer that which he expressed at the Tuileries than what he told Las Cases on St Helena. Yet not even the most ungifted Bonaparte could avoid being interesting on such a stage in such an era. It was the last time the armies of France were able to make and unmake not just sovereigns but whole countries. The way in which a poor, untalented, immigrant clan latched on to its mighty brother and gatecrashed the world of crowned and anointed royalty, let alone of great nobles with sixteen quarterings, is without parallel. In the 1980s it is a virtue to be of obscure origin, and difficult to understand what it was like to be a parvenu two centuries ago. This neglected aspect, the very real sense of social ambition felt by all Bonapartes including the Emperor himself, adds another dimension to an extraordinary family saga.

1

'In the time of the King, my Uncle'

'I will do you Frenchmen all the harm I can.'

NAPOLEON AT BRIENNE

'Who does not pity the noble chamberlain that confesses his
blood to have run cold when he heard Napoleon – seated at
dinner at Dresden among a circle of crowned heads – begin a
story with, "When I was a lieutenant in the regiment of La
Fères." Who does not pity Napoleon when he is heard
speaking of some decorations in the Tuileries as having taken
place "in the time of the king, my uncle"?'

LOCKHART, *The History of Napoleon Buonaparte*

In 1768 the Most Serene Republic of Genoa ceded Corsica to King Louis
xv of France. A French army landed and by the following mid-summer the
island was effectively part of France. 1769 was also the year in which a
Corsican patriot gave birth to a child who was christened Napoleone.

France's new acquisition was a wild, barren, rocky land of eagle-
haunted mountains and forests, with no roads save goat tracks. Fear of
North African pirates had driven the inhabitants into the hills so that the
plains were deserted and covered by impenetrable heathland. The island's
sole resources were sheep, goats, vineyards, olive, orange, lemon and
mulberry groves, and chestnut trees. Barter was the normal currency in the
countryside. The handful of small coastal towns were scarcely more than
fortified fishing villages. Corsicans were hard, dour men, small of stature,
often fine featured and noted for piercing eyes. Both coastal folk and hill
people had the traits associated with mountain dwellers, being generous
hosts and loyal friends, tough fighters and merciless enemies – Corsican
vendetta was a byword throughout Italy for sustained ferocity, magnan-
imity was unknown, the pardoning of any injury or insult considered
shameful. These frugal and suspicious islanders rarely laughed and had
little time for music. They were famed for extraordinarily deep family
loyalties – when a father died young his eldest male child automatically
took over his responsibilities as head of the family. Women were little
regarded and not allowed to sit at table with the men, but they knew that
every one of their male relations would fight to the death in their defence.
The seventy-seven families of Corsican gentry were almost indistinguish-

able from the peasants, who called them by their Christian names, living very similar lives whether as mountain chieftains or in the little coastal towns on their rents, generally wearing brown homespun garments made from the wool of their own flocks.

Napoleon told a contemptuous Metternich, 'The Bonapartes are a good Corsican family, little known, for we have hardly ever left our island.' Metternich adds that he 'laid great stress on his aristocratic birth and the antiquity of his family'. In fact he descended from a Florentine patrician family whose ancestry could be traced back to the eleventh century, the first Buonaparte to establish himself in Corsica being Francesco 'the Crossbowman' who settled at Ajaccio in 1490. Yet if technically noble the Buonapartes were at best half-savage squireens, scarcely more than peasants with coats of arms.

Carlo Maria Buonaparte, Napoleon's father, was born in 1746. A miniature of him in his thirties portrays a sharp-faced little Italian with thick, black eyebrows and a coarse, weak mouth. He had unusually polished and amiable manners for a Corsican and was plainly popular. Fond of ostentation, he must have enjoyed his nickname of 'Carlo il Magnifico'. Extravagant and self-indulgent, he none the less lacked neither determination nor subtlety where the interests of his family were concerned, and these latter qualities may have been instilled by his uncle the formidable Luciano Buonaparte, who was Archdeacon of Ajaccio. For a Corsican, Carlo was a man of unusual culture and well before the conquest learnt to speak French fluently. Moreover, in 1769 he procured letters patent from the Archbishop of Pisa confirming that he was both a nobleman and a Patrician of Florence. This seemingly pretentious gesture showed quite extraordinary foresight, as proof of nobility was to mean everything under the new French régime. There were many sorts of French noble, from the enormously rich magnates who dominated Versailles and Parisian society down to the humble little hedge squire who pushed his own plough, but in theory all shared the same privileges: exemption from other men's tax burdens together with a monopoly of the principal posts in the army, the administration, the Law and the Church.

In 1764 when he was eighteen Carlo married the fourteen-year-old Letizia Ramolino. She belonged to a noble family of Genoese origin and her stepfather, a Swiss called Francesco Fesch, was a captain in the Genoese navy, while her mother came from a notoriously ferocious mountain clan – in her youth Letizia carried a stiletto in her belt. She was a considerable beauty with falcon features, huge and flashing black eyes, and dark chestnut hair. Like most of her countrywomen she had had little education and was barely literate. She could not speak French and when she learnt to do so spoke with a thick Italian accent. She never

6

overcame her dislike of the foreign race who were to be her son's slaves and he may well have been thinking of her when he wrote that Italians were 'a people essentially hostile to the French, from prejudice, from habit down the centuries, from instinct'. Her superstition was matched only by her avarice.

The Casa Buonaparte, near the cathedral, was in the oldest and poorest part of Ajaccio. If undeniably patrician, it is none the less a barrack-like dwelling of the utmost plainness, four floors of buff-coloured masonry built in the seventeenth century, whose rooms are dark despite high windows. Carlo's mother and Archdeacon Luciano lived downstairs, a cousin who had married a man named Pozzo di Borgo at the top, so Carlo and Letizia only had the two floors between. They had a single indoor servant, the housekeeper *Mamuccia* Caterina.

In January 1768 Letizia gave birth to her eldest son to survive, Giuseppe, one day to be King Joseph of Spain. The French invasion began in August the same year. Although hopelessly outnumbered, the Corsicans exploited their difficult terrain and won several small victories. Letizia, six months pregnant with the baby who would one day be Emperor of the French, insisted on riding out with Carlo to join the patriot army. However, in May 1769 the Corsicans were bloodily routed at Ponte-Nuovo on the banks of the Golo river in north-eastern Corsica. Cut off from her husband, Letizia had to escape from the battle by herself. Eventually Carlo found her in the wilderness. Despite her being pregnant they galloped through the pinewoods and up into the mountains, to hide in a cave on the remote Monte Rotondo with a handful of other fugitives. They dared not light a fire, living on bread and chestnuts brought by shepherds. Fortunately a messenger came to the cave after a fortnight with news of an amnesty.

There was one last adventure before the couple came home to Ajaccio. The almost mother-to-be's mule slipped from the bank into a fast-running river beside which she was riding – Letizia coolly swam it downstream until they could land. At Ajaccio, on the Feast of the Assumption of the Virgin Mary (15 August), Letizia gave birth to a boy, who was delivered by *Mamuccia* Caterina for want of a midwife, on a sofa in the *piano nobile*. The baby, remarkable for its large head and disproportionately small body, was called Napoleone after Carlo's uncle, who had been killed in the recent fighting.

Shortly after the birth of his second son Carlo went off to Pisa to obtain that all-important confirmation of nobility. Characteristically, when he returned, he gave a party to celebrate – no less characteristically for the rest of her life his wife recalled bitterly that it had cost them nearly two years' income. Even so the investment in nobility speedily paid dividends. In 1770 Louis xv promulgated a decree by which Corsicans who could prove nobility and residence in the island for two hundred years were given the same privileges as French noblemen. Carlo's membership of this fortunate group was established by a certificate from 'the principal nobles of Ajaccio'. When the new States General of Corsica met for the first time in 1772 he was elected one of the Council of Twelve Nobles. Henceforward he styled himself 'Carlo *de* Buonaparte'.

The early childhood of Napoleone and his brothers and sisters was little different from that of the children of a rich peasant. Flour, wine, oil, fruit, all came from the family property. The *cucina* was basically maize *polenta*, fish, occasional game, cheese of ewe's and goat's milk, olives, figs, cherries and chestnuts – wheaten bread was more of a luxury than that made from chestnuts. Nevertheless Carlo added a new dining-room. He had important guests to entertain, notably the French Governor, the Comte de Marbeuf, who was an old bachelor. Boswell, who had been his guest, wrote, 'One of the most agreeable characters in the world is a Frenchman who has served long in the army . . . gay without levity and judicious without severity. Such a character was the Count de Marbeuf, of an ancient family of Brittany.' He appears to have taken a genuine liking to Carlo, a quarter of a century younger than himself, and to his pretty wife. With his fluent French, intellectual tastes and steadily growing library, M. de Buonaparte must have seemed unusually civilized company for Corsica.

Letizia was always busy with her children, four of whom died in infancy though others soon followed. When it rained she shut her brood up in what would today be called a playroom, where they could play, wrestle, scream or draw on the walls to their hearts' content – on fine days they explored the countryside on ponies, escorted by an aunt. Sometimes, however, the boys joined their social equals, the *Ajaccini*, against the *Borghigiani* or guttersnipes in vicious little street battles fought with sticks and stones, limping home bruised and bleeding. The Buonaparte brothers learnt their first letters from the nuns of Ajaccio and from a writing master, the Abate Recco, all of whom found Napoleone unmanageable and troublesome, always in fights.

There were unpleasant family quarrels among the grown-ups. Carlo sued Letizia's mother and stepfather for not having paid her dowry to him ten years after they had been married, and was successful. He again went to law when his cousin Maria Pozzo di Borgo, who lived on the top floor of the Casa Buonaparte, emptied a chamber-pot over him. This seemingly comic dispute turned into a vendetta – in years to come Maria's son, Carlo Andrea, would enter the service of the Russian Emperor and set his master against Napoleone.

At their most prosperous Carlo and his wife had an annual income of 13,000 livres – well over £500 a year in English money – from three houses, and from wine, corn, olive oil and other farm produce. (Apparently some of the wine was excellent.) They also owned a mill and charged a fee to local peasants who were obliged to grind their corn there. However, not only did Carlo waste large sums on ostentation and gambling – the small Napoleone was once sent into a tavern to persuade him to stop – but he simply spent his income as it came in. Under the circumstances Letizia taught her children the importance of a good appearance, that it did not matter how one lived behind closed doors but that outside it was essential to be seen wearing a smart coat and riding a good horse. Meanwhile there was the growing expense of a steadily increasing family, Luciano (Lucien) being born in 1775, Maria Anna (Elisa) in 1777, Luigi (Louis) in 1778, Maria Paola (Pauline) in 1780, Maria Annunziata (Caroline) in 1782 and Girolamo (Jérôme) in 1784.

Nobility saved the day. Presumably on M. de Marbeuf's advice, Carlo took out a 'certificate of indigence' testifying that he had insufficient means to provide his children with suitable education. The French Crown thereupon agreed to educate them in France as noblemen.

Marbeuf's help with Carlo's certificate has been uncharitably ascribed to the charms of Letizia, 'the most striking woman in Ajaccio' according to the Governor's secretary. For a time Napoleon himself would question his paternity, on the grounds that none of his forebears had possessed any military talent to bequeath to him. In fact Letizia was unshakeably faithful to her husband, a fidelity confirmed by her refusal to marry again when a most attractive young widow.

Carlo knew what he was doing in cultivating the Governor. M. de Marbeuf was not just the most important man in Corsica but also uncle to the Archbishop of Lyons, the royal almoner responsible for state bursaries. Giuseppe received a bursary to attend a seminary in France, Napoleone another to go to a military academy and Maria Anna one to go to the best girls' school in France – at a time when most Corsican young ladies were barely taught to read and write. Letizia's half-brother, Giuseppe Fesch, secured a similar bursary, being among the twenty Corsican seminarians sent to France for superior training as the island's future higher clergy.

In 1778 Carlo de Buonaparte, re-elected as one of the Council of Twelve Nobles, was chosen to be a member of a Corsican delegation to King Louis XVI. He took ten-year-old Giuseppe and nine-year-old Napoleone with him, to begin their life in their new country. Fesch went too. They left Ajaccio on 17 December. Letizia saw them off at Bastia, where they had travelled in Marbeuf's carriage. They spent a night in a miserable inn at the port, sleeping on mattresses laid out on the floor. *En route* from Corsica they visited Florence where – as a Patrician of Florence – Carlo was able to procure a letter of introduction from the Habsburg Grand Duke Pietro Leopoldo to his sister Queen Marie Antoinette. Then they went on to France. Years later Napoleone told General Bertrand, 'While we were passing through Villefranche, Father remarked, "How stupid we are to be so proud of our own country. We speak grandly about the Main Street of Ajaccio yet here in one French town alone there's a street every bit as fine." ' Nevertheless Carlo thoroughly enjoyed himself at Versailles, buying a dozen embroidered waistcoats for the visit despite 'indigence'. Admittedly he had something to celebrate, having been informed by the Minister for War that Napoleone had been granted a bursary and a place in the military school at Brienne as a 'Royal Pupil' whose expenses would be paid by the King. All that remained was to obtain the certificate of nobility necessary for admission. This the Judge of Arms of France duly issued without demur in March 1779.

His two sons did not enjoy being transformed into little Frenchmen at a church school in Autun. Their fellow pupils jeered at the wild young foreigners for being unable to speak French and laughed at their outlandish manners. A master, the Abbé Chardon, reporting on Napoleone, says that after only three months 'he has learnt enough French to talk quite well and can even write little essays'. Soon he had to leave Autun, where he had at least the support of Giuseppe – now Joseph – and go to Brienne. An eye-witness records that while the former wept and Napoleon did not, the younger boy was in fact more upset, but controlled himself.

Brienne was far more daunting than Autun. The penniless young Corsican was looked down on by the scions of great French families, mocked for his uncouth accent and dislike of games – as he put it, subjected to 'a cascade of disdain'. He reacted by taking an exaggerated pride in his native island. On more than one occasion he promised them, 'I will do you Frenchmen all the harm I can.' He was far from outstanding at his studies except for mathematics. Nevertheless, the gloomy, introspective, undersized boy showed an unmistakable talent for leadership in organizing his companions' war games – there was a famous snowball fight in which he led the juniors to victory against the seniors. Probably Joseph was much more unhappy at Autun, studying to be a priest while slowly realizing that he had no vocation.

In 1782 Napoleon's parents visited him at Brienne. Carlo was suffering from mysterious stomach pains and attacks of nausea, the reason for this second expedition to France being the need to consult doctors. Even his wife's iron-hard constitution had been overwhelmed by a vicious bout of puerperal fever after the birth of her eleventh child (Maria Annunziata, the future Caroline Murat) and she had accompanied her husband in order to take the waters at Bourbonne-les-Bains. None the less, the two invalids made a splendid impression on the college. Carlo was in a silk suit, with powdered hair and a court sword, while Letizia wore a costly white silk dress ornamented by fashionable panniers.

Napoleon is unlikely to have been deceived by his parents' air of opulence. The previous year he had written to his father, 'If you or my patrons can't let me have sufficient funds to keep up a more respectable appearance at this college, then please write and ask for me to be sent home and as quickly as possible. I am tired of looking like a beggar and being jeered at by impertinent schoolboys whose one claim to be my superior is a rich background.' Rather than endure such mockery he would prefer to be apprenticed to a trade, and abandon any pretensions to nobility. Carlo was away so Letizia answered, enclosing a draft for 300 francs but at the same time warning him that if ever he wrote such a letter to his parents again, they would have nothing more to do with him. She also said that in any case Carlo and she were unable to help him. Indeed, they were now in serious financial difficulty and Carlo was resorting to planting mulberry groves (in the mistaken belief that he would be subsidised by the Crown), and suing the Jesuits for the return of a legacy although their order had been suppressed a decade earlier.

Despite his worries M. de Buonaparte continued to ensure that his children were educated as nobles. In 1783 Luciano (Lucien) was brought to Autun to join Joseph and learn French, escorted to the school by his uncle Fesch – now the Abbé Fesch – but the War Minister refused to give the boy a bursary to go to a military academy until Napoleon had left Brienne, as there was a new regulation that brothers must not hold bursaries at the same time. His father therefore had the added burden of having to pay fees for Lucien's first half-year at Brienne, which he entered in 1784. Then Joseph decided that he was not cut out for a clerical career. When Carlo came to Autun to take Lucien away to Brienne, his eldest son told him he wanted to leave the school and go to a military academy instead.

One cannot help pitying the unfortunate father. He had only been able to pay for his third visit to France by borrowing 25 louis (£25) from the garrison commander at Ajaccio, Letizia having offered the family plate as security for this pathetically small loan. It was not just that Carlo had to see Lucien safely installed at Brienne and escort Maria Anna (Elisa) to her convent school at Saint-Cyr. The most important reason was that his health was failing fast and he needed to see the specialists again.

Napoleon's concern for the careers of his entire family dated from a very early age indeed, to judge from a letter written by him to Fesch after his father's second visit to Brienne in mid-June 1784. He writes in glowing terms of nine-year-old Lucien, saying that he has forgotten Italian and already speaks good French. He laments the fact that Joseph is abandoning a clerical career. 'He has had a churchman's education and it is very late in the day to think of changing. His Lordship the Bishop of Autun would undoubtedly have given him a fat living and he would certainly have become a bishop himself. What a help to the family that would have been! His Lordship has done everything he possibly can to make him persevere, promising him that he will never regret it. However, if he really does insist on being a soldier, then I shall have to give him my support . . . While it is all very well wanting to be a military man, in what branch of the service is it to be?' He continues that at bottom his brother is idle and frivolous, unfit to be either a soldier or a sailor. 'One last try must be made to persuade him to enter the Church. If he won't, then my dear father ought to take him back to Corsica where he can keep an eye on him and make him go in for the Law.' The writer of this letter was fifteen years old.

In the event Joseph insisted on going into the army, and Carlo thought it might be possible to find him a place at a military academy, either Brienne or Metz. Napoleon suggested that his brother should join him at Brienne so that they could study together for the entrance examination for the artillery. But in October 1784 Napoleon was admitted to the Ecole Militaire in Paris.

Carlo had left the capital the previous month to return to Corsica. He was so weak that he could not find sufficient strength to visit Brienne and say goodbye to Napoleon and Lucien. He got as far as Montpellier, accompanied by Joseph and the Abbé Fesch, intending to consult the medical faculty there, which was famous throughout Europe. Too exhausted to travel further, he took lodgings in a wretched inn but was rescued by a Corsican friend of Letizia, Mme Permon, who moved him into her house. Here he lingered over Christmas and into the New Year. In terrible pain this 'irreconcilable enemy of religion' returned to the faith of his childhood and could not see enough of priests. On 24 February 1785 he was plainly so desperately ill that his brother-in-law gave him the Last Sacraments. He cried out again and again for Napoleon to come and defend him. He died the same evening, not yet thirty-nine. The doctors performed an autopsy – in those days a most unusual proceeding – and discovered, as they had suspected, cancer. He was buried in the cemetery of a local Franciscan friary.

Much later Napoleon condemned his father for his attachment to the nobility. Carlo, however, had had the foresight to realize that nobility provided a sure means of rising in the world. Although about to be discarded by a new social order, it none the less served the Buonaparte children very well indeed. Not only did it procure them an extremely good and otherwise unobtainable education, but it transformed these wild young Italians from over the sea into civilized Frenchmen, admitting them into an entire new world of opportunity. They all owed a very great deal to the social acumen of 'The Noble Sieur Carlo de Buonaparte'.

2

The Buonaparte Revolution

'Can one be revolutionary enough? Marat and Robespierre, those are my saints!'

NAPOLEON TO BARRAS, AUTUMN 1793

'You know, my dear friend, that I live purely for the pleasure that I can give to my family.'

NAPOLEON TO JOSEPH, SEPTEMBER 1795

Thanks to Carlo, the Buonapartes' membership of the *ancien régime* was beyond question. They were nobles and they were privileged; even in civilian dress Napoleon and Joseph wore swords to distinguish them from bourgeois. Yet their hopes of advancement were far from glittering. The social structure of pre-revolutionary France was almost geological and they were among the lowest strata of its ruling class. Any brainless fop from Versailles who bore a great name had infinitely better chances of promotion than some brilliantly gifted but obscure officer. Napoleon said afterwards that he might have become a general at most in the old days – he could never have aspired to be a Marshal of France.

Nevertheless he was happy enough when he began his military career, well paid for a boy of his age. In November 1784 when still only sixteen he joined the Regiment of La Fère as a lieutenant. It had the reputation of being one of the most efficient artillery regiments in the entire French army and he was proud to wear its blue uniform with red facings, proud of his brother officers – he considered these noblemen 'the best and most worthwhile people in the whole world'. His good opinion was not always reciprocated. At least one officer remembered him as being at this time a ranting windbag, admired only by ladies because of his 'sombre, intent, Italian gaze'. He had 800 livres a year, augmented by a royal bounty of 200 livres and a lodging allowance, so that his income was £40 or £50. Unfortunately much of this had to go to Corsica where his family needed every sou it could lay its hands on.

Carlo had left his widow in desperate straits. At the very most she had 1200 livres a year on which to support herself and her younger children. As well as these four, she was looking after Uncle Luciano now bedridden – admittedly his contributions made it just possible for the household to survive. But, as her son recalled on St Helena, 'she was managing everything, running everything'. Servantless, Letizia did both the cooking and the washing herself. It was too much for her health – a poisoned finger refused to heal. She did not have Joseph to help her since he was at Pisa reading Law. As soon as he could, in September 1786, Napoleon returned to his family who met him when he landed at Ajaccio. He was horrified by his mother's situation and insisted on her writing to Joseph at Pisa – just about to return, having obtained his degree – to tell him to bring back a really good indoor servant. Joseph soon arrived, bringing the excellent Saveria who remained in Letizia's service for forty years.

Napoleon grew extremely attached to the old Archdeacon, the Buonaparte patriarch. Uncle Luciano's resources – gold and silver coin saved sou by sou and hoarded inside his mattress – had kept the family from ruin. He still enjoyed his clerical revenues, though Fesch now performed his duties at the cathedral. The old man was a figure of considerable authority, the peasants frequently asking him to settle disputes. We have Napoleon's own testimony that Archdeacon Luciano had been a second father to him and that it was his advice which put the family finances on a sound footing again – so much so that Letizia and her children were able to leave Ajaccio during the hot summer months and spend them at a country villa.

After more than twelve months Lieutenant Buonaparte returned to France for an audience with the Controller-General of Finances, seeking reimbursement for Carlo's outlay on the royal mulberry groves. He was unsuccessful. He soon secured another leave of absence from the Minister of War 'for the recovery of his health', and was back in Ajaccio by New Year's Day 1788. He returned to France in June, rejoining his regiment which was in garrison at Auxonne. He often wrote home to complain of lack of letters from the family. He also repeated a promise to have young Luigi to live with him and be responsible for his education. He had few friends and no romantic attachments, except for an early and innocent flirtation with a girl called Caroline Colombier whom he met while garrisoned at Valence.

The States General met at Versailles in the spring of 1789 and Napoleon was an enthusiastic supporter of the Revolution. He believed that it meant the rebirth of France, and also the rebirth of Corsica in which he was far more interested. He obtained leave of absence in September that year, rushing back to Ajaccio where he would stay for nearly eighteen months. His principal interest, and that of Joseph, was politics. What they wanted was a Corsica ruled by Corsicans but allied to the new revolutionary France. Their mother sympathized enthusiastically, even going to the horrific expense of entertaining their political friends in Carlo's much deplored dining-room. Mirabeau, who then dominated the French Assembly, announced that he was ashamed at having fought against General Paoli – the Corsicans' exiled leader – and that the General should be invited to return to Corsica as Military Governor. Meanwhile the two brothers were whipping up ill will against royalists and French troops. In December 1789 the commandant of Ajaccio wrote to the Minister of War in Paris to complain of Lieutenant Buonaparte. 'This young officer was educated at the Ecole Militaire, his sister is at Saint-Cyr and his mother has received countless kindnesses from the Government. This officer had much better be with his regiment since he spends all his time [here] stirring up trouble.' Paoli returned in July 1790, to be elected unanimously President of the new Corsican Assembly. The following month Joseph was elected President of the Ajaccio town council. However Paoli soon came to disapprove of the Revolutionary Club of Ajaccio, whose leaders were the Bonaparte brothers, loud in their vociferous denunciation of priviledge, aristocrats, royal lackeys and everything to do with the *ancien régime*.

Napoleon returned to France in January 1791. As always, even when with his regiment, he helped his family. He could not do much for Luciano, who had left Brienne after only a year, attending the seminary at Aix for a time with some vague idea of a career in the Church but doing little work and soon going home to Ajaccio despite every attempt by Napoleon and his mother to dissuade him. The thirteen-year-old Luigi was a different matter. Napoleon took the boy back to Auxonne, housing him in his dressing-room. Not only did he keep Luigi but he educated him. He cooked the food himself – notably a sustaining but very cheap broth – while teaching his brother French, mathematics and geography. He wrote to Fesch that

> Monsieur Louis [is] a hard worker, as much from natural inclination as from a sense of duty, and full of good intentions. All he has to do is go on in this way. He has already acquired a genuine French manner, very correct but animated. He goes out into society, greets acquaintances gracefully and does the courtesies with the grave and dignified air of a man of thirty. Every woman round here is in love with him.

The boy did not enjoy this regime as much as Napoleon, hinting in a letter to Joseph that he wanted to go home.

When Lieutenant Buonaparte's regiment was moved to Valence he took Louis with him. They lived as before. Napoleon tried to make him join in his own daunting programme of reading, which ranged from astronomy to Merovingian history, from Racine and Corneille to Rousseau, from law and statistics to English politics. Everywhere he went, the Lieutenant brought a trunkful of books. He was still working at his French, trying to eradicate his Italian accent. He avoided local society as too royalist. In June 1791, a week after their arrival at Valence, Louis XVI fled from the Tuileries – only to be brought back ignominiously from Varennes, an event which turned Napoleon into a complete republican.

In October news came to Valence that Archdeacon Luciano was dying. The brothers rushed home. They found the old priest fully conscious on his gold-lined mattress and very tetchy – although deeply pious he told Fesch not to pester him when the latter entered his room in a surplice and stole. Years later Napoleon joked that his uncle's deathbed reminded him of Jacob and Esau. 'You, Joseph', said the Archdeacon, 'are the eldest but Napoleone is the real head of the family. Never forget it.' He added, 'You, Napoleone, you're going to be a big man.'

He left 5,000 francs all of which was quickly spent on buying votes to make Napoleon a lieutenant-colonel and second-in-command of a regiment of Corsican Volunteers. Paoli was already irritated by lengthy epistles from the precocious Luciano Buonaparte telling him how to run Corsica, and also angered by the latter's wild speeches in the Revolutionary Club. In the spring of 1792 during religious riots at Ajaccio Napoleon's troops fired on the rioters – who had Paoli's sympathy – and tried to occupy the citadel. The French commandant refused and three days of street fighting ensued. Then, having antagonized both Paoli and the French garrison, Napoleon left for Paris which he reached at the end of May.

He was promoted to captain after an anxious two months off the active list. On 10 August this convinced democrat witnessed the storming of the Tuileries and the massacre of the Swiss Guard. 'How could they let that rabble get in?' was his comment. 'They ought to have mown down four or five hundred with cannon and the rest would still be running.' It was a dangerous climate for aristocrats, even of the humblest sort, and Maria Anna Buonaparte was in genuine peril at her convent for young ladies. In September, her brother obtained papers from the municipality of Versailles enabling him to remove her and take her home. They had some anxious moments on the way, being stopped and made to show their passes again and again and deny that they were aristocrats.

Napoleon and his sister reached Ajaccio safely in October, whereupon he resumed his rank as a lieutenant-colonel of Corsican Volunteers. However, old General Paoli did not like the way the Revolution was turning out – nor did he like the elegant French Commissioner, the former Marquis de Sémonville, who was staying at the Casa Buonaparte. Then in April Lucien Buonaparte, in a speech to the Republican Club at Toulon, denounced Paoli as a tyrant who ought to be guillotined. In consequence the Committee of Public Safety in Paris ordered the General's arrest. Paoli replied by ordering Napoleon to be captured 'dead or alive'. He was caught but escaped. His mother prepared to defend her house until a message from Napoleon reached her: 'This country is not for us.' Leaving young Maria Annunziata and Girolamo with her own mother, Letizia and Fesch took Louise, Maria Anna and thirteen-year-old Paoletta through the fields by night to their farm at Milelli, where they stayed in the open country till dawn. In Ajaccio the Casa Buonaparte was sacked while one of their farms on the outskirts of the town went up in flames. Paolists were hunting for them, so they hid in the bushes near the ruined tower of Capitello – on the far side of the bay from Ajaccio – where Letizia had arranged a rendezvous with Napoleon. Luckily, he arrived in a ship within a few hours. After embracing his mother, a weeping Napoleon took the party off in a longboat. Finally they reached Calvi, still held by republican troops, found lodgings and were joined by the two youngest children. But Calvi itself was threatened and it was clear that within a very short time the General would drive the French out of the island. The only refuge left was the mainland. On 11 June 1793 the Buonaparte family took passage on a coaster sailed by a noted blockade runner – they had to risk the English fleet – and left Corsica for good.

They reached Toulon two days later, to be welcomed by Lucien. Despite his youth he was already a prominent figure in the Jacobin Club which dominated the city, a key Mediterranean port and the French navy's arsenal. The Terror was in full swing, with its attendant horrors: a guillotine whose blade rose and fell ceaselessly, mobs brandishing heads on pike points, mutinous crews in the harbour threatening to hang their officers, the constant threat of denunciation. It was just as well for the Buonaparte family that they were penniless and had suffered in the cause of the Revolution, that the passports of Letizia and her daughters described them as 'dressmakers'. Napoleon rejoined his regiment at Nice while Joseph went to Paris to try to obtain compensation. The former was able to draw 3,000 francs in back pay. The latter secured a grant of 600,000 francs from the Convention, though not one sou arrived. Their mother left after only a few days, no doubt thankfully, and took lodgings in the little town of La Valette. She had got out just in time. Toulon rose against the Terror in July, to let in Admiral Hood and the British navy while hunting down revolutionaries such as Lucien, who fled. Letizia too had to flee from La Valette, taking to the open road and having to beg for food. Luckily Joseph was able to install her in two rooms at Marseilles, though there was no furniture in them and she had to queue for soup at the municipal soup kitchen. He was able to help because Napoleon had persuaded a Corsican acquaintance, the Deputy Cristofero Saliceti – a former ally against Paoli and one of the Republic's Commissioners for War – to employ him as his secretary. In early September Saliceti engineered Joseph's appointment as an Assistant Commissary of the Republic with the Army of the South on a salary of 6,000 francs. Lucien had to be content with a post as a commissariat storekeeper in a village at a mere 1,200.

Then Joseph found the 'rich girl' of his dreams. Mlle Julie Clary was trying to obtain Saliceti's good offices on behalf of her family, several of whom were suspected of counter-revolutionary activities, and in particular of her dying father, a silk merchant, some said a soap boiler, possibly of Irish origin. Joseph stepped in and ensured that everyone was safe. Julie was short, horse-faced and afflicted with pimples, but she was kind-hearted, extremely intelligent and, most important of all, going to inherit over 80,000 francs. Joseph introduced this promising young creature to his mother, who at once approved of her and her inheritance. Soon there was an engagement.

Meanwhile Saliceti was doing even more for the clan. Having visited the republican forces besieging Toulon, on 26 September 1793 he reported to the Committee of Public Safety in Paris that 'Captain Dommartin having been wounded, we were left with no one to command the artillery, but we have had an amazing piece of good fortune. We stopped Citizen Buonaparte (a well-qualified captain in the same arm) who was on his way to join the Army of Italy, and ordered him to take Dommartin's place.' At first Napoleon was frustrated by unprofessional superiors who resented his dedication – he invariably slept on the ground next to his guns – but in the end his dynamism prevailed. Not without considerable hardship and daunting setbacks he captured the English redoubt on a promontory overlooking and commanding the port, from where, firing red-hot cannon-balls 'to burn the ships of the despots', as he put it, they could prevent the enemy fleet from entering or leaving harbour. The British were forced to evacuate Toulon on 18 December. He had seen savage hand-to-hand fighting, been bayoneted in the leg, had horses shot beneath him, been laid low by fever, and captured an enemy general. What mattered in the immediate future was that he won the favour of another of the Republic's Commissioners for War, Paul de Barras, who had him promoted. He was just twenty-four years old.

In January 1794 Brigadier-General Buonaparte was posted to the Army of Italy, in command of its artillery. Headquarters were at Nice – then an Italian city, 'Nizza la Dolce' – so he installed his mother at the Château Sallé, a pretty little house in the country near Antibes. She impressed the locals by her democratic behaviour in washing the family laundry in a stream that ran through the garden, despite receiving a lavish allowance from her son. Plainly she did not expect such good fortune to last.

By this date two former warrant officers from Gascony, both future members of the Bonaparte clan, had begun to see golden prospects. In 1787 a regiment of light horse, the Chasseurs à Cheval of Champagne, had picked up an unlikely recruit when halting at Toulouse. Their new trooper was a seminarist who had fled from his seminary after running up petty debts he could not pay. He was twenty years old, and his education helped him become the regiment's quartermaster sergeant within two years, though he then left to serve behind the counter of his cousin's draper's shop. At the Revolution he rejoined the army and, on being elected a lieutenant in October 1793, wrote home, 'Since despotism has expired everything looks bright for me.' The name of this would-be priest turned swaggering cavalry officer was Joachim Murat. The second, Jean Bernadotte, the son of a lawyer's clerk at Pau, had been elected a lieutenant as early as March after eleven years in the ranks. He too had written home, to his brother in July 1793, 'I hope to become a captain soon. At present I am fourth lieutenant here. But these considerations do not give me so much pleasure as the thought of Liberty, of which today I know the precious worth.' He had 'Death to Tyrants' tattooed on his arm, a reference to kings.

Barras, who admittedly hated him by then, writes in his memoirs that at this time Napoleon was a ferocious republican. 'Marat and Robespierre, those are my saints', said the little gunner. Referring to a pamphlet which Buonaparte had published recently, Barras adds, 'It is impossible to imagine anything more Jacobin than the principles of that hellish tract.' He also compares Napoleon with the arch-revolutionary Marat. Beyond question Napoleon was an ultra-Jacobin at this date. As he put it smoothly when on St Helena, 'I was then very young and my opinions were not yet settled.' Barras records wryly that, during the banquet given by the revolutionary committees to the commissioners to celebrate the recapture of Toulon, Buonaparte 'already playing that double game second nature to him, alternated between the dinner from the commissioners, at which he was so proud and privileged to be present, and that for the *sans-culottes* in the next room, constantly going in there as though to apologize for not being with them'. Barras further tells us how when the new brigadier-general joined the Army of Italy

he made friends with the younger Robespierre and with Ricord and his wife, who became his patrons. From the very beginning of his Italian service Buonaparte, still a very junior general officer scheming to rise by any means whatever, and who considered women a most effective means, danced attendance on Mme Ricord since he knew that her husband had considerable influence over his colleague, the younger Robespierre. He heaped attentions on Ricord's wife, handing her her gloves and fan, holding her bridle and her stirrup with the deepest respect when she mounted her horse, taking her for walks hat in hand, and appearing to be in constant terror lest she should meet with some accident.

Certainly this was most uncharacteristic behaviour.

There is no doubt that Napoleon was in constant touch with the Jacobins in Paris and completely trusted by them. We know from his own account that he considered the elder Robespierre, Maximilien, to have been a scapegoat: 'Robespierre had more foresight and policy than is generally realized.' Augustin (the younger) Robespierre took a great fancy to the 'patriot' brigadier-general, whom he considered to have 'transcendent talent'. In Thermidor (July) 1794 he invited him to accompany him when he reported back to Paris in his capacity as the Republic's representative to the Army of Italy. Napoleon shrewdly declined the invitation.

He was busy all this time organizing coastal defences and preparing for a campaign against Piedmont. He appointed Louis a *sous-lieutenant* on his staff so that he could continue his lessons. The boy saw real fighting when he accompanied his brother during some skirmishes with the Pied-montese in the foothills of the Alps, and to give him still more experience Napoleon posted Louis to a coastal battery at Saint-Tropez.

Lucien – now styled Brutus Buonaparte to demonstrate his republican fervour – was busily proving that Napoleon was not the only Jacobin in the family. In his capacity as President of the Revolutionary Committee of his village of Saint-Maximin he had over twenty of his neighbours thrown into prison on suspicion of disaffection towards the Republic. His brother can have had no objections to such behaviour, but in April 1794 Brutus-Lucien took democratic principles too far by marrying the village innkeeper's sister. At twenty-one Catherine Boyer was two years older than he and – worse than not being able to read or write – she was penniless. He did not ask his family's permission. Letizia, barely literate herself, later feigned a liking for the pretty little brunette, but Napoleon and Joseph found it difficult to forgive their brother. Even during a revolution one has to think of one's family's place in society.

These were the months when the Terror was at its height. No doubt for the Committee of Public Safety and for its supporters – such as the Buonaparte brothers – it was no more than a species of martial law necessary for the Republic's survival, but thousands perished horribly for no other reason than their class or their religion or mere suspicion, and thousands more lived in constant fear.

Among the victims was the former Vicomte de Beauharnais. Alexandre de Beauharnais, a garrulously enthusiastic Jacobin and General of the Republic who had commanded the Army of the Rhine, was arrested in March 1794 and imprisoned in the Carmes, where the walls were still stained with blood from the massacres of the previous September. Here he stayed in daily expectation of hearing his name called for trial and execution until guillotined on 19 July. Ironically his wife Joséphine was confined with him, although they had long been separated. Despite his vile treatment of her, she had done her best to save Beauharnais, an act which had led to her own arrest. Expecting to follow him to the scaffold, she moaned and wept throughout her incarceration, but found consolation in a torrid affair with another prisoner, the personable young General Hoche.

However, on 10 Thermidor [23 July] 1794 Robespierre and his supporters were overthrown in a *coup* organized by Barras. It succeeded because the entire Convention went in fear of their lives. Among those beheaded with the Incorruptible was his brother Augustin, the admiring friend of Brigadier-General Buonaparte. On 8 August Napoleon was arrested as a Robespierrist and confined in the Fort Carré at Antibes, not far from his mother. His papers were seized – there was a possibility of a capital charge. Lieutenant Junot, who had served under him as a sergeant during the siege of Toulon, offered to arrange his escape but he declined. In the event General Dumerbion, his commanding officer, persuaded the investigating commission that France could not afford to lose so able a soldier and he was declared innocent. For the time being he was allowed to retain his command.

In August 1794 Joseph secured the family fortunes by marrying Julie Clary. She insisted on a ceremony performed by an outlaw priest who had refused to swear allegiance to the Republic. It was worth the risk since speculations as to her wealth were gratifyingly confirmed while her sweet nature soon endeared her to the family. Her soldier brother-in-law described her as 'the best woman that ever lived'.

It was lucky for the Buonaparte brothers that one at least was prospering, for in May 1795 Napoleon was deprived of his Army of Italy post. Instead he was offered an infantry command in the Vendée, a step down. When he refused it his name was removed from the active list and he was placed on half pay. He was reduced to living in a cheap hotel in Paris wearing a shabby uniform and muddy boots. Gloves, then an essential, he disdained as a luxury. Joseph sent him remittances but not enough. He was so poor that when dining out he wrapped the money for his bill in a piece of paper to conceal how little he was spending. He could no longer afford to keep Louis, for whom he managed to find a place in the Artillery School at Châlons. There were days when he contemplated suicide. In desperation he considered a career in the Turkish service – once in the Sultan's employ he was going to have Joseph appointed French Consul at Chios.

In June, just after his dismissal, Napoleon wrote to Joseph on whom he was now largely dependent,

> Whatever may happen to you, remember that you cannot possibly have a warmer friend than I, one to whom you are more dear or who is more sincerely anxious for your happiness. Life is a mere dream that fades. Should you go away and suspect that it may be for some time, let me have a miniature of yourself. We have lived together for so long and been so close that our hearts have become one – you know more than anybody how completely mine belongs to you.

This letter was prompted by a request from Joseph's wife for a miniature of Napoleon which he was having painted for her sister Désirée, with whom he had fallen in love.

Désirée Clary was 'a cheerful little Marseillaise' with huge dark eyes, an enchanting smile and the strong accent of her native city. She was genuinely in love with him – on one occasion she hid under his bed. She was also ambitious. On St Helena he told General Bertrand, 'Désirée had ability and was eager for me to be successful.' There seemed very little prospect of his being so, in the summer of 1795.

His situation was not helped by Lucien. Denounced as a Robespierrist, the half-starving storekeeper was arrested at Saint-Maximin a full year after Thermidor. He had made many enemies in the village. Letizia wrote a shrewd letter to the Convention's representative to the Army of Italy, Citizen Chiappe, saying that she could not understand why her son had been denounced since there were no émigrés at Saint-Maximin and no one had died because of him. After a fortnight Lucien was released. The incident can have done his brother's reputation no good.

'When I was young I was a revolutionary from ignorance and ambition', Napoleon admitted to Metternich long afterwards. Even if he abandoned Jacobin principles, Jacobin manners left their mark on him. Metternich remarked in the 1790s how the French had been changed by the Revolution: 'The highest polish and an elegance one could scarcely hope to imitate have been replaced by the utmost slovenliness, extreme amiability by a dull, sinister air.' Napoleon was neither slovenly nor sinister but his language had become coarse, frequently foul, and try as he would, he could never shake the habit off. He always remained almost incapable of speaking politely, let alone pleasingly, to a woman, habitually asking the greatest lady the most intimate questions as though she were some barrack-room slut.

The Buonaparte clan had been Jacobins of the deepest dye. They had adopted extremist principles and *sans-culotte* manners from a greedy desire for advancement, from a misguided belief that that was the way in which the wind was going to blow – in short, from the purest opportunism. Now, led by the brother who was their family genius, they would change to politics which if seemingly revolutionary were none the less anti-Jacobin. All they wanted was to rise to the top of society.

3

The Ascent Begins – The Directory

'Our family shall want for nothing.'

NAPOLEON TO JOSEPH, NOVEMBER 1795

'Napoleon had a strong tendency to the superstition of
fatalism, and he always believed that his fortunes were bound
up in some mysterious manner with those of this graceful
woman [Joséphine]. She loved him warmly, and served him
well. Her influence over him was great, and it was always
exerted on the side of humanity. She, and she alone, could
overrule, by gentleness, the excesses of passion to which he
was liable; and her subsequent fate will aways form one of the
darkest pages in the history of her lord.'

LOCKHART, *The History of Napoleon Buonaparte*

During the autumn of 1795 Napoleon's career suddenly began its comet-
like ascent. Hitherto there had been an element of equality, of mutual
self-help, almost of partnership, in his relations with his family. Now he
emerges as its supreme patron. Henceforward until the creation of the
Napoleonic Empire in 1804 the other members of the Buonaparte clan
were to devote their energies to amassing wealth and establishing
themselves in France's new society – the most money-conscious in the
West since Roman times.

General Buonaparte was five feet six and a half inches tall and, until he
was thirty, alarmingly thin. In the fashion of the day he wore his hair in
'spaniel's ears' (cut square under the ears and falling to his shoulders)
which gave him a vaguely absurd air. However, there was nothing absurd
about his deep-set, grey eyes, large and feverish with a peculiar, often
somewhat gloomy, look – they could charm but they could also terrify. A
woman who knew him in 1795 told Stendhal long afterwards, 'Had he not
been so thin as to have a sickly air which was quite pitiful to see, one
would have realized that he had unusually delicate features. The lines of
his mouth in particular were full of charm.' As his success grew and as
they grew older, Joseph and Jérôme attempted to emphasize their very
slight facial resemblance to him. Neither could convey even a hint of their
brother's overwhelming presence.

In August 1795 the Convention introduced a new French constitution,
the Executive Directory, with five Directors (all regicides), advised by an

upper and a lower chamber – the Ancients and the Five Hundred. Two-thirds of the membership of the Convention remained members of the new chambers without having to submit to re-election. But by now many Frenchmen were tired of the Revolution and wanted a return to monarchy. Seeing there was no hope of electing their representatives, they decided to try force. By early October not less than 20,000 royalist National Guards in Paris controlled large areas of the capital and were preparing to march on the government at the Tuileries. A White Terror threatened. The Republic's army was demoralized and mutinous and the Directors realized that they had very few friends indeed. In desperation they appointed the First Director, Citizen Barras, as Commander of the Army of the Interior on 4 October. Barras at once released from prison and armed several hundred extremist 'guillotine lickers' and looked for Jacobin officers, arresting the ineffectual General Menou for negotiating with the insurgents. He told the Committee of Public Safety, 'I have just the man you want – a little Corsican officer.' But Bonaparte could not be found at his lodgings or in any of the cafés or eating houses he frequented – later Barras suspected that his protégé had been bargaining with the other side. When he was located Barras secured his services by appointing him second-in-command.

By then it was nine o'clock on the evening of 13 Vendémiaire (5 October). Napoleon, without the cannon which he needed, knew that the National Guard's artillery was parked at the Place des Sablons and guarded by a mere fifteen men. He ordered the nearest body of cavalry to secure the forty guns and bring them to him at the Tuileries. They did so at the gallop under their major, Joachim Murat. In consequence, when the insurgents attacked at just after four o'clock in the morning they were blown off the streets by grapeshot; when they took refuge in the church of Saint-Roch government troops went in after them with the bayonet. The fighting was over by the end of the day, hundreds of the insurgents having been killed, many of them well-known royalist guerrillas. At two o'clock the following morning General Buonaparte, who had had his horse killed under him, wrote to Joseph that all was quiet. 'As usual, I have not been hit.'

Barras was so impressed that within three weeks he had Napoleon promoted to General of Division, then to full General and GOC of the Army of the Interior. The Director is said to have told his colleagues, 'Promote this man, or he will promote himself without you.' He was twenty-six years old. He now had money in abundance, being rewarded with large sums by the Directors in addition to his pay. He moved from his shabby lodgings in the Marais to a splendid town house, drove out in an expensive carriage and began to drop old friends. By the end of

November he had sent his mother 60,000 francs (£2,400), writing to Joseph that 'our family shall want for nothing'. He moved Letizia and his sisters out of their wretched Marseilles garret into a superb apartment in the best house in the same street. He gave Joseph money to invest in Genoese privateers. He engineered Lucien's appointment as secretary to Citizen Fréron – one of the Directory's most important officials, charged with stamping out reaction in the South – and then as a Commissary with the Army of the North in the Netherlands. Louis was commissioned as a lieutenant in the 4th Regiment of Artillery immediately after 13 Vendémiaire, joining his brother's staff the following month as ADC and military secretary. The eleven-year-old Girolamo, transformed into Jérôme, was brought to Paris and sent to the most expensive and most fashionable school, where Napoleon visited him frequently and made sure he did not suffer from that agonizing shortage of pocket money which he himself had known at Brienne. Fesch, who had left the priesthood for the time being, acquired the immensely lucrative post of a Commissary to the Army of Italy. He seems to have been the clan's acknowledged financial adviser. On 17 November 1795 the General wrote to Joseph at Genoa,

> I have just received 400,000 francs for you. I have given it to Fesch who will pay it into your account. [Napoleon adds in the same letter] I may install the family here [Paris]. Let me have much more news of you and your wife and of Désirée. Goodbye, my good friend, I am all yours. My only worry is the knowledge that you are so far away and to be deprived of your company. Were not your wife pregnant, I would try to persuade you to come and spend some time in Paris.

Yet despite his new eminence General Buonaparte appears to have still felt financially insecure. No doubt he remembered his short-lived prosperity under Robespierre. He decided to copy Joseph and make a rich marriage. Désirée Clary, Joseph's sister-in-law, had become his mistress and he seems to have thought that she might make him a suitable wife. However, her relations considered 'one Corsican in the family quite enough'. In any case she was only eighteen and at this date Napoleon preferred more mature women. Barras helpfully introduced him to Mlle Montansier, definitely overripe. By her own admission she was old enough to be the little General's mother but she possessed over a million francs. (Her wealth was genuine – she owned a combined theatre and brothel in the Palais Royal.) He invited her to meet Letizia and his brothers, suggesting a visit to Corsica. Nothing came of this, so he transferred his suit to the recently widowed Mme Permon, the same Corsican lady who had sheltered his dying father in Montpellier, under the impression that the late Permon had left a vast fortune – in fact he died penniless – which he tried to secure by a double proposal, that the widow's son should marry his sister Pauline and that, as soon as her mourning was over, he would marry her. He was twenty-six, his intended bride well over fifty. Initially stupified, the *veuve* Permon burst into peals of laughter, to the mortification of her suitor who sternly told her to think it over. He called several times to see if she would change her mind, finally storming off in a rage.

During his wooing of Mme Permon, presumably to make her jealous, he had spoken of yet another lady: 'People have introduced me to a woman who is charming, good-natured and agreeable, and who belongs to the Faubourg Saint-Germain. My Paris friends are all very much in favour of my marrying her.' The Faubourg was the world of the old aristocracy and he was almost certainly referring to the *ci-devant* Victomtesse de Beauharnais, one of the smartest women in Paris. Joséphine de Beauharnais was not, however, the sort of person a young man would care to introduce to his mother. There were lurid rumours that, with her friend Thérèse Tallien, she had danced naked before Barras.

The fall of Robespierre had brought in a new society, flashy, vulgar, profligate. Its leaders were venal politicians, ruthless bankers, gamblers and speculators, madams and whores. Money was everything in a world as decadent as it was now. Yet if vicious it was undeniably cheerful. Even Napoleon had written in July 1795, when his prospects were gloomiest and he had contemplated suicide, 'Everything which can make life pleasant and delightful is available in abundance. One has no time to be depressed or to think among so many gay and amusing people. Ladies are everywhere, in the theatres, out driving, in the libraries.' Citizen – once Vicomte – Barras typified the Directory, a former career soldier and man of pleasure from Provence who had been a bankrupt in 1789, corrupt, without beliefs or principles of any sort, a total opportunist but extremely amusing company. His house was always thronged by shady stockjobbers and 'actresses'.

The regime had an extremely sinister side embodied by the icily formidable Minister of Police Joseph Fouché, who like Barras had voted for the execution of Louis xvi. (He was known as 'the Butcher of Lyons' because he had sent 2,000 people to their deaths there beneath the guillotine or before the firing squad during the winter of 1793–4.) A small, white-faced, thin-lipped but fine-featured man, his dreadful glassy stare – at once seemingly both sightless and all-seeing – never failed to inspire terror. Always exhausted from overwork, this foul-mouthed former cleric and schoolmaster was one of the most effective police chiefs in history.

Citizeness Tascher-Beauharnais – the prefix *de* was bad form these days – was another flower of the Directory, the widow of General Beauharnais who had been guillotined under the Terror. A Creole, she had become the eternal Parisian with all the nuances of sophistication, chic and frivolity conveyed by the word. The new age was ideally suited to adventuresses, a time when lovers could procure them wealth and position. If ladies were attractive and ready to prostitute themselves, then truly glittering careers lay open to them. Joséphine's affair with General Hoche had ended abruptly after they emerged from prison, when he caught her *in flagrante* with one of his grooms (a gigantic Alsatian). Nevertheless her warm Caribbean blood ensured her success with quite enough other men of power and influence, her patrician manners proving an aid rather than a handicap. Thirty-two, she was not really pretty, without good features, and with teeth so bad ('like cloves') that she had trained herself to smile without showing them. Yet she was clearly most alluring – apparently what the French calle a *belle laide* – and knew how to make the most of her assets, which included fine, silky, chestnut hair, magnetic, dark blue eyes with amazingly long lashes, a genuinely sweet smile, brilliant skin, a seductively graceful carriage and a warm, husky, drawling Creole voice so musical that servants would pause for the pleasure of listening to it. There was something exotic about her – she was the nearest thing in eighteenth-century France to a Southern belle. She dressed superbly, wore her jewels with an air, surrounded herself with flowers, masses of flowers. Moreover, the aristocratic citizeness was totally amoral, with an expertise in bed of a sort hitherto unexperienced by the farouche young General Buonaparte.

At her pretty little house in the rue Chantereine, rented from the actor Talma's wife, she gave intimate dinner-parties where delicious food and superlative wines were served to the accompaniment of perfectly chosen music. The guests included all the rich and famous of the day. Barras, inevitably one of her lovers, was often present. Fouché, who had spies in every smart brothel and gaming hall in the capital, paid her for any useful gossip she might hear, her initial advance being 24,000 francs – as the Police Minister said, 'She saw all Paris.' Although up to her ears in debt and living on the very brink of bankruptcy, she contrived to give an impression of considerable wealth.

It seems that after 13 Vendémiaire Parisians were ordered to hand in all weapons and that Joséphine's fourteen-year-old son Eugène came to ask Napoleon's permission to keep his father's sword. The General gave leave with some amiability whereupon the boy's mother called to thank him. It is clear that the citizeness recognized a man with a brilliant future when she saw one. She would have known all about General Buonaparte from her friend and fellow adventuress Mme Tallien, who was Barras's favourite mistress and one of the most notorious courtesans in Paris – the General had also made advances to Thérèse Tallien, rebuffed in such a way as to make him a laughing-stock. By the end of 1795 he was writing naïvely passionate letters to Joséphine. Her daughter, the thirteen-year-old Hortense, met her mother's new admirer in January 1796 at a dinner-party given by Barras (to celebrate the third anniversary of Louis XVI's execution). She remembered his face, 'handsome, very expressive, but strikingly pale', now he 'talked eagerly and seemed wholly absorbed in my mother'. She did not like him at all, suspecting at once that he wanted to marry Joséphine.

In contrast, Hortense's brother, Eugène de Beauharnais, seems to have taken a fancy to Napoleon from the very beginning. He himself was obviously a most likeable boy, and good-looking – apart from a slight squint and Joséphine's horrible teeth. Under the Terror all children of noble birth had been forced to learn a trade, in a statutory attempt to degrade them, and having chosen to be apprenticed to a carpenter, he worked for his master without complaint. Then, when still only thirteen, he had spent a year as orderly to his mother's friend General Hoche in the frightful campaign in the Vendée against the Chouans' 'Catholic and Royal Army'. Despite the horrible atrocities he must have witnessed, this experience, together with the memory of his soldier father, had made him long for a military career.

Citizeness Beauharnais realized that Buonaparte was hers for the taking when expensive gifts began to arrive. She also guessed that, misled by her opulent life-style, he believed her to be extremely rich. She confided in Barras that she did not really care for 'that little puss-in-boots', who 'belonged to a beggarly family of no consequence', though on the other hand he did have a brother who had brought off 'a great marriage' at Marseilles. 'I thought that it would be wise not to tell him the truth about my cruelly embarrassed circumstances', she explained to Barras. 'He is under the impression that I still have plenty of money and thinks that I have great expectations from Martinique. Don't let him know that it isn't true, dear friend, or you'll spoil everything.' Her lawyer Raguideau cautioned her against such a step. 'Can you be so foolish as to marry a young man who has nothing but his cloak and his sword?' Eventually she decided that 'puss-in-boots' was a reasonable investment, in view of his rich brother and of Barras's patronage. For his part Napoleon afterwards admitted frankly that he had proposed to Joséphine 'only because I thought she had a large fortune'. Within four months of their first meeting they were married in a civil ceremony on 9 March 1796, Barras and the Talliens being the witnesses. Her husband recalled, 'I really did love her. I had no respect for her.' He had not even dared to tell his mother, let alone ask her to the wedding – for once in his life he may have known the meaning of fear. Unquestionably it was a *mésalliance*, even if she provided him with a smart house in Paris and a base in what then passed for fashionable society. She was extravagant to the point of profligacy, an insatiable lover of luxury. Her only virtues were that she was genuinely kind-hearted and an unusually loyal friend. However, as Lucien points out, 'Barras gave her a dowry, namely the supreme command of the Army of Italy.' General Buonaparte was nominated to the post on 2 March, exactly a week before his marriage.

En route for his headquarters at Nice Napoleon visited his mother at Marseilles. Letizia had to accept Joséphine as her daughter-in-law even if, without having seen her, she considered her 'an old woman with grown-up children'. The fact that the lady was of infinitely higher social origin, a *ci-devant* vicomtesse who would not have condescended to meet the *veuve* Buonaparte in the days before 1789, did not help matters. Joséphine had written a letter for her husband to give to her new mother-in-law. Letizia wrote in her reply: 'It could not, of course, add to the charming impression which I had already formed of you. My son has told me of his happiness, which is enough to ensure not only my consent but my approval. My own happiness lacks nothing but the pleasure of meeting you. I already look on you as one of my children.' Almost certainly Napoleon dictated his mother's letter. Down the years Letizia and her brood were to intrigue against 'that widow' with unflagging hostility. After all, Joséphine had captured the architect of the family fortunes. She was always vulnerable since she would never be able to give him a child.

At Marseilles the General had to listen to his mother's worries about the sixteen-year-old Pauline. She had acquired the most unsuitable lover possible in Stanislas Fréron, Lucien's chief. Once a blood-stained hatchet man of Robespierre, who had organized massacres at Toulon, he was also a dandified, forty-year-old, syphilitic libertine – he kept an actress in Paris, now about to present him with their third bastard. Pauline begged her mother to let her marry this handsome, inveterate womanizer, Lucien and Maria Anna being foolish enough to encourage her. Ironically, Fréron – in his eagerness to climb on to the Buonaparte bandwaggon – overreached himself by trying to enlist Joséphine's support. Citizeness Buonaparte, conscious of newly acquired respectability, warned her husband that Pauline would demean herself by marrying such a man and promised to do everything she could to prevent the marriage. Napoleon had to be careful, however, since Fréron was an ally of Barras. Only in May 1796, when he had become more powerful, did he intervene. He could write to Joseph, 'I don't intend that Fréron should marry her. Tell her, and let him know too.'

General 'Bonaparte' reached Nice at the end of March 1796. Although he had signed himself 'Buonaparte' on his marriage licence, he now altered his name, presumably to keep the troops from worrying about being commanded by an Italian. (But nothing could ever stop his mother calling him 'Poleone'.) His army consisted of 38,000 ragged, shoeless, unpaid men who had spent the last four years in miserable conditions, skirmishing fruitlessly on the southern slopes of the Alps. His message to them was in essence, or so he later suggested, 'You need clothes, boots and bread. The enemy has plenty of everything. It is up to you to win. You want to, you can. Forward!' Luckily the army included some truly superlative commanders. Among these was the recently promoted Colonel Murat, who with Gascon impudence had offered his services as a cavalry ADC – the General had accepted, though he can scarcely have guessed that this flashy *beau sabreur* would prove to be one of the bravest captains of horse in history. There were other future Marshals of France, such as Masséna, Lannes, Marmont and Augereau. The latter's comment on his new chief was, 'The little bugger actually frightened me – I can't explain just what I felt when he looked at me.' For General Bonaparte cowed and dominated these hard-bitten veterans. Despite the shabbiness and demoralization of their troops he proceeded to launch a devastating offensive.

In early April the Army of Italy's headquarters were moved to Albenga. Here General Bonaparte was joined by Joseph who spent the next fortnight with him. Louis was on his staff, working as hard as any other ADC. They witnessed the start of their brother's first full-scale campaign. He faced 31,000 Austrian and 25,000 Piedmontese regulars, crack troops. He sent Masséna into the attack at Montenotte on 12 April 1796 and in this opening engagement the French inflicted 3,000 casualties on the enemy. Within a fortnight Napoleon had stormed the key mountain passes, cut off the Piedmontese army and forced their king to sue for peace, and driven the Austrians into a hasty retreat. His extraordinary success was largely due to his strategy of dividing the enemy and destroying isolated detachments one by one, switching troops to an unexpected point with maximum speed and without warning. In this way he was able to concentrate overwhelming masses of men against opponents whose overall numbers were much greater than his own.

On 24 April Bonaparte sent Joseph back to Paris, carrying dispatches for the Directory announcing his victories, and the Piedmontese request for an armistice, together with twenty-one captured enemy colours. His brother was given further valuable information to communicate verbally. As Napoleon intended, all this made Citizen Joseph Bonaparte a person of importance. In addition Joseph had an introduction to Joséphine. 'My brother is bringing this letter to you,' wrote her husband. 'I'm extremely fond of him and I hope you will be too – he's worth it. Born really kind-natured and thoroughly sound, he has countless good qualities. I'm writing to Barras to have him made consul at some Italian port. He wants to settle down with his little wife, away from the rough and tumble of the political world. I recommend him to you warmly.' One may be sure that Joséphine was charming to her brother-in-law, though she would not agree to return immediately with him to her husband at the front. One may be equally sure that she failed to charm Joseph, who had been counting on a match with his wife's sister Désirée to build an even stronger bond between him and his gifted brother. Joséphine was receiving visits from the newly promoted General Murat, who had come with dispatches announcing fresh victories, and got on very well with the handsome cavalryman – some said too well. They were seen breakfasting, dining and supping together in the Champs-Elysées, all on the same day. Before leaving the capital, Joseph bought property outside Paris as an investment, made influential friends and let it be known he wanted to be an ambassador. He and his sister-in-law, whose luggage filled several carriages, did eventually set out for the Italian front at the end of June. *En route* she made determined advances to Junot, which the embarrassed Colonel only repulsed by flirting desperately with her lady companion.

During Joseph's absence Napoleon had stormed the bridge of Lodi with a daring infantry charge, in which his reckless bravery earned him the nickname 'The Little Corporal' among his troops. It was this engagement which, he said, convinced him that a great destiny lay before him. He had then driven the Austrians out of Lombardy, capturing Milan where he set up his new headquarters in May. He was blockading the key Austrian fortress of Mantua when in July a formidable new enemy commander-in-chief, the veteran Field-Marshal Count von Würmser, counter-attacked on two fronts in an attempt to relieve it. A series of ferocious campaigns ensued.

When Joseph and Joséphine reached Milan they found Napoleon and his staff in the Palazzo Serbelloni. The poet Arnault calls it 'one of Milan's most splendid . . . the palace of the King of Cocagne', comparing the General's drawing-room to the foyer of the Paris Opéra. 'Never did a headquarters look more like a court. It was a forerunner of the Tuileries.' Yet it was not princely enough for the great man, who moved to the Villa Crivelli at Mombello outside Milan where his salons and a huge marquee in the gardens were thronged with officers, civil servants and army contractors. He kept semi-regal state, dining in public and driving out with an escort of 300 red-uniformed lancers from General Dombrowski's

Polish Legion. Soon Mme Bonaparte was presiding like a queen. She acquired a bosom friend in Marchesa Visconti, General Berthier's mistress and a Milanese version of Mme Tallien, who played the role of lady-in-waiting. Napoleon was shocked by the Marchesa. 'Good God! What women! What morals!' Joséphine had brought not only her dog Fortuné – she insisted on its sharing her bed with Napoleon, whom it bit on their wedding night – but also a Captain Hippolyte Charles, a foppish hussar with a nice taste in practical jokes and 'the face of a whore'. When her husband found out, he thought of having the Captain shot; eventually he arranged for him to be cashiered and sent home.

Nearly all the Bonaparte clan visited Mombello at one time or another, Caroline and little Jérôme coming for their school holidays. Louis, normally so gay and lively, was oddly moody. Fesch was there too, making a fortune out of army supplies and dabbling very profitably in usury.

Only Lucien stayed away. Busy though he was, General Bonaparte nevertheless found time to write in August to Lazare Carnot, the Directory's President, complaining about him.

> One of my brothers, a commissary of the War Department at Marseilles, has gone to Paris without permission. The young man has intelligence of a sort, but he is also ill-balanced. All his life he has had a mania for meddling in politics. At a moment when it is perfectly obvious that a large number of people would like to damage my reputation and are using all kinds of intrigue to give colour to stupid and harmful rumours, I ask you to help me by ordering him to rejoin one of the armies within twenty-four hours. I would prefer it to be the Army of the North.

No one could accuse Napoleon of favouritism since that particular army was suffering reverse after reverse. At the General's request Carnot had already posted Pauline's unwelcome suitor, Fréron, to it. However, Napoleon added, 'May I recommend to you my brother [Louis], the aide-de-camp whom I sent to you just before the battle of Lonato? This brave young man deserves the good opinion which I am sure you will have of him.' Indeed Louis made such an excellent impression when reporting on the situation at the front that Carnot had him promoted to captain and presented with an expensive brace of pistols.

The General soon had cause to complain again about Lucien, who had sent Carnot a foolish missive.

> You will have seen, merely from reading my brother's letter, how hare-brained the young man is [he wrote]. He was in trouble several times in '93, notwithstanding my repeated warnings. He wanted to play the Jacobin, and it was lucky for him that he was only eighteen and had his youth as an excuse. Otherwise he would have found himself with that little band of ruffians who disgraced their country. It would be dangerous for him to go to Marseilles, not

only on his own account but for the good of the public. He would undoubtedly fall into the hands of intriguers, and he has some very unsavoury connections in the area. Now that Corsica has been liberated you would do me a great favour by ordering him there if he is not prepared to stay with the Army of the Rhine. He might be of some use to the Republic.

Joseph had already left Milan for Corsica, which the English had recently evacuated. Old Paoli had left even before, this time for good. The island's new regime was more than anxious to win the favour of a brother of the famous Corsican General, so that he was able to pack the administration with his friends. He recovered all the family properties, including the Casa Buonaparte. It had been occupied by an English officer called Hudson Lowe, whose name would one day be only too well known. Napoleon wrote to Joseph from Milan, 'Whatever happens, I want the house to be in a really good state and worthy to live in. . . . Do what you can to make the street more imposing.'

The Italian front grew critical once more in November 1796. The Austrians were trying desperately to relieve Würmser, who had himself been forced to take refuge in Mantua. Bonaparte routed them amid the marshes around Arcole. It was essential to capture the bridge of Arcole. During the action the General seized the tricolour to lead the charge, but, running towards the bridge along the causeway over the marshes, fell into a dyke. He would have drowned had not Louis pulled him out. The boy had already distinguished himself by carrying a vital order from his brother through a hail of bullets. When he got back Napoleon told him, 'I thought you'd been killed.' The storming of the bridge of Arcole captured popular imagination and the little General became even more of a hero in France.

Yet 1797 proved still more glorious. The Austrians made a final attempt to save Würmser at Mantua in January, but amid snow and ice Bonaparte broke them at Rivoli, inflicting 14,000 casualties and driving them in headlong retreat. (He owed much to General Murat's handling of his cavalry.) Würmser surrendered the following month whereupon the French marched on Vienna. That excellent commander the Archduke Karl barred their way, but after three further defeats the Emperor sued for peace in April. Napoleon then went on to occupy Venice in May, overthrowing the ancient republic.

The court at Mombello continued to flourish. The mannish Maria Anna, scraggy, sour-faced and evil-tempered, arrived there. 'The most disagreeable woman I have ever known,' remembers Mme d'Abrantès. 'Mme Bacciochi was never nice to her mother, but who was she ever nice to? I have never met anyone with a sharper tongue.' Maria Anna now had a husband and she brought him with her. He was a Corsican Major named Pasquale Bacciochi, whom she had married on May Day 1797 at Marseilles where he had been a lodger in the house rented by Letizia. Fifteen years older than his bride, tall, plump and heavy-faced, amiable enough but irredeemably stupid and totally insignificant, he was another petty nobleman from Ajaccio and closely related to the unloved Pozzo di Borgo cousins – his family were strong Paolists. There was always something slightly comic about him, even his surname which translated means 'Kiss Eyes', while Lucien complained of his doing 'nothing but scrape his violin'. Letizia insisted that the marriage should be regularized by a religious ceremony. Privately the Bonapartes regretted the match – Metternich says in his memoirs, 'Napoleon would have preferred a brother-in-law not quite so destitute of intellect' – but they none the less gave Maria Anna a dowry of 40,000 francs. No doubt Bacciochi sometimes regretted it himself – his young wife's tongue could upset even her brother. She spoke rapidly and brusquely in a dry, acerbic voice, with no trace of an Italian accent if Lucien is to be believed, though she had charm of a sort when she cared to use it. Both she and Bacciochi changed their Christian names – she from Maria Anna to Elisa, he from Pasquale to Félix (or Felice later). The following year they had a son, Félix Napoléon, who only lived six months.

One day in June the General, working in his study at Mombello, heard noises coming from behind a screen. Investigating, he found one of his staff officers on top of Pauline and, so Sémonville informs a friend, insisted on his marrying her at once. The wedding was celebrated with the full rites of Holy Church, Pauline too receiving a dowry of 40,000 francs. Her husband was Victor Emmanuel Leclerc, twenty-five, small, slight and colourless, the son of a rich miller from Pontoise. In those days he seemed a reasonable catch. Napoleon promoted him to brigadier-general a fortnight before the wedding. Leclerc made himself a laughing-stock by aping his brother-in-law's mannerisms, wearing his hat sideways and walking up and down with his hands behind his back. While plainly enjoying being married, Pauline remained 'as much a madcap as ever', according to Arnault. A son was born in 1798, to whom she gave the odd name of Dermide, taken from the epic *Ossian*.

Occasionally Joséphine was difficult. A cavalry officer, Baron Carrion-Nisas, who saw her in October 1797, says, 'Mme Bonaparte is neither young nor pretty. She has beautiful manners and is good-natured. She appears very fond of her husband who seems deeply attached to her. She cries frequently, several times a day, for the most trivial reasons.' Perhaps she missed Captain Charles. Though not unimpressed by Napoleon, she was flattered by her nickname, 'Our Lady of Victories'.

In September 1797 General Bernadotte arrived from the Army of the

Rhine with 20,000 reinforcements. He soon fell out with his new brother officers, challenging General Berthier to a duel. Many were angered by his reintroduction of 'Monsieur' in place of 'Citoyen', which particularly upset the more sincere republicans. However, Napoleon concurred – a significant pointer as to how the wind would blow on a future day.

General Bonaparte's achievements appeared all the more brilliant in the light of the Army of the North's abject retreat. Napoleon had not only conquered Northern Italy, he had saved his country. The Directory would have preferred to play down his victories but did not dare. He was a national hero.

The Directors had none of Robespierre's uncomfortable idealism. In their eyes the Revolution's principal purpose was to ensure the prosperity of themselves and their supporters, the 'notables' or *honnêtes gens* as they were known sarcastically. These were the wealthy bourgeois and renegade aristocrats who secured high office, bought 'national' (i.e. confiscated) property or made fortunes from purveying shoddy equipment and stale provisions to the troops.

Citizen Joseph Bonaparte, now a Deputy for Corsica in the Council of Five Hundred, was all too typical of the *honnêtes gens*. After a profitable if dangerous few months in Rome as French Ambassador at a salary of 60,000 francs in gold, he returned to Paris at the end of 1797 to devote himself to his business interests. It was rumoured that he had obtained a share in the jewels, gold and works of art secretly extorted as 'tribute' (blackmail) from the Papal States, but that the entire shipment had been lost at sea. Nevertheless he was becoming a very rich man indeed.

His cautious mother preferred to go home to Corsica. Her arrival at Ajaccio in July 1797 was a joyous occasion. She was greeted by an artillery salute while the entire town was illuminated in her honour. Having received compensation of nearly 100,000 francs from the Directory, she redecorated and refurnished the Casa Buonaparte, and installed a new staircase. She wrote to Joseph's mother-in-law – 'Citizeness Clary, rue Gay, Marseilles' – asking for red and yellow wallpaper, white window cord, four armchairs and a sofa in damask, and three small clocks. Fesch, grown very pompous, joined Letizia and began buying property. Brother and sister clearly intended to spend the rest of their days in their beloved island.

General Bonaparte's victories were consolidated by the Treaty of Campo Formio, dictated by him in October 1797. The Emperor ceded Belgium and the left bank of the Rhine, besides recognizing the Cisalpine Republic, the puppet state which the French had set up in place of the former regimes at Milan, Modena and Bologna. The Directors presented the Army of Italy with a flag bearing the inscription

This army has taken 150,000 prisoners; captured 170 enemy colours, 540 cannon and howitzers, 5 bridges, 9 ships of the line, 12 frigates, 12 corvettes and 18 galleys; given liberty to the peoples of the North of Italy, Corcyra, the Aegean Sea and Ithaca; sent to Paris the masterpieces of Michelangelo, Guercino, Titian, Paolo Veronese, Correggio Albano, the Carracci, Raphael . . . triumphed in 18 pitched battles; and fought 67 actions.

When Napoleon returned to Paris on 5 December he was given a Roman triumph. The street where he lived in Joséphine's little house, the rue Chantereine, was renamed rue de la Victoire. More important, even if he had made his troops suffer dreadfully – one French soldier scrawled on an Italian wall, 'To be a real fighting man one needs the heart of a lion, the feet of a goat and the stomach of an ant' – he had won their undying loyalty.

His position seemed unassailable. Another royalist threat – there had been a royalist majority in the autumn elections – had been pre-empted by the *coup* of Fructidor (September), which purged reactionary deputies and re-enacted the laws against émigrés. From a distance he had played a major part in organizing the *coup*, sending Augereau to carry it out, and he had been delighted by its success. Now that he was back in Paris he was lionized in the salons, impressing everyone by a combination of soldierly bluntness and careful charm. Joséphine was in her element.

She was soon in trouble with her husband. Hippolyte Charles was working for the merchant house of Bodin of Lyons and lodged at the senior partner's house in Paris. In March 1798 Joseph informed Napoleon, no doubt with relish, that not only was Joséphine in contact with Charles again but that she had procured a purveyor's contract with the Army of Italy for his firm. Hysterically, she denied everything, offering her husband a divorce if he wanted one and threatening suicide. He believed her.

The General's next task was to have been the invasion of England, but in February 1798 he reported that such an operation would be impracticable. Instead he proposed to occupy Egypt and strike at England's wealth; from Egypt the French would be able to disrupt English communications with India. The Directory were impressed and he sailed with an expedition in May. *En route* he captured Malta, taking its knights by surprise. In July he occupied Cairo. However, on 1 August at the battle of the Nile Nelson blew the French fleet out of the water off Aboukir. Bonaparte and France's best troops were trapped in a distant land. His mother did not despair. 'My son will not die miserably in Egypt as his enemies are hoping,' she declared. 'I know that a higher destiny lies before him.'

Joseph, who had seen him off at Toulon in May, was joined by Lucien at Paris in April 1798. Now himself a deputy for a Corsican district and eager to take part in the Five Hundred's debates, he moved into Joseph's house. Louis had been going to the devil amid the capital's more vicious pleasures, so Napoleon had dragged him off to Egypt, much against his will. Eugène de Beauharnais, Joséphine's son, was also with the Army of Egypt, as a *sous-lieutenant*. His sister Hortense was at school at Saint-Germain with Caroline Bonaparte. It was the smartest academy for young ladies in France and run by Marie Antoinette's former woman-of-the-bedchamber, the excellent Mme Campan.

Joséphine, who had never ceased to see Hippolyte Charles in secret, renewed her torrid affair with him now that her terrifying husband was out of the way. Supporting himself by shady business deals (from which he eventually made a fortune) Charles was delighted to rediscover a rich mistress, even if she was nine years older than he. A swarthy little man with jet-black hair, who dressed to impress his women friends – Joséphine said she was convinced 'no man before him ever really knew how to tie a cravat' – he was an accomplished womanizer and unfailingly cheerful, very different from a gloomy Corsican. All the smart ladies of the day, including Mmes Récamier and Tallien, fell for him despite his provincial manners. His protectress introduced him to the most useful people in Paris society. Needless to say, her in-laws saw to it that rumours of his wife's infidelity reached General Bonaparte amid the Egyptian sands.

'Women! Deceiving me like this!' he shouted. 'Woe betide them – I'll exterminate her whole band of puppies and fops. As for her, divorce!' At the end of July 1798 he wrote to Joseph, 'I am suffering great personal unhappiness – the veil has at last fallen from my eyes. . . . It is a wretched state to be in, to have all one's thoughts centred on another person.' (He seems to have been regretting Désirée.) His stepson Eugène wrote to warn his mother, adding, 'You know, Mama, that I don't believe it, but the General is certainly very upset. However, he's friendlier than ever towards me. It looks as though he's trying to tell me by the way he behaves that children aren't responsible for their mother's faults.' Napoleon's letter and Eugène's were intercepted by English ships and, on the Cabinet's instructions, were published in London.

Napoleon consoled himself as best he could. No less than six Circassian ladies – reputedly the most beautiful in the Mameluke harems – proved on inspection to be too fat for his taste. Luckily he found a young Frenchwoman, a cheerful little blonde with hair down to her knees and violet eyes, Mme Fourès – nicknamed 'Cleopatra' by the troops – whose rounded form looked particularly well in naval uniform. 'Bellilotte', as Bonaparte called her, had spent her youth in Paris selling hats. As David did with Uriah the Hittite, he tried to get rid of her husband by sending him on dangerous missions, though Lieutenant Fourès returned from them with embarrassing frequency. The General ordered Eugène, who was becoming a hard-working and most useful officer, to act as Cleopatra's escort when she drove out in her carriage.

In his absence Joseph was head of the family. Rich and influential, he was much sought after. However, he took little part in politics – quite content with a regime so indulgent to speculators – and devoted himself to increasing an already large fortune. He spent nearly 100,000 francs on purchasing and renovating an hôtel in the rue du Rocher. Near what is now the Gare Saint-Lazare but in those days still in the fields, it had been built by Jacques-Ange Gabriel (architect of the Petit Trianon) for Mme Grandi, one of the stars of the Opéra, on behalf of a rich banker who had perished during the Revolution. In October 1798 he bought a château and estate of 589 hectares at Mortefontaine near Chantilly, paying 258,000 francs – its previous owner, the banker Duruey, had been guillotined. It included a park, woodlands and ornamental lakes, Citizen Bonaparte adding a theatre, an orangery with grottoes, and statuary. Lucien also acquired a château, Le Plessis-Chamant near Senlis, as did Pauline and Leclerc at Montgobert in the Aisne.

Napoleon was none the less the richest member of the clan. He had extracted countless millions from the treasuries of Northern Italy, which he placed in secret deposits. On his instructions Joseph bought Malmaison for his wife. The château, on the banks of the Seine to the west of Paris near Bougival, was charming with an elegant home farm and pretty gardens covering over 20 hectares. At reckless expense Joséphine speedily turned it into a love-nest for herself and the amusing Charles. Glasshouses and artificial lakes were constructed, together with aviaries and a private zoo containing lions, zebras, chimpanzees, kangaroos and flying squirrels. She also created the first English rose-garden in France, with 197 varieties. Her ensuing debts were enormous, compounded by Joseph, managing her financial affairs at his brother's request, who kept her short of ready money and stole 30 million francs out of her allowance – or so she complained to Barras, still a friend. Joseph avoided her as much as he could, while keeping her under constant surveillance.

Joseph resigned his seat in the Five Hundred to pay more attention to business matters, but would always take time off from money-making to help with family problems. In the summer of 1798 he received a further letter from Egypt. 'I do hope Désirée will be happy if she marries Bernadotte,' wrote Napoleon. 'She certainly deserves to be.' General Bernadotte, a prominent member of the Jacobin *Club du Manège*, appeared to have a considerable future in politics – in July 1799 he would be appointed Minister of War. Tall and slight, thick black hair surmounting a colourless face with a huge hook nose, it was said that he had Moorish blood. Despite having attended a Gascon village school and spent his formative years in a sergeants' mess, he had polished up his manners, though he spoke with a thick country accent like Murat. He was able, energetic, ruthless and a good liar but with plenty of charm, one of nature's political soldiers. Désirée, clever and ambitious, was clearly attracted by a man who obviously had a distinguished career in front of him. (She had been very upset when she heard of Napoleon's marriage, writing, 'You have made my life a misery, yet I am weak enough to forgive you.') Joseph approved highly of this useful match which would neutralize a potential rival of his brother by bringing him into the clan. The couple were married on 17 August 1798, the wedding being attended by Joseph and Lucien and their wives.

Louis returned from Egypt in March 1799 after a hair-raising voyage during which his ship was chased by British frigates. On the way he found time to visit Corsica and spend three weeks with his mother, who was recovering from a bout of malaria. He persuaded her to accompany him to Paris where Joseph placed an entire floor of the smart new house in the rue du Rocher at her disposal. Apart from a brief visit many years later, Letizia had left Corsica for ever. Perhaps she was relieved to go – the island was still bitterly divided between former Paolists and French supporters, the name of Bonaparte arousing real hatred in certain quarters.

Paris too was far from peaceful. Politically the Directory was lurching from side to side like a ship in a storm – turning against Jacobins just as it had turned on royalists. It had lost the magnificent position secured at Campo Formio, encouraging England, the Empire, Russia, the Two Sicilies, Piedmont and Turkey to declare war. At home, finances were in chaos, inflation causing many bankruptcies, while the poor suffered far more misery than before the Revolution. (In 1794 the gold franc was quoted at 75 paper francs – at the end of 1795 it was worth 2,000 paper francs and by 1798 80,000.) In August 1799 a forced levy on the rich of 100 million francs infuriated the new ruling class. Panic-stricken, the Directors closed the *Club du Manège* and dismissed the government's Jacobin ministers – including Bernadotte. The Directory was now a regime with very few friends indeed. As early as September 1797 Napoleon had hinted to Talleyrand and Sieyès that it could not last long. Joseph and Lucien had come to share his opinion. In speech after speech in the Assembly, though with more caution than in his Jacobin days, Lucien constantly criticized the Directory and was elected President of the Five Hundred.

Suddenly, in October 1799, news reached the Bonapartes that their chief had returned from Egypt and landed at Fréjus. Napoleon had had an even more exciting voyage than Louis, only just escaping from two blockading English squadrons. *En route* he too had stopped briefly at Corsica, where Uncle Fesch obligingly changed his Egyptian gold sequins into French paper francs. Joseph, Lucien and Louis rushed south to meet him. On the way back to Paris they brought him up to date with the political situation. Abroad an Austro-Russian army had entered Milan, General Jourdan was being driven back across the Rhine and the British were about to invade Holland. At home the Directory was on the verge of collapse.

They also confirmed Joséphine's infidelity. When the General reached the rue de la Victoire early in the morning of 16 October his wife was not there. Alerted by Fouché, she had driven to meet him but had missed him on the road. His mother, sisters and sisters-in-law called on him at once, urging him to move to the rue du Rocher – Letizia spoke of *la putana*, the whore. Fortunately for Joséphine he declined and stayed at the rue de la Victoire. On reaching home two days later she found herself locked out. Well-experienced in handling unreasonable men – though it is hard to imagine any human being more terrifying than an angry Napoleon – she did not lose her nerve. Lying prostrate in tears on the staircase outside, she sent in Eugène and Hortense to plead for her: 'Do not abandon our mother, she will break her heart.' Her husband, nothing if not a Latin, succumbed. When Lucien called the following morning he found her in bed with his brother, beaming. The reconciliation was complete. The family were furious, particularly Pauline and Letizia, though the latter was wise enough to say nothing. They had all hoped for a divorce and Elisa was so rude and spiteful that Joséphine could never again bear the sight of her. Only Joseph's sweet-natured wife, Julie, took no part in the unpleasantness. But Joséphine had triumphed. In any case there was much to distract a difficult husband.

Within a fortnight of General Bonaparte's return to Paris Lucien arranged a secret meeting at his house in the rue Verte with the Director Sieyès, who wanted a *coup d'état* which would install a new and firmer form of government. Sieyès was supported by Talleyrand and Fouché, a villainous trio of ex-clergymen who knew a real soldier when they saw one. They had considered using Bernadotte, but decided that 'while he looks like an eagle, he is in fact a goose'. In any case, Bernadotte was too much of a Jacobin (though he also flirted with the royalists). Napoleon himself had the impression that the Jacobin General did not like him, suspecting that 'if he grows ambitious, he will try anything'. Understandably, Napoleon was nervous; if the *coup* failed he would lose his head, and his family would be ruined. However, Sieyès assured him that the Ancients, the upper chamber, were going to co-operate, while Lucien, as President of the Five Hundred, promised that his chamber would meet at Saint-Cloud to eliminate any threat from the Paris mob. Barras was to be trapped into resigning.

Bonaparte was still uneasy. Sieyès was his pet aversion, while the veteran revolutionary referred to him as 'that insolent little man'. It was essential to obtain the generals' support and, if most of them gave it immediately, the Jacobin Bernadotte refused to join in what he called a rebellion. He had already urged Napoleon's arrest for deserting his command in Egypt. Joseph, who had already played a useful part in lobbying busily but discreetly for allies, apparently persuaded his brother-in-law not to warn the Directors of the impending *coup* – when the day came he took him out to lunch in the country outside Paris so that he was unaware of what was happening. The ordinary soldiers' loyalties lay with Bonaparte. As soon as they had learnt of his return, three dragoon regiments of the Paris garrison petitioned for the honour of being reviewed by him and officer after officer called to assure him of his personal support. Napoleon took the plunge, though throughout the *coup* he carried a brace of pistols.

On 18 Brumaire (9 November) the Council of Ancients, persuaded by Lucien that there was going to be a popular rising in Paris, obligingly adjourned the meeting of both chambers from the Tuileries to Saint-Cloud on the following day. In addition, it appointed General Bonaparte GOC of all troops in the capital, with orders to protect Saint-Cloud. On 19 Brumaire Napoleon came very close to failure. He was not accustomed to dealing with noisy politicians who shouted back. His speech to the Ancients went badly enough, but it was still worse when he addressed the Five Hundred. He was greeted with yells of 'Down with the tyrant! Down with the dictator! Outlaw him!' The General could not make himself heard. One of the deputies hit him while another threatened him with a pistol. He turned pale and, almost fainting, left the hall to take refuge with his soldiers outside. Lucien saved the day. As President he exercised his right to call on armed intervention to deal with unruly behaviour. Drums rolled, then grenadiers with fixed bayonets, led by Murat and Pauline's husband Leclerc, burst in and forced the deputies to jump out of the windows into the garden where they fled through the dusk. A cowed remnant of the members of both chambers met at nine o'clock the same evening under Lucien's chairmanship and passed a motion which appointed Citizens Bonaparte, Sieyès and Ducos as a provisional 'Consulate' in place of the Directory.

Mme Permon, despite her rejection of Napoleon, had again become a close friend of Letizia and her daughters. Mme Permon's daughter, Laure – Junot's future wife, better known as the Duchesse d'Abrantès – tells us that on the evening of 19 Brumaire they had gone to the Opéra Comique (then the Théâtre Feydeau). Suddenly the actors stopped and the man playing the principal part came to the front of the stage and announced in a very loud voice, 'Citizens, General Bonaparte has just escaped assassination at Saint-Cloud by traitors to their country.' Pauline immediately gave a piercing scream and burst into tears. After she had calmed down, the party hastened to Lucien's house, where they were told what had happened. The news reached Caroline at her school in Saint-Germain in an even more dramatic way. Though she was only seventeen General Murat was wooing her. He sent troopers with a letter telling her of the coup: 'Bonaparte and Murat have saved France.' Arriving after dark, their horses' hooves and clanking sabres terrified the poor head-mistress, Mme Campan, who had dreadful memories of the Terror. 'Imagine the effect of four horse grenadiers knocking on the door of a girls' school in the middle of the night', says her schoolfriend Hortense de Beauharnais in her memoirs, 'but Caroline saw it as a proof of love.'

Letizia and her daughters can scarcely have realized the implications of what had taken place. A new constitution was to come into effect in December, in which Sieyès confidently expected to play the leading part. He was mistaken, following Barras into gilded obscurity almost at once. At thirty Napoleon Bonaparte had become First Consul and supreme ruler of France. The Bonaparte family had acquired semi-regal status.

4

Almost a Royal Family – T█

'It was at the Luxembourg, in the salons of wl█
did the honours so well, that the word *Madam*█
again. This first return to traditional French c█
a number of sensitive republicans, but things █
carried still further at the Tuileries by the intro█
Votre Altesse on state occasions and of *Monseigneur* in the
family circle.'

BOURRIENNE, *Mémoires sur Napoléon*

'All Napoleon's family then possessed fine country houses,
which they filled with guests. Joseph had Mortefontaine,
Lucien Plessis, Mme Leclerc Montgobert. At Mortefontaine
parties on the lakes, public readings, billiards, literature,
ghost stories sometimes genuinely mysterious, a perfect ease
and liberty, lent charms to the passing hour.'

DUCHESSE D'ABRANTÈS, *Mémoires*

In theory there were three Consuls, in practice only one – the First Consul.
An elaborate constitution could not hide the fact that France was now a
military dictatorship. However, Napoleon knew just what the French
wanted: a return to the Catholic faith, an end to the brigandage terrorizing
the countryside, and sound finance. He was assisted by two of the
shrewdest politicians living, Fouché and Talleyrand. He retained the
former as Minister of Police and made the latter his Foreign Minister.
Charles-Maurice de Talleyrand, once Bishop of Autun, was to serve him
for eight years and as long as this white-faced, club-footed renegade
supported a regime its durability was beyond question.

Bourrienne, Napoleon's friend and private secretary during this period,
is the only close witness who has left an account of how his master
transformed the Consulate into a monarchy. He tells us: 'To sleep at the
Tuileries in the bedroom of the Kings of France was all that Bonaparte
wanted, since everything else would follow in due course', adding that he
quickly 'began to find the Luxembourg too small for him.' (The
Luxembourg had been the Directors' official residence.) It took the First
Consul precisely a hundred days to transfer his residence. Gradually the
trappings and etiquette of royalty were reintroduced. He adopted a
spectacular red velvet suit as the uniform of his office – previously velvet

45

banned, as undemocratic – while the Consular Guard gave him
al salute. In Bourrienne's words, 'It was Bonaparte's constant aim
face the republic, even in the slightest trifles, and to prepare things in
uch a way that when the customs and ceremonies of monarchy had been
restored, only the word for the regime itself would need to be changed.'
Indeed he went so far as to tell Joséphine what she should wear,
frequently expressing disapproval of low-necked dresses because they
were insufficiently regal. Yet Napoleon was still dazzled by his own
success. During the first few days he spent at Malmaison at the beginning
of the Consulate he amused himself by adding up the little estate's
revenue, about 8,000 francs a year. 'Not bad', he commented. 'But to live
here one needs an income of at least 30,000 francs.'

Bourrienne records that he never saw the First Consul happier than
when in Malmaison's pretty gardens. He played leapfrog with Eugène
and Hortense. The latter had begun to overcome her dislike of him,
though at the age of thirteen – just after he had become her stepfather –
she had written to ask him why he had bothered to marry, since he had
such a low opinion of women. The rapprochement was watched by
spiteful eyes.

Needless to say, it was a period in which the Bonaparte family rose
spectacularly in the world. Its members' hatred of Joséphine increased as
her husband's affection for her grew. They had reason to be frightened –
she was in favour of restoring the monarchy as it had been before 1789, of
Napoleon's playing the role of General Monck (who had restored the
Stuarts in Britain) and becoming Constable of France. This prospect was
dreaded by the Bonapartes, who hoped to become princes and princesses.
They continued to build their enormous fortunes: real estate, works of art
and diamonds. The head of the clan began to distribute the spoils of office
as soon as he attained supreme power. Joseph was created a Senator and
appointed one of three plenipotentiaries then negotiating with the United
States, Lucien was made Minister of the Interior, and Louis was
promoted to colonel in a dragoon regiment. Murat, now a member of the
family, was given command of the Consular Guard and of an Army.

Joachim Murat, thirty-two in 1799, was undeniably a glamorous figure
with thick, jet-black curls, dark-blue eyes and good features marred only
by a coarse, sensual mouth. Deeply respected by his men, more often
than not he charged with them in the front rank. Unfortunately, despite a
certain cunning, he was far from intelligent, while a streak of the draper's
assistant remained all too obvious: he was unmistakably vulgar besides
speaking with a strong Gascon accent. Like Bernadotte he too had been
an ardent Jacobin. When Robespierre fell he had been cashiered and
arrested as a terrorist. As late as December 1796 he was complaining

about the prevalence of aristocratic manners and titles in the Army of Italy, in a letter to Barras – whom, with characteristic obtuseness, he regarded as the coming man. But he had re-established himself and cultivated the Bonapartes carefully, including Joséphine who encouraged his pursuit of Caroline and allowed them to meet at the rue de la Victoire. The First Consul had wanted his younger sister to marry a general who would be of political use, such as Moreau or Lannes. Moreover, Joachim was a little too common for the supposed enemy of class prejudice. 'Murat is an innkeeper's son,' grumbled Bonaparte. 'In the high position to which fortune has raised me, I simply cannot let my family marry into a family like that.' His brothers agreed. His attempts to dissuade her show that as yet he still did not understand young women. 'One day you'll learn just what it is to sleep with a man who has no idea of manners, when you find yourself alone with him without your nightdress and the man is there stark naked', he warned her.

In the end Joséphine, hoping that she might acquire an ally, persuaded Napoleon to give his consent. The wedding, a civil ceremony, took place at the Luxembourg on 18 January 1800 in the presence of the entire Bonaparte clan including even the Bernadottes – Louis alone being absent, on active service with his regiment. There was a reception at Mortefontaine the following day. Caroline's brothers gave her 40,000 francs in gold as a dowry, together with an elaborate trousseau and jewels which cost 12,000 francs. Joachim immediately began to emulate his in-laws. He bought an estate at Villiers near Neuilly-sur-Seine in 1800 and another, Motte-Sainte-Héraye in the Deux-Sèvres, in 1801 – paying 470,000 francs for the latter. Next year he bought a magnificent town house in Paris, the Hôtel Thélusson – built for a millionaire banker before the Revolution – between the rue de la Victoire and the rue de Provence, and one of the capital's finest mansions. Fesch, who now handled his business interests, had it done up at vast expense. 'But don't let this frighten you since you can always make an excellent re-sale', he told his new nephew after they had spent half a million francs. General Murat can hardly have saved such sums out of his pay – some of it undoubtedly came from his brother-in-law, while he seems to have taken substantial bribes in return for government posts and contracts in the Cisalpine Republic.

Napoleon's brothers were now in positions where they could demonstrate their aptitude for public affairs. They had none. Joseph, fat, round-shouldered and undistinguished looking, was much more interested in his investments. In 1801 he would be sent as a plenipotentiary to negotiate both a peace with the Austrians and a concordat with the Church – all the real work was done by professional diplomats. He was none the less swollen with self-importance. The First Consul offered to make him President of the Cisalpine Republic, with Milan for a capital, but he made so many conditions that the offer was withdrawn. He was perfectly happy in Paris, where he held court and patronized men of letters. In 1801 he moved from the rue du Rocher to the Hôtel Marbeuf for which he paid 60,000 francs – not only was it the former town house of the Marbeuf family, patrons of his Corsican childhood, but, with a garden which ran as far as the Champs-Elysées, it was an excellent speculation.

Lucien was a disaster as Minister of the Interior, leaving all the work to his civil servants – he had a stamp engraved with his signature so that they could sign documents for him – and constantly criticizing his brother's policies. When his poor little wife died in May 1800 he shut himself up in his country house and refused to deal with any official business for a fortnight. His instincts were essentially those of a third-rate politician with a weakness for inept intrigue. At the end of 1800 he published a pamphlet, *Parallèle entre César, Cromwell et Bonaparte*, which argued that in the event of the First Consul's death he should be succeeded by one of his brothers. Napoleon had every intention of establishing a dynasty but did not want to show his hand quite so soon. He was furious with Lucien, and even more so for having had the pamphlet printed on his Ministry's official paper and for calling Fouché – the police chief, who had drawn his attention to the pamphlet – a 'bloodstained cutthroat' in his presence. He demanded his resignation, whereupon their mother intervened. In consequence Lucien was appointed French Ambassador to Madrid the day after his resignation and allowed to take his best friend Bacciochi, Elisa's husband, as his secretary. For, perhaps surprisingly, of all his sisters he was closest to Mme Bacciochi. 'In those days I loved my sister Elisa tenderly', Lucien writes in his memoirs. With uncharacteristic kindness she had nursed his wife Christine on her deathbed and had then been a mother to their two small daughters. She returned his affection since it was he who had achieved the difficult task of finding her a spouse.

In Spain Lucien kept a magnificent establishment and gave sumptuous parties whose ostentation impressed even the Spaniards. He acquired a mistress with an unsavoury reputation, a German adventuress who called herself the Marquesa de Santa Cruz. He accepted suspiciously lavish gifts from the Spaniards. The King presented him with his portrait, telling him to unpack it personally in private; inside the case were diamonds worth half a million francs. In April 1800 Lucien angered his brother by suggesting, at the King's prompting, that the First Consul should divorce Joséphine and marry his daughter the Infanta Isabella. ('Why should I get rid of my excellent wife', Napoleon asked on another occasion, 'just because I've become a greater man than I used to be? If I'd been imprisoned or exiled, she would have stood by me.') Lucien gave further cause for annoyance by allowing Portugal quite unjustifiable concessions in a treaty which he negotiated in the same year, after receiving still more diamonds from the Portuguese. At the end of 1801 he abandoned his post, returning to Paris without permission. He then sold his diamonds in Amsterdam, investing the proceeds in London and in the United States. He now possessed an enormous fortune. He left public life and took the huge Hôtel de Brienne in the rue Saint-Dominique (today the French War Office) at an astronomical rent of 12,000 francs a year, where he held court rather like Joseph. His highly unpresentable mistress was installed in the country at Le Plessis-Chamant, Elisa paying frequent visits there to lend respectability – Lucien was said to be fonder of her than of la Santa Cruz.

If we are to go by portraits, Lucien was tall and swarthy with an oddly small head, his nervous little face gazing out short-sightedly. He genuinely believed that 18 Brumaire had been all his own work and that the First Consul owed his exalted position entirely to him. Yet since then his sole contribution to his brother's regime had been to identify those in the assemblies who opposed it and to deliver aggressively propagandist speeches on state occasions. Only his women folk – who admittedly found him most attractive – really thought that Lucien had ability.

Lucien was one of Joséphine's most outspoken and most venomous enemies. She responded by supplying Fouché, her old paymaster, with details of her brother-in-law's more discreditable activities in order to undermine his standing in Napoleon's eyes. She also warned her husband constantly against taking Lucien's pernicious advice. Her discreet counter-offensive undoubtedly contributed to his enforced resignation as Minister of the Interior in 1800. The clan blamed 'that widow' for setting brother against brother and hated her more than ever. They never ceased intriguing to persuade the First Consul to divorce her, but were hampered by his belief that he could not father a child, an impression which was sedulously encouraged by his wife.

The younger Bonaparte brothers were turning out to be no more effectual than Joseph and Lucien, though at least they had the excuse of youth. Louis, now a general, was constantly on leave on grounds of ill health, dabbling in literature or simply day-dreaming. He suffered from a vicious and undiagnosed disease, probably gonorrheal in origin, inducing rheumatic attacks which would eventually cripple him. He was no more healthy mentally than he was physically, being afflicted by fits of jealousy and delusions of persecution which, it has been suggested, may have sprung from suppressed homosexuality. Napoleon nevertheless continued to nurse great hopes of him, genuinely believing that he might one day become his successor even if admitting reluctantly that despite heavy-lidded good looks, there was 'something vacuous' in Louis's appearance – *quelque chose de niais*.

Persuaded by Joséphine trying to strengthen her own position, the First Consul decided most unwisely that his stepdaughter Hortense de Beauharnais – who had grown up into a beautiful and sweet-natured though somewhat feckless woman – would make Louis an excellent wife. Horrified by the prospect, Louis took refuge at his lonely château of Baillon, deep in the woods outside Paris. In his own ineffectual, complicated way he was deeply in love with Hortense's poverty-stricken and unsuitable young cousin, Emilie de Beauharnais, whose stepfather was a negro. Napoleon hastily married her off to a favourite staff officer, Major Chamans-Lavalette, an ex-priest, which made Louis more miserable and self-pitying than ever. In the end this irritable hypochondriac with perpetually gloomy eyes was forced to marry the unhappy eighteen-year-old Hortense, who accepted him to please her mother to whom she was devoted. She had had flirtations with other young men who, understandably, she found far more attractive. In a last attempt to stop the marriage Lucien informed Louis that she was expecting a baby by Napoleon.

The ceremony took place on 4 January 1802 in the salon of the house in the rue de la Victoire and was conducted by the Papal Legate, Cardinal Caprara, Archbishop of Milan. Hortense was very pale – she had been crying – and her pallor was accentuated by the white wedding dress, a bouquet of orange blossoms and a single string of very fine pearls (a present from her mother). Joséphine, who may have felt a certain guilt, wept throughout and continued to do so for days after. When the service was over, Murat and Caroline stepped forward to have their own marriage blessed by the Cardinal. 'This double ceremony made a most disagreeable impression on me,' says Hortense. 'The other couple were so happy. They were so much in love with each other.' The whole clan was present, save for Jérôme away in America, and all were angry at Louis for marrying a Beauharnais, especially Caroline, who in any case was always jealous of her old schoolfriend. Joseph, Lucien, Elisa and she were one day to be proved right in seeing it as a victory for Joséphine, whose future grandson was to be the Emperor Napoleon III. The First Consul gave the bridegroom (whose declared wealth was already 180,000 francs) the house in the rue de la Victoire, and the bride a dowry of 250,000 francs to which Joséphine added another 100,000. Hortense's new sisters-in-law must have been very well aware that this was far larger than their own dowries.

Jérôme, seventeen in 1802, fresh-faced with curly black hair but with too short a neck and a thin, mean mouth, was the spoilt brat he remained for his entire life, yet at this time the First Consul could deny him nothing. Since the age of fourteen he had been going on wild shopping sprees in Paris, the bills being paid by his brother or Joséphine with unflagging good humour. After Marengo he asked Napoleon for the sword he had worn during the battle and was given it at once. Appointed a subaltern in the cavalry of the Consular Guard, he promptly fought a duel with another young officer and received a bullet in the chest which the doctors were unable to extract. (It was taken out only in the reign of his nephew Napoleon III.) After a long convalescence, spent partly at the Tuileries, his brother made him enter the navy. 'Get up the rigging,' Napoleon exhorted him in a letter. 'Learn all the ship's ropes. When you put into port at the end of this voyage I want to hear that you've become just as handy as any salted jack tar.' Jérôme was eight months at sea on Admiral Ganteaume's flagship during 1801, and when the Admiral captured a British man-of-war was sent on board to receive the enemy captain's sword. Returning to Paris he was treated as a hero, constantly lecturing the First Consul on maritime warfare. He then went to serve in the Caribbean. At Martinique he ran into his brother-in-law General Leclerc, Pauline's husband, who was *en route* for the island of San Domingo (today the Dominican Republic and Haiti). The General was scandalized to see the young naval officer wearing a dashing hussar uniform of sky blue and scarlet.

Another member of the clan was prospering rather more than he expected. On receiving the news of 18 Brumaire Bernadotte had fled in disguise and hidden with Désirée – dressed as a boy – for three days in the forest of Sénart. There was good reason for the Jacobin General's alarm. After the *coup* Bonaparte complained bitterly to Bourrienne, 'That Bernadotte! He wanted to betray me. Yet his wife has plenty of influence over him. I thought I had done quite enough to win him over – you were there and you know. I am sorry that I tried so hard to please him. He will have to leave Paris.' Nevertheless Bernadotte went unscathed – he now belonged to the clan. Soon he was in command of the Army of the West, and a senator with lucrative emoluments. The First Consul became godfather to Désirée's son, choosing for him the outlandish name of Oscar, which he took from his favourite epic, Macpherson's *Ossian*.

Napoleon's first priority for France was reconciliation. He abolished the laws against émigrés, allowing them to return and hold public office and serve in the army, while at the same time guaranteeing security of tenure to those who had purchased confiscated property. A royalist rising in the West was speedily suppressed, but everyone who surrendered was treated with hitherto unheard of clemency. The First Consul's publicly declared aim was, 'No more Jacobins, moderates or royalists, only Frenchmen.' Churches were reopened, all priests in prison being released. Robbery and brigandage were put down efficiently and mercilessly. He began the country's financial salvation, replacing worthless banknotes by a sound gold and silver currency and establishing the Bank of France.

Abroad he did his best to make peace. Unfortunately the Austrians were determined to keep Northern Italy, the British intent on driving the French out of Egypt. On the Rhine the very tough and able General Moreau was holding back the Austrians, but in Italy the outnumbered Masséna was besieged in Genoa and would obviously have to surrender in the not too distant future. Bonaparte decided that only he himself could save the Italian front. He crossed the Alps in May 1800 through the snows of the Great St Bernard Pass, coming down behind the enemy commander Baron Melas and cutting off his retreat. The Austrians were taken completely by surprise when Napoleon entered Milan. He dispersed his army to hold the river crossings and prevent the enemy from escaping, whereupon Melas, an experienced and formidable opponent, concentrated his own forces so that when he attacked the French on 14 June near the farmhouse of Marengo it was with over 30,000 men. Napoleon had less than 24,000 troops and far fewer cannon. Despite some heroic fighting, in particular by his 800 Consular Guardsmen, he was very nearly overwhelmed. Just in time, General Desaix arrived with 5,000 men to turn defeat into victory at the cost of his own life. The First Consul returned to an ecstatic reception in Paris. His generals were to drive the Austrians out of Italy by the end of the year.

After Moreau defeated the Austrians decisively at Hohenlinden and the French reached the gates of Vienna, the Emperor sued for peace. At Lunéville in February 1801 he accepted terms similar to those negotiated at Campo Formio, besides recognizing France's puppet states, the Batavian (Dutch), Cisalpine (Italian) and Swiss Republics. The English were now isolated and finding the war alarmingly expensive, while the French troops in Egypt had been overwhelmed and were no longer a threat. Accordingly, in March 1802 England made peace at Amiens, Joseph acting as France's chief plenipotentiary.

Joseph could not resist speculating on the rise of government stock, which he believed would take place on the announcement of peace. The reverse took place and he lost so much money that, according to Bourrienne, 'he could not satisfy the engagements in which his greedy and silly speculations had involved him'. The sum was so large that not even his brother could lend it to him. Talleyrand saved the day by suggesting an adroit manipulation of the state sinking fund.

It was the first time for ten years that France had not been at war. Another welcome peace came into effect shortly afterwards. The Concordat with Rome, while giving security to those who had bought clerical property during the Revolution, arranged for the clergy to be paid by the state; the state would nominate bishops, and priests had to pray for the First Consul in their services. The versatile Fesch, who had resumed his priesthood – abandoning gambling, dancing and going to the theatre, though not speculations – played an important part in the negotiations and became Archbishop of Lyons in 1802. The following year he was created a cardinal and appointed France's Ambassador to Rome.

Napoleon did not leave the New World out of his calculations. He tried to recover San Domingo (modern Haiti) in the Antilles, France's richest colony before 1789, sending his brother-in-law Leclerc against the black dictator Toussaint l'Ouverture. But although Toussaint was defeated and captured, the French were eventually driven out of San Domingo for good. Napoleon also sold Louisiana to the United States for 80 million francs, in later days justifying the sale with the words, 'It is in the interests of France that America should be strong.' In reality President Thomas Jefferson had made him understand that if the French stayed in Louisiana, the United States would join Britain in the war which was about to break out. Undoubtedly he had hoped, if only briefly, for a French Empire in the Americas. However, these far-off reverses scarcely detracted from the Consulate's popularity at home.

The First Consul was fonder than ever of his chastened – if still irredeemably pleasure-loving – consort, though he would never again trust her alone with another man. She was under Fouché's constant surveillance, so much so that sometimes she fancied herself a prisoner in the Tuileries. Bonaparte himself, introduced by her to the pleasures of physical love, was sleeping with a variety of actresses procured by his valet Constant, in particular the great *tragédienne*, Mme Georges, whom he first saw on the stage of the Comédie-Française in the role of Clytemnestra. Even so, he continued to relax at Malmaison.

Meanwhile his wife ran up astronomical debts. Talleyrand informed him that creditors were beginning to grumble, that there were stories about her extravagance all over Paris. Napoleon ordered Bourrienne to find out just how much she owed. Joséphine told him to say it was 600,000 francs though it was well over a million. She explained that she did not dare admit the full sum to her husband. 'I can't do it, Bourrienne. I know him. I couldn't face his rage.' She was said to order 900 dresses a year – at her giddiest, Marie Antoinette had bought no more than 170 –

and a thousand pairs of gloves. Bourrienne discovered a bill for 38 hats in one month alone, another of 1,800 francs for feathers and another of 800 for scent. He persuaded the tradesmen to settle for half but she was incorrigible. She purchased a superb necklace of fine pearls, once the property of the late Queen, to replace a diamond one which Napoleon had given to Caroline as a wedding present. At first she was too frightened to wear them. When eventually she put them on, he immediately asked, 'Where did you get those pearls? I never saw them before.' She answered, 'You've seen them a dozen times – it's the necklace the Cisalpine Republic gave me, which I always wear in my hair.' He believed her. Bourrienne adds that 'her hopeless extravagance caused permanent disorder in her household'. Nevertheless she was the perfect hostess for the First Consul's semi-royal court. Metternich, who met her a few years later, observes that not only was she extremely kind-hearted, but she possessed 'quite extraordinary social tact'. She had a remarkable memory for names and faces.

Bonaparte was obsessed by the Bourbons. Bourrienne tells us that whenever the exiled princes were mentioned 'he would experience a sense of inward dread and speak of the need to build a wall of brass between France and them'. Although her husband seldom listened to her advice, Joséphine was brave enough to contact the princes secretly. For a time the beautiful Duchesse de Guiche acted as a link between the Bourbons and Mme Bonaparte, dancing graceful attendance at the Tuileries and Malmaison, but her mission was discovered and she was banished. Napoleon did not object to his wife's politics nor to their being public knowledge – he hoped they would keep the royalists quiet. Joséphine genuinely wanted a restoration. It was not simply that she cherished ambitions of shining at a refurbished Versailles as a duchess and wife of the Constable of France. She feared that if her husband founded a throne and dynasty as his family were urging then she might be divorced to make way for a bride who could provide him with an heir – as she herself could not. In fact from the very beginning of the Consulate Napoleon was planning to set up a new monarchy. But he had to proceed cautiously for fear of arousing both royalist and republican opposition.

At first Louis XVIII thought that the First Consul would summon him home. In February 1800 he wrote to Bonaparte, 'Save France from her own violence. . . . Restore her King. . . . You will always be needed by the state', and, shortly after, 'Fix your reward and say what you want for your friends.' Napoleon answered, 'You must not think of returning to France – you would have to march over a hundred thousand dead bodies.' This was not quite true. Many Frenchmen would have welcomed King Louis back, on terms. The supporters of the Bourbons realized that the First Consul was hostile to their cause and on Christmas Eve 1800 they tried to blow him up with an 'infernal machine' as he was driving to the Théâtre-Français to hear Haydn's *Creation*. Napoleon had gone in front in one coach with three generals while Joséphine, Hortense and Caroline – who was pregnant – followed behind in another. A barrel of gunpowder concealed in a cart exploded in the street killing or maiming thirty-five bystanders. The First Consul was saved by the accident of his coachman's being drunk and driving too fast, the women owed their lives to Joséphine's delaying to rearrange her beautiful cashmere shawl to best effect. At the theatre she and Hortense trembled for the rest of the evening, unable to hide their tears, though tough little Mme Murat showed no emotion whatever. The royalists continued to plot Bonaparte's assassination. He had every reason to fear the Chouans – royalist guerrillas – who held out in Western France for several years.

The regime grew steadily more monarchical. From the start there were military reviews to the music of stirring marches in the Place du Carrousel or on the Champs de Mars, taken by the Consul in his red uniform. The glittering Consular Guard, with its horsemen in yellow, was one of the sights of Paris. Every few days there were dinner-parties for 200 at the Tuileries while balls at the Opéra – a feature of Parisian life under the *ancien régime* – were reintroduced and attended by Joséphine, as they had been by Marie Antoinette. Court dress for men, with silk knee-breeches and cocked hats, reappeared in 1801. In 1802 Napoleon was appointed First Consul for life by a cowed Senate, and then given the right to nominate his successor. In the same year he founded the Legion of Honour to take the place of the old royal orders of knighthood. In 1802 also he became President of the Cisalpine Republic – soon to be the Italian Republic – and Protector of the Helvetic Republic. In 1803 coins bearing his effigy were struck. His birthday, 15 August, became a public holiday. His sword hilt was adorned with Louis XVI's diamonds. His wife acquired ladies-in-waiting recruited from France's noblest families, such as Noailles or La Rochefoucauld, her husband graciously remarking, 'Only that sort of people know how to be servants.'

The entire Bonaparte clan began to put on fresh airs and graces in the emergent court at the Tuileries. Joseph was no longer addressed as 'Citoyen Bonaparte', but as 'Monsieur Joseph' – which was not too dissimilar from the 'Monsieur' accorded to the king's eldest brother under the *ancien régime*. Within two years of 18 Brumaire they were grumbling at the lack of deference paid to them. Lucien told Count Roederer, at a supper-party at Le Plessis-Chamant in December 1801, that

> Joseph is just as disgusted as I am by the way in which he [Napoleon] treats us. My mother is in a state of nerves every time she has to go to the Tuileries. Elisa has to put up with unpleasant remarks at each visit and comes back with tears in her eyes. We are given no sort of precedence at table and have to sit down among the aides-de-camp; and, following the example of the Consul, ambassadors are taking the same liberties. Only recently Azara [the Spanish envoy] relegated Joseph to the end of the table, which is perfectly scandalous. Joseph is less demanding than I am, but he feels it even more.

The Bonapartes took little time in coming to regard themselves as – if not a royal family already – a royal family in waiting.

Yet Napoleon was ill at ease. Joséphine recalls that he could not help feeling 'almost overawed when he went into the late King's study'. When retiring he would sometimes say to her, 'Come, my little Créole, come and sleep in your master's bed.' At heart he always remained a parvenu, never quite knowing how to behave. His manners were atrocious, even – especially – towards women. According to Bourrienne, who saw a lot of him during this period, 'He seldom said anything agreeable to females and frequently made the rudest and most extraordinary remarks. To one he would say, "Heavens, how red your elbows are!" To another, "What an ugly hat!" Or he might say, "Your dress is none of the cleanest. Do you never change your gown? I have seen you wearing that at least twenty times!" ' Bourrienne adds that he had an 'invincible antipathy' to fat ladies.

At fifty Letizia still looked astonishingly young and pretty, till she opened her mouth – she had lost all her teeth. She lived in her brother Fesch's house in the rue du Mont-Blanc having declined her son's offer of the Luxembourg palace, a somewhat incongruous residence for the former mistress of the Casa Buonaparte. Later Metternich heard that 'Napoleon's mother cared for nothing but money. Neither her turn of mind nor her tastes inclined her towards social elevation. She had an immense income but without her son's explicit instructions would have done nothing save invest it.' She found it difficult to adapt and went on speaking Italian. When she spoke French it was with the thickest of accents. Nevertheless the most powerful man in Europe and the tamer of the French Revolution still went in awe of his mother.

Elisa, the family bluestocking, was the best behaved of his sisters – for the time being. She filled her elegant little town house, the Hôtel Maurepas, with men of letters, scientists and artists. Painters like David, Isabey and Gros were always there. She also adopted an *académicien*, the poet and orator Louis de Fontanes, as her particular friend, with whom she corresponded regularly. They do not seem to have been lovers – her charms were probably too angular even for the sycophantic Fontanes. No less of a literary lion than René de Chateaubriand graced her salon and she persuaded Bonaparte to take his name off the roll of proscribed émigrés. She also indulged in theatricals with Lucien, notably a performance of Voltaire's tragedy *Alzire* in which she played the title role in pink silk tights – the First Consul complained of her appearing 'almost naked on a mountebank stage'. She founded a society of literary ladies, designing a special dress for them which she wore herself. (Laure Permon describes it as a mixture of Jewish, Greek, Roman and mediaeval.) Bacciochi cut an odd figure in such cultivated circles. His ties with Lucien lessened after the latter's departure from Madrid, and a job had to be found for him. Accordingly he was given command of a demi-brigade and posted to a garrison town. Elisa was glad to be rid of him, but visited him from time to time in the role of self-appointed colonel-in-chief to decide which of his officers should be promoted or retired, treating them with the same exaggerated arrogance she showed to the ladies of the Tuileries. The unhappy Bacciochi lived in constant terror of his wife who found his stupidity intensely irritating.

Pauline was unquestionably the worst behaved of the sisters. Forced to accompany her husband Leclerc to San Domingo (Haiti), she was heartbroken at having to say goodbye to her latest lover Pierre Lafon, an actor at the Comédie-Française. Cruel tongues said that the First Consul was packing off his wild young sister to put an end to all too many scandalous love affairs. Sémonville, an old friend from her Corsican childhood, told Baron Mounier, 'I was one of her lovers. There were five of us sharing her favours in the same house before she left for San Domingo . . . the greatest hussy imaginable but the most tempting.' On one occasion she spent three entire days in bed at Saint-Leu with the future Marshal Macdonald, their bedroom having been provided with food and drink. She was also a nuisance at the Tuileries, publicly putting her tongue out at Joséphine. She wept at the prospect of leaving Paris, complaining to Laure Permon, 'How could my brother be so hard-hearted, sending me into exile among savages and snakes? In any case I am ill – I shall die before I get there.' Laure told her that she would be very pretty dressed as a Creole whereupon her sobs grew less hysterical. 'Do you really think, Laure,' she asked, 'that I shall look prettier, prettier than usual, in a Creole turban, a short waisted gown and a striped muslin petticoat?' Consoled, she set sail with her baby son in December 1801. At San Domingo she showed surprising courage, even when it seemed as though the negroes would capture the capital, refusing to be evacuated. She also became mildly interested in voodoo, expressing a wish to meet 'Baron Samedi', though the interview never materialized. Leclerc did his best against the blacks but died of yellow fever within the year. After tearfully placing her hair in his coffin, which accompanied her, she returned to France and was back by New Year's Day 1803. She set up house in the rue du Faubourg-Saint-Honoré at the Hôtel de Charost, purchased from the Duchesse de Charost for 400,000 francs, which speedily acquired the name 'Pauline's nest', her splendid horses and carriages attracting much admiration. (Today the house is the British Embassy.)

For all her beauty the *veuve* Leclerc was an embarrassment to the regime and not only because of her lovers, from whom she caught a venereal disease, presumably gonorrhea, fortunately soon cured. Her conversation, in a strong Italian accent, was almost insanely frivolous, her manner disconcertingly abstracted if amiable, and her eyes had a disquietingly vague expression. Her clothes, on which she spent vast sums, were noticeably odd. She went to fortune-tellers, in particular to those who consulted the Tarot cards or who read patterns in egg-white dropped into a glass of water.

In August 1803, less than a year after Leclerc's death – despite Napoleon's pleas for a longer, more seemly, period of mourning – Pauline married again, the wedding being celebrated by the Papal Legate Cardinal Caprara. In rank and fortune the bridegroom was the biggest catch so far secured by the Bonapartes. Prince Camillo Borghese, Prince of Sulmona, Rossaro and Vivaro, Duke of Ceri and of Poggio Nativo, and Baron Crapolatri, was the richest man in Italy and owned the most beautiful diamonds in Europe. He had adopted republican principles to save the family fortunes, his brother taking the side of reaction for the same reason, both being in complete agreement with each other. Camillo was twenty-eight years old, swarthy and diminutive but elegant, the first man to wear court dress at the Tuileries since Louis XVI's time. Shortly after her marriage the new Princess made an unexpected call on Joséphine at Saint-Cloud, wearing the entire Borghese collection of diamonds sewn on to a green velvet dress, knowing that, taken by surprise, her hated sister-in-law would be dressed in only a simple muslin frock.

On reaching Rome Pauline took a dislike to the Borghese Palace (now the Caccia Club) and to Roman society. She found the Black (Papal) nobility as stiff and cold as her husband's palazzo, failings of which she herself could never be accused. Moreover, if not exactly impotent, Camillo was apparently not much good in bed. He had homosexual and transvestite tendencies. Even before leaving Paris, when Laure Permon wished her a happy honeymoon, she had replied, 'What, a *honeymoon* with that idiot!' Soon she was complaining to her uncle the Cardinal, 'I wish I had stayed Leclerc's widow on only 20,000 francs a year instead of marrying such a eunuch.' In 1804, pleading ill health, she escaped to Florence where she commissioned Canova to sculpt two statues of her as *Venus Victorious*, at her own suggestion naked save for a little drapery. When a lady gasped at her daring to pose in the nude, she answered, 'Why not? There was a perfectly good fire in the studio.' Prince Camillo was horrified by the statues and had them locked up in the attic of his palace. She began to stray. Angrily, the First Consul declared that he would never receive her at the Tuileries without her husband.

Caroline's spouse, Joachim Murat, was given command of the Army of Observation (a kind of 'fire-brigade' force) at the end of 1800, although Joseph had wanted it for his brother-in-law Bernadotte, whom Napoleon still distrusted, with reason. He then spent the next few years in Italy where he became commander-in-chief in 1801 and was soon receiving pay and lavish allowances, which together amounted to 84,000 francs annually. From the very beginning of their marriage Caroline, who paid frequent visits to Paris, seems to have been discreetly unfaithful to him – as he was to her, with less discretion. In June 1800 Lucien reported in a letter to Joseph that, although pretending to the General that she was staying at her brother's house, in reality she was living somewhere else in the capital. 'Her husband is a fool whose wife ought to punish him by not writing to him for a month.' Lucien does not reveal the name of Caroline's mysterious lover. However, the marriage survived and when at Milan she lived like royalty with Murat in a splendid palace. Moreover they quickly had three children, two boys and a girl, whom Caroline often took back to their hôtel in Paris with its great salon, green salon and purple salon, showily opulent rooms which were always thronged by glittering cavalry officers dancing attendance on their General's tough little wife. Murat was appointed Military Governor of Paris in January 1804, with suitably increased allowances, and immediately engaged the best chef in that capital of chefs. Caroline had her portrait done by the veteran painter of royalty, Mme Vigée-Lebrun – now very much in fashion again – whom she infuriated. Dressmakers and hairdressers kept on coming in throughout the sittings to add fresh touches to Mme Murat, maddening the unfortunate artist who, to add insult to injury, had been forced to accept only half her usual commission. The friend of Marie Antoinette and of Maria Carolina of Naples tells us in her memoirs that when the last sitting was over she remarked deliberately, in a voice loud enough for Caroline to hear, '*Real* princesses are much easier to paint.' Even so, her subject must have been delighted with a very flattering portrait which disguised short legs and an excessively large head, and gave her a radiant smile.

Few people can have been surprised that the marriage of Louis and

Hortense was proving a disaster. Even Napoleon admitted it had only taken place 'because of Joséphine's scheming'. As for Letizia, Lucien informs us in his secret memoirs, 'Our mother was plainly furious at the alliance. She saw it as a triumph for a family which she detested.' Later Louis was to claim that he had been bullied into marrying the girl. Within a few weeks he had abandoned her, first for the army and then for various watering-places. With Lucien's vicious innuendo (that she was expecting a baby by the First Consul) in mind he forbade her to give birth to a child before nine months were up. As it was, she bore a son after only eight months, Napoléon Charles, who – since Joseph had only daughters – was the ultimate heir of the Bonaparte dynasty. Save for the First Consul, the entire clan insisted on regarding the baby as a bastard. Not without prompting Louis eventually rejoined his wife, to make her thoroughly unhappy. Because of his disease he was in constant pain and his hands and forearms were partially paralysed. At home he behaved as a neurotic tyrant obsessed with Hortense's imaginary infidelity – every night he searched her rooms with a candle, looking for lovers. Napoleon rebuked him for 'treating a young woman as though you were drilling a regiment'. Vague and impetuous, she was the last girl in the world to submit to a rigid marital discipline.

As if to spite his brother's pretensions, Lucien contracted another unsuitable marriage. Napoleon suggested that he go to Florence as resident French envoy with a view to marrying the widowed Queen of Etruria (a new state made up of Tuscany and Parma). He was offering him a throne, even if the lady was notoriously ugly. To the First Consul's surprise and irritation Lucien declined. Nevertheless he was given the senatorship of Trèves (Trier) with a salary of 25,000 francs and the castle of Poppelsdorf on the Moselle, which had its own theatre and a fine art gallery. Lucien recruited a team of art experts to fill the gallery with Flemish paintings. However, he refused the office of Treasurer to the Senate lest it affect his 'rights to the Consular succession'. Joseph had refused the Chancellorship for the same reason. Napoleon was therefore all the more astonished when he learnt that on 26 October 1803 Lucien had not only married a Mme Alexandrine Jouberthon in a civil ceremony but had also legitimized a five-month-old son by her. Daughter of a lowly tax official in Normandy, the bride was the widow of a bankrupt speculator who had bolted to San Domingo and whose death had not yet been confirmed – there was a possibility of bigamy. Red-haired and blue-eyed, Alexandrine was clearly most attractive. Elisa wrote to her intellectual friend Louis de Fontanes, 'The lady is quite lovely, as gay as she is beautiful – and as greedy as she is gay.' After installing her in a house which could be reached from the Hôtel de Brienne by a secret passage and having evicted the German adventuress from Le Plessis-Chamant, Lucien had married her in a religious service the day after she gave birth to their first child. A match with the *veuve* Jouberthon was scarcely a dynastic alliance, yet, as he knew very well, his son was another potential heir to the First Consul. Joseph tried to stop Alexandrine from using the name Bonaparte for the time being. At first Lucien agreed, then he changed his mind. Napoleon was enraged. He asked their mother to intervene but, if Lucien's secret memoirs are to be believed, Letizia took the side of her younger son, saying, 'He is no more obliged to ask your permission to marry than you have any right to tell him to marry whom you choose.' There was a shouting match between the two brothers during which, so Baron Chaptal tells us, the First Consul reproached Lucien for having married a widow, whereupon the latter retorted, 'You married one yourself. But mine is not old and smelly.' In December Lucien and his wife left Paris to travel in Switzerland and Italy. He told Joseph, 'Don't try in any way to make peace between me and the First Consul during my absence. I leave with hatred in my heart.'

Soon after, Letizia also left Paris. There was a certain coolness between her and Napoleon. During the squabble over Lucien's marriage she had reminded the First Consul pointedly that he had not asked her consent for his own marriage. She hated Joséphine more than ever. The latter, more shrewdly than might be expected, had recovered all the ground lost while her husband was away in Egypt and made herself indispensable as a hostess at the Tuileries. She responded to the Bonapartes' unrelenting enmity by reviving her old alliance with Fouché, whom she supported in every way she could. They blamed her for Lucien's dismissal. Their mother was only too pleased to leave the enforced company of 'that widow'.

In March 1804 Cardinal Fesch wrote to the First Consul describing Letizia's reception in Rome.

> Yesterday I presented her to the Pope at the Quirinal, together with her daughter [Pauline] and Mme Clary [Joseph's mother-in-law], wearing court dress and being greeted with full ceremonial. The Swiss Guard escorted her to the first antechamber, where she was received by the gentlemen-in-waiting and the Noble Guard presented arms. . . . The Roman nobility call on her ceaselessly. The Dean of the Sacred College has asked all cardinals to pay their respects to her within twenty-four hours.

It must have been a relief to her to speak Italian again to all and sundry – her spoken French was vile and she could not write the language of her son's subjects. For a time she stayed in what is today the Palazzo Torlonia, near the Spanish Steps, bought by Lucien who had not yet arrived. When he came she moved in with Fesch at the Palazzo Falconieri in Via Giulia. Fesch was justified in telling his nephew, 'I really believe Rome is the place which suits her best.' She never lost her love of the Eternal City.

Out of the blue came yet another marital disaster. Jérôme was becoming bored by a sailor's life in the Carribean. Already his love of pleasure was so notorious that he was known as 'Fifi' throughout the French navy. He decided to visit the United States, landing at Norfolk, Virginia, in July 1803. He went to Washington where he was received by President Jefferson, then to Baltimore. Here he met Miss Betsy Patterson, the nineteen-year-old daughter of a Baltimore shipowner and banker. Her father came from Ireland but was the antithesis of those Catholic Irishmen who have always been so close to the French. William Patterson was a Presbyterian Ulsterman, Scots in name and ancestry. The son of a Donegal smallholder, he had arrived in America in 1766 when only fourteen, entered a shipping office and made a fortune gun-running for Washington's army during the War of Independence. He had married Dorcas Spear, sister-in-law of the influential Senator Samuel Smith and was supposed to be the second richest man in America. (President Thomas Jefferson described him as 'a man of great worth and respectability', his family as standing 'among the first in the United States'.) Betsy was three months older than Jérôme and, to judge from both portraits and contemporary accounts, stunningly beautiful, with a svelte, wasp-waisted figure, pink and white complexion and wonderful brown eyes – indeed she bore a certain resemblance to Pauline Bonaparte. A lively, high-spirited girl, she fully deserved her nickname, 'The Belle of Baltimore'. She spoke adequate French while Jérôme could speak barely a word of English.

Betsy was more than just a Southern belle. Even if she quarrelled with him, she was very much her father's girl, with all his ambition, drive, business sense and flair for making money – she had spent long hours watching in his counting-house. At this date she may have been inexperienced, but she was far from naïve and her favourite reading was La Rochefoucauld's *Maxims*, most worldly of observations on the human race. She hated Baltimore so much that she contemplated suicide, and afterwards admitted that she would have married the devil to escape. She longed to visit Europe. She saw more than escape in Jérôme, whose shallowness she probably divined from the beginning. For her, marriage to him meant marriage to the brother of the most powerful man in the world, a seemingly brilliant investment for a dazzling future. Moreover, with her personality and intelligence she would be an asset to the Bonaparte clan and provide them with valuable links with the New World.

Jérôme tricked the French chargé d'affaires into lending him all the money he needed and on Christmas Eve 1803, although she was a Protestant, he and Betsy were married according to the rites of the Catholic Church by Dr Carroll, first Archbishop of Baltimore. When the news reached France – via the columns of a British newspaper – Napoleon was enraged, although only a few years before he would have regarded such a marriage as a triumph. Jérôme wrote to his mother, 'I am looking forward to introducing my beloved wife to you', but for once Letizia did not oppose her elder son in a family matter. He told the French chargé to stop lending the boy money, to order him to come home immediately on a French ship, to ensure that no French officer allowed 'the young person' – i.e. Betsy – to come on board his vessel and to make it perfectly clear that should 'Miss Patterson' try to land in France she would be sent back to America. In the event Jérôme did not dare return to France until 1805. While one can only feel sorry for Betsy, his superior in every way, it is easy to understand why the marriage angered his brother.

These family upsets were all the more irritating since there was so much to occupy the First Consul. At home the state was able to balance its budget for the first time for sixty years. Abroad, however, the Peace of Amiens turned out to be a mere armistice. In May 1803 war with England started again and despite earlier reservations Napoleon began to build up an invasion fleet at Boulogne, where he concentrated an 'Army of England'. The thoughts of Downing Street turned to assassination. 'The atmosphere was full of daggers.'

The most dangerous royalist of all, Georges Cadoudal, a ferocious veteran of the Vendée, was brought to France by an English boat with the utmost secrecy. His plan was simple enough. He would kill the First Consul, whereupon a Bourbon prince would arrive to negotiate a merciful restoration. Cadoudal reached Paris safely with a small band of dedicated followers, but the police were waiting for them and they were captured in March 1804. Their trial took place in June, Cadoudal being guillotined. In February the police had discovered that General Pichegru – a former tutor of Napoleon's at Brienne – was involved and arrested him. General Moreau, supposedly a staunch republican, was implicated too and also arrested. Pichegru was then found strangled in his cell – officially by his own hand, in reality by secret agents. 'His death was considered necessary,' says Bourrienne. The hero of Hohenlinden, Moreau could not be disposed of so easily and was banished, taking refuge in the United States. Bernadotte was undoubtedly implicated in the plot as well but was forgiven yet again for Désirée's sake.

There was a paranoiac side to Napoleon. 'Am I a dog to be killed in the streets?' he shouted. 'My would-be murderers are regarded as something holy. They threaten my life, so I will make war on war!' He was not a Corsican for nothing and saw the situation in terms of vendetta – if the Bourbons tried to kill him, then he would kill a Bourbon. (In his will he would leave money to a man who had tried to assassinate Wellington.) Talleyrand and Fouché encouraged him. The ablest of the exiled princes of the blood was the young Duc d'Enghien, last heir of the Princes of Condé, who was living just across the French frontier in the neutral Duchy of Baden to be near an adored mistress. On the night of 14 March 1804 he was seized by a raiding party of 300 French dragoons and taken to the fortress of Vincennes. Here he was court-martialled, quite illegally, and shot in the moat by a firing squad at dawn a week after his abduction. Murat signed the death warrant (receiving a grant of 100,000 francs from the Civil List shortly after).

Despite all the bloodshed of recent years the French were horrified. Joséphine wept openly, without trying to conceal her feelings. Even the Bonaparte women felt for her. Elisa wrote a letter of protest, drafted for her by her literary friend M. de Fontanes. Letizia, although well used to Corsican vendettas, was appalled. It was probably after returning from Italy that, according to Joseph, 'in tears she reproached the First Consul bitterly, while he listened in silence. She told him it was an atrocity of which nothing could ever absolve him, that he had yielded to treacherous advice from men who were his secret enemies and who were only too pleased to blacken his name by such a wicked act.' Exceptionally her son appears to have been embarrassed. He bestowed a pension of 120,000 francs on her, besides commissioning Gérard to paint her full-length portrait. She did not change her opinion.

There was more to Enghien's murder than vendetta, however. Not only did it strike terror into the Bourbons and their supporters, but it reassured the 'notables' of the new establishment – who included many influential regicides – that whatever form Bonaparte's regime might take, it would never become a counter-revolution. Just before he was guillotined Georges Cadoudal had prophesied, 'I came to make a king and instead I have made an emperor.'

Bonaparte did not quite dare to make himself King of France. Instead he tried to fuse the Revolution and the past in a new type of monarchy, taking for his model Charlemagne's revival of the Roman Empire in the West. His own Napoleonic Empire was able to emerge because its creator had crushed all opposition, France having been transformed into a totalitarian state, terrorized by the Ministry of Police, by the High Police and by the half dozen other police forces of a vast network of oppression brilliantly co-ordinated by Fouché. There was nobody left to organize any opposition. Moreover, Napoleon enjoyed the backing of all those who had bought up confiscated estates, the 'notables', who feared the sovereignty of the people no less than a Bourbon restoration. As Jean Tulard observes, 'The founding of the Empire signified a dictatorship of public safety in favour of the well-to-do who had profited from the Revolution.'

5
Princes and Princesses – The Empire

'You ought to have stayed First Consul. You were the only one in Europe, and look at the company you are in now.'

LAZARE CARNOT TO NAPOLEON

'The distribution of favours and fortunes, and afterwards of kingdoms, among the whole following, seemed to come strangely from the son of the Revolution, particularly when one thinks of the excessive greed, envy and inefficiency only matched by self-conceit, displayed by that peculiarly unpleasant set of people.'

PIETER GEYL, *Napoleon For and Against*

On 18 May 1804 the Senate proclaimed the First Consul 'Napoleon I, Emperor of the French Republic'. Joseph was nominated as his heir, after which the crown would go to Louis, since the former had only daughters. Both were created Princes of the Empire with annual allowances of a million francs. In addition, Joseph was appointed Grand Elector, to preside over the Senate as the Emperor's representative on certain great occasions, with the Luxembourg palace for his residence and another third of a million francs for expenses. The *ancien régime* dignity of Grand Constable was revived for Louis, with a third of a million francs for expenses too. As yet Lucien and Jérôme received nothing, nor did Napoleon's sisters, though Murat obtained the ancient office of Grand Admiral. The old title of Marshal of France was brought back, among those on whom it was bestowed being Joachim and Bernadotte. There was a whole host of accompanying dignitaries: an Arch-Chancellor and an Arch-Treasurer of the Empire, a Grand Marshal of the Palace, a Grand Master of the Horse, a Grand Chamberlain, a Grand Master of Ceremonies and a Grand Huntsman. Fesch became Grand Almoner. There were countless chamberlains and lesser court officials.

The First Consul's transformation into an Emperor was ridiculed by other European rulers. They were not going to be impressed by the liturgical pantomime of the imperial coronation which was about to take place at Notre-Dame. Nor were the notables.

The Consulate had been one of France's golden ages. It is sometimes compared with the reign of King Henri IV who like Napoleon had reunited a country ruined by sectarian violence, giving it peace and prosperity, and who is still remembered with affection by the French. But unlike Napoleon Henri had died before he could embark on aggressive adventures abroad. By contrast the Empire which grew out of the Consulate was to be an age of glory bought at the cost of ultimate disaster. It is revealing that the Emperor thoroughly enjoyed games of chance – invariably cheating – yet was a very bad chess player. His insecurity expressed itself in the most basic way. Fouché tells us that he kept a vast hoard of gold in the Tuileries vaults under the Pavillon de Marsan, amounting to nearly 500 million francs – saved from the 2,000 millions of foreign currency which France had extorted from conquered countries – and watched it increase day by day with the glee of a gangster gloating over his loot.

Insecurity did not stop the Bonapartes from exploiting the situation. In 1806 Jérôme referred, in a letter to Lucien, to 'our family and that of the Bourbons'. As Pieter Geyl points out,

> Nothing is more remarkable than the ease with which the Bonapartes accustomed themselves to their grand position . . . a dizzying ascent, but they did not in the least suffer from vertigo. They never seemed to realize that without their brother's genius they were nothing. Napoleon was sometimes capable of reminding them, bluntly and angrily. For instance, when Joseph tried to stress his 'rights' by threatening to stay away from the imperial coronation and attacked Napoleon in his most tender spot, his jealous sense of power . . . 'If you stay away, you are my enemy,' he said to Joseph, 'and where is the army you can bring against me? You lack everything, and if it comes to that I shall destroy you.' Joseph submitted, but how many times had Napoleon given in, and how often would he do so again, to his unreasoning weakness for his family – call it a Corsican weakness or not.

Napoleon's brothers were obsessed by the fantasy that they or their children would succeed him on the throne. At one moment Joseph grew so over-excited that he fired a pistol at the Emperor's portrait, screaming abuse at 'the tyrant'. He was outraged by Napoleon's proposal to adopt Louis's son Charles-Napoléon – Joséphine's grandson – as his heir, clinging desperately to his 'rights' as eldest brother. For his part Louis refused to make way for his son. On the other hand Lucien – who had returned to Paris – would not hear of his son by Mme Jouberthon being excluded and again left for Italy in a fury. In the end a compromise was reached. The succession was to go first to Joseph and then to Louis, then to their male descendants, though the Emperor reserved the right of adopting as his heir any prince of the imperial family who had reached the age of eighteen. He also stipulated that his successor must be a soldier and, for Joseph to qualify, announced that the latter had 'expressed to me his wish to share in the dangers of the army encamped on the shore at Boulogne so that he can share in its glory'. He then furnished him with a totally spurious record of military service, alleging that he had served in the campaigns of 1793–4 and been wounded at the siege of Toulon. Joseph went off to Boulogne for a few weeks, where he seems to have spent his entire time with the town's ladies of easy virtue. Disguised in a wig and spectacles, he first visited Mme Fagan, 'a charming lady from Dunkirk' patronized by several generals including Soult. He had at least four other mistresses there, among them an actress, a friend's wife and the wife of a young officer. In response to Napoleon's gesture he graciously agreed to allow his own wife Julie to carry the Empress Joséphine's train at the forthcoming coronation, together with Elisa, Pauline, Caroline and Hortense, while sniggering at the ludicrous costume he himself was going to have to wear for the occasion.

During a state banquet at Saint-Cloud on 18 May, after the proclamation of the Empire, it was announced that not only had Joseph and Louis become princes but that their wives were princesses and Imperial Highnesses. Elisa and Caroline remained without titles. One of Joséphine's ladies-in-waiting, Mme de Rémusat, who was present, tells us:

> Mesdames Bacciochi and Murat appeared dumbfounded by this distinction between themselves and their sisters-in-law. Mme Murat in particular could scarcely conceal her resentment. . . . During dinner she was so little in control of herself that, when she heard the Emperor address 'Princess' Louis [Hortense] several times, she was unable to keep back her tears. She swallowed several large glasses of water in an attempt to recover herself and to seem to eat something, but in the end she was overcome by sobs. . . . Mme Bacciochi, older and with more self-possession, did not cry, but adopted a curt and cutting manner, treating the ladies-in-waiting with marked hauteur.

Elisa and Caroline went home in a fury – no doubt they saw it as yet another victory for Joséphine.

The very next day, so Mme de Rémusat – who was in the adjoining room – informs us, Caroline had a private interview with Napoleon in the Empress's boudoir. (Elisa shrewdly stayed at home, knowing just how much he disliked her.) Screams and sobs were heard. Caroline 'demanded to know why she was being condemned, she and her sisters, to obscurity, to public contempt, when strangers were being heaped with honours and titles'. The Emperor replied coldly, 'To listen to you, one would think that I had robbed you of the inheritance of our father the King.' Caroline played a last card, falling rigid to the floor in a faint. Astonishingly, one of the hardest men in the world surrendered to this hackneyed feminine stratagem. The following day the official journal, the *Moniteur*, announced, 'The French Princes and Princesses have been given the title of Imperial Highnesses. The Emperor's sisters will bear the same title.' In addition Bacciochi was speedily promoted to general and created a senator.

The clan's mother was not going to be left out. She was so upset that she left Rome to take the waters at Lucca. On 9 July Fesch wrote to Napoleon on her behalf, complaining that his lack of letters to her was making her feel ill. Furthermore, 'Your mother would like a title, a formal rank. She is very distressed that some people are calling her "Majesty", or "Empress Mother", while others only address her as "Imperial Highness" like her daughters. She is impatient to learn what has been decided for her.' Letizia was not invariably sensible. After lengthy discussions with experts on etiquette who had survived from the old days of Versailles, her son decided on the style 'Madame, Mère de Sa Majesté l'Empereur', which the imperial court soon abbreviated to 'Madame Mère'.

She was far from satisfied and decided not to attend the coronation. Her sons Lucien and Jérôme – the latter still in disgrace because of his American marriage – were not recognized as imperial princes. Nor did they receive invitations to the coronation.

Up until the last moment the Bonapartes tried to prevent Joséphine from being crowned at the forthcoming ceremony. Early in November the Emperor complained bitterly about his family to Count Roederer, one of his Counsellors of State.

> Apparently you forget that my brothers are nothing without me; they are great men only because I have made them great. Everything that the French have heard about them has been heard from me. There are thousands of people in France who have done the state better service. . . . I have never regarded my brothers as the natural heirs of my power. I merely saw them as suitable men to stop that power from collapsing during a minority.

He was particularly cross with Joseph. 'When I went off to Egypt I entrusted him with my entire property. He has not yet rendered an account of it. . . . What does Joseph really want . . . does he think the state should pay him two million a year to stroll through the streets of Paris in a smart coat and a top hat?' Napoleon was determined to stand by his wife. He was furious that Joseph should 'dare to tell me that her coronation is against his "interests", that it would enhance the claims of Louis's children against his own'. He added,

> They [the Bonapartes] are jealous of my wife, of Eugène, of Hortense, of everyone near me. All I can say is that my wife has nothing but diamonds and debts. Eugène hasn't even 20,000 francs. I'm fond of those children because they always do their best to please me. . . . My wife is a sweet-natured woman who doesn't do them any harm. She merely wants to play at being Empress for a bit, to have beautiful diamonds, smart dresses and all the fashionable luxuries. Yes, she's going to be crowned all right! She will be crowned if it costs me 200,000 men!

There was yet another objection to Joséphine's being anointed. She had never been properly married, at least in the eyes of the Church. Accordingly on 1 December a secret religious ceremony took place, conducted by Fesch – no doubt unwillingly.

The coronation took place on 2 December 1804. Some ladies of the court had their hair done at 2 o'clock in the morning in order to be in time at Notre-Dame. The streets were crowded, though spectators seemed more curious than enthusiastic. The unfortunate Pope Pius VII had to wait for several hours on a throne in the freezing cathedral, opposite a rather larger throne for the Emperor at the other end. Before setting out from the Tuileries at 10 o'clock Napoleon took Joseph by the arm, dragged him before a looking-glass and said, 'Joseph! If our father could see us!' Their finery was certainly dazzling, the Emperor's purple velvet coat being girded with a white and gold silk sash and topped by a short purple cloak embroidered with golden bees (his new emblem) while Joseph was in a white silk tunic embroidered with gold and a trailing, ermine-lined mantle of flame-coloured velvet powdered with the golden bees – both wore floppy seventeenth-century hats with turned up brims and ostrich plumes, and a plentiful supply of diamonds. Joséphine's gown was of white satin embroidered with the bees, beneath a court mantle of purple velvet – she had taken the inspired precaution of having her face painted by the miniaturist Isabey. 'The Empress, ablaze with diamonds and her hair in a thousand ringlets in the style of Louis XIV's day, did not look more than twenty-five,' says the loyal Mme de Rémusat. 'She had on a diamond tiara, necklace, earrings and belt of great value, all of which she wore with her accustomed elegance.' The entire court were in velvet cloaks embroidered in gold or silver, creations of Isabey who had personally designed every costume, and the best actors and actresses of the day had been hired to teach them how to wear the clothes.

The imperial couple set out for their crowning in a coach of glass and gilt with seven wide windows and, on the roof, four eagles bearing a crown. Before his ceremonial entry into Notre-Dame Napoleon paused to put on a vast mantle of purple velvet embroidered with the golden bees and lined with ermine. A simple wreath of gold laurel leaves encircled his head. 'He looked like an ancient coin', comments Mme de Rémusat. After the Emperor and Empress had processed in, the bearers of the regalia entered. Berthier, in green as Grand Huntsman, bore the orb, Eugène de Beauharnais, also in green but with a red dolman as Colonel-General of the Chasseurs, bore the ring, Bernadotte, in dark blue as Marshal of the Empire, bore the chain, Kellermann and Pérignon, also in dark blue as honorary marshals, bore the crown and sceptre, and Talleyrand, in scarlet as Grand Chamberlain, bore the case for the mantle. Two orchestras struck

70

up a march and then the Mass began.

After the Pope had anointed the Emperor's head, arms and hands, Napoleon took the crown from the altar and placed it on his own head. He then crowned the Empress, who burst into tears. 'When the moment came for her to proceed from the altar to her throne, she had a sharp exchange with her sisters-in-law, who were carrying her train so reluctantly that I thought the newly crowned Empress would be brought to a complete standstill', Mme de Rémusat tells us. 'Sparkling with innumerable precious stones', the women of the Bonaparte clan were plainly furious, especially Pauline, and even Julie, Joseph's amiable wife. Napoleon saw what was happening and hissed 'a few, sharp, firm words' at them, after which Joséphine was able to ascend her throne. The climax of the Mass was a superb *Vivat Imperator in aeternum*. It was followed by two ceremonies which symbolized the paradoxical nature of the new regime. Napoleon swore on the Gospels to maintain the territory of the *Republic*, after which a herald proclaimed, 'The Most Glorious and August Emperor Napoleon has been consecrated and enthroned Emperor of the French', a formula almost identical with that used after the coronation of a King of France. Between 2 and 3 o'clock in the afternoon the imperial party began its return to the Tuileries, arriving there after dark by the light of countless torches. The Emperor was so elated that he would not let Joséphine take her crown off, insisting that she wear it at supper.

It was only a decade since the execution of Louis XVI. Mme de Rémusat admits that the cheers from the crowd 'were not exactly rapturous outbursts' and that throughout the ceremony the wretched Pope 'wore the look of a victim resigned to his fate'.

The pantomime was repeated at Milan the following spring. This time Joséphine was not crowned but watched from a gallery as Napoleon again placed the crown on his head – the ancient iron crown of Lombardy – with the noble words, 'God gave it to me, woe unto him who touches it.' Avrillon, Joséphine's favourite personal maid, says, 'The ceremony was simply gorgeous.' In June 1805 the Emperor-King appointed Eugène de Beauharnais Viceroy of Italy. Eugène was still only twenty-three yet he proved an immediate success as a satrap, encouraging his stepfather in the unfortunate delusion that all the other members of the clan would make equally effective rulers.

The Viceroyalty of Italy had been turned down by Lucien, who refused to abandon the widow Jouberthon and continued to insist that his children by her should have 'dynastic rights' with the title of Imperial Highness. When Napoleon brusquely declined to give way, Lucien retired sulkily to a luxurious exile in his beautiful palace in Rome. The Emperor persisted in trying to break up the marriage – he wanted his brother to be available for some useful foreign princess – while Lucien complained ceaselessly to the family that without his efforts the Empire would never have come into existence. When Uncle Fesch joined in, he received a savage rejoinder from Lucien who wrote, 'At least have the sense not to compare me to Jérôme and spare me the useless embarrassment of your cowardly advice. . . . Hide your degrading ideas beneath your cardinal's purple and tread the road of ambition in silence.'

Indeed Jérôme was all submission by contrast, only too eager to abandon his wife if it would please Napoleon. He had sailed from Baltimore in March 1805 – in the *Erin*, a fast clipper commissioned by his father-in-law – accompanied by his wife and her brother William. When they landed at Lisbon they were met by the French Ambassador, who informed them that 'Miss Patterson' would not be allowed to enter France. 'Tell your master', Betsy told him proudly, 'that "Madame Bonaparte" is ambitious and demands her rights as a member of the imperial family.' Jérôme then persuaded her to go on to Amsterdam while he went and argued with his brother, who was then at Milan. The Emperor refused to see him unless he submitted unconditionally. By early May Jérôme's resistance had collapsed and he wrote a grovelling letter of surrender. Most unwisely, Betsy took refuge in England where at Camberwell in July she gave birth to a son, who was christened Jerome Napoleon Bonaparte. The Emperor told the father firmly, 'Your union with Miss Patterson is null and void in the eyes of both religion and the law.' Even though the Pope declared that it was perfectly valid in the Church's eyes, Jérôme gave up. He wrote to Betsy, saying how much he loved her and their son, and asked her to go home to Baltimore and trust him. By July he had rejoined the French navy, commanding a small squadron at Genoa. Characteristically, he promoted himself to full captain without any official authorization and wore the uniform. He received a sharp reprimand from his brother for his presumption. He then took his ships to Algiers, from whence he returned with 200 ransomed French and Italian galley slaves whose liberty had already been secured by the French Consul. When he came back he was most undeservedly hailed as a hero by the French press and promised promotion by his brother. In the mean time he went to Paris for a round of wild dissipation. Occasionally he wrote to Betsy – whom he called 'Elisa' – in Baltimore.

The other Elisa played her cards much better than any of her brothers or sisters. She knew very well that although she resembled him most Napoleon liked her least – even feared her, if Metternich is to be believed. Moreover, her idiotic husband Bacciochi was infuriating everyone by his ridiculously haughty airs. Yet she was constantly trying to persuade her old ally Lucien to break with la Jouberthon, which must have pleased the

Emperor. 'In staying close to Napoleon or in accepting a throne from him, you could be so useful,' she wrote to her favourite brother at Rome. 'Do think again about the prosposals being made to you. Mama and all of us would be so happy if we could be politically united as a family. Dear Lucien, do it for us who love you.' On the other hand she made it quite clear that she wanted to live as far away from Paris as possible and encouraged the Emperor to long fervently for her departure by making herself as unpleasant as only she knew how – specializing in vicious remarks at Joséphine's expense. She got her way. Fouché had something to do with it, pointing out to his master that it would put an end to two extremely unsavoury love affairs which were causing scandal all over the capital, both lovers being financiers of the shadiest sort. At the end of March 1805, in the same proclamation in which he assumed the crown of Italy, Napoleon created her hereditary Princess of Piombino, announcing with unusual honesty that he was bestowing this little state on her 'not from fraternal tenderness but out of political prudence'. As consort her nonentity of a husband – who according to Metternich suffered from an 'entire lack of intellectual faculties' – received the title of Prince Felix I, but it was Elisa who ruled. On the coast opposite Corsica, Piombino had only 20,000 inhabitants. However, in June the same year she was promoted to Princess of Lucca and Piombino, the ancient republic of Lucca with some adjoining territory being given to her. Her elevation made her an object of envy to the entire Bonaparte clan.

> On the day we learnt of Elisa's nomination to the Principality of Lucca, my husband and I called on his other sisters [Hortense remembers]. We began with Caroline who, with a very forced laugh, said to us, 'Well! So Elisa is now a sovereign princess. She is going to have an army of four men and a corporal. It really is a fine thing!' Vexation showed through her flippancy. Princess Borghese made no attempt whatever at hiding her feelings. 'My brother only cares for Elisa and is not interested in the rest of us,' she said, most unjustly. 'As for me, I don't want anything since I'm an invalid, but it's not fair to Caroline.'

(In reality Pauline hated Caroline, whom she always called by her old name of Annunziata to annoy her.) Princess Borghese then proceeded to pick a quarrel with Hortense, accusing her of being able to obtain anything she wanted from the Emperor.

The Murats were particularly envious. They grew even angrier when Eugène de Beauharnais was made Viceroy of Italy. Not content with being created Grand Admiral of France and then in February 1805 a prince and a Serene Highness Joachim had confidently expected to rule in Milan. Yet he and his wife were doing very well indeed. Princess Caroline's New Year's gift from the Emperor for 1805 was 200,000 francs. A few weeks later, when her second daughter was born, he presented her with the Elysée

Palace (today the official residence of the President of France), and then gave her sums totalling nearly a million francs to buy out the tenants and market gardeners who had settled there during the Revolution – which was now beginning to seem a very long time ago. In any case she had an annual allowance of 240,000 francs from the Civil List. Her husband's official income was nearly 700,000 francs, though of course he also had his estates and investments. Masson estimates that during the first year of the Empire the couple's total income was approximately a million and a half francs. Joachim began to build the château of Labastide-Murat near his birthplace. His brother André, still a humble farmer, was soon to be created a Count of the Empire. However, it was always impossible to satisfy the greed and ambition of the Murats.

After the wrangling over her title during the proclamation of the Empire, Caroline decided that nothing further was to be gained from an alliance with Joseph – let alone with Lucien. Accordingly, she worked assiduously at pleasing the Emperor. Seeing that he was casting lustful eyes on her pretty young lady-in-waiting Mme Duchâtel, she obtained her confidence and did her best to procure the girl for her brother, while Murat pretended to be in love with her to deflect suspicion from Napoleon. Their joint efforts proved only too successful. Less dramatically, she gave lavish parties for the Emperor and the court, taking special pains to observe punctiliously his new etiquette, however preposterous, since she knew that he set great store by it. She assumed what was meant to be a suitably regal manner, which her gratified brother described as 'worthy of a queen' – Mme de Rémusat calls it 'stilted'. At her urging Joachim accepted every task demanded of him, from carrying Joséphine's crown at the coronation to opening the Senate. All this made the Empress increasingly uneasy, since she now recognized the Murats as being among her most dangerous enemies. A shrewder observer was equally alarmed by Joachim's steady advancement, if only because he was so incapable off the battlefield – according to Mme de Rémusat, Murat joked in that yokel's accent of his, 'Moussu de Talleyrand would like to have me broken on the wheel.' He was probably speaking no more than the truth. But Caroline, who had acquired a formidable ally in Fouché, was a match even for Talleyrand.

No doubt it came as a relief to Napoleon that, alone among his sisters, Pauline simply wanted to enjoy herself in Paris, giving ball after ball at her Hôtel de Charost. She remained shallow to the point of inanity and lived purely for pleasure, which for her consisted of lovers, parties and the care of her person, whose loveliness was well attested. Laure d'Abrantès says, 'It is quite impossible to imagine her perfect beauty.' Countess Potocka, by no means lavish with praise, tells us that 'as well as the most delicate and regular features imaginable, she possessed a truly admirable figure –

admired a little too much'. The bluff General Thiébault considered her 'a magnificent creature who had the most seductive air and the prettiest form nature ever made; and one that was not exactly niggardly in displaying its charms'. She frequently received admirers in her milk baths, for which she was carried to and fro by her giant black servant Paul – popularly rumoured to have been a king in the Congo – who also showered her with water from a hole in the ceiling. When friends remonstrated she explained in her girlish way that 'a negro is not a man'. She was only too happy when her boring Borghese husband, now running to seed and developing a large paunch, went off to try his hand at being a soldier as a colonel in the Horse Grenadiers of the Imperial Guard. Nor was she unduly distressed when her only child by Leclerc, Dermide Louis Napoléon, died at the age of eight in 1806 – she was not at the little boy's deathbed in the house where he was boarded out, despite a Bonapartist legend that she spent his last hours with him in tears. In Mme de Rémusat's words again, 'The Princess Borghese, alternating between physic and amusement, meddled with nobody.' Her favourite country retreat was the Petit Trianon at Versailles, once Marie Antoinette's fabled refuge. From 1805 until 1807 her principal lover was her chamberlain, Count Auguste de Forbin, an aristocratic dilettante whose father had been lynched by a Lyons mob and who, having lost his estates, earned a scanty living as a would-be fashionable portrait painter. She paid his debts and in return he ran her household and tried to interest her in books. From contemporary medical evidence it would appear that the count's private parts were as big as those of a stallion, which would ultimately have regrettable consequences. However, the couple appear to have led a genuine idyll for two years. In the end, Forbin tired of his mistress's exhausting demands – and such little ways as throwing the odd volume at his head – to the point of going to Fontainebleau and begging Napoleon to send him to the front on active service.

The Emperor also effected a reconciliation with his august mother, only slightly mollified by her new title, who more or less blackmailed him into satisfying even her rapacity for the time being. She was given a household of 200 courtiers with the Duc de Cossé-Brissac (bearer of one of the proudest names in France) as her chamberlain, a bishop assisted by two chaplains as her almoner, a former page of Louis XVI as her first equerry and a baron as her secretary, together with nine ladies-in-waiting. Characteristically, she complained about the expense of such a staff. In addition, she received vast new revenues and money to buy the enormous Hôtel de Brienne from Lucien to serve as her Paris residence. Her country residence included one wing of the Grand Trianon at Versailles (formerly the Dauphin's apartments), which she disliked and never used, and the immense seventeenth-century château and extensive estate of Pont-sur-

Seine near Troyes. Napoleon paid for the redecoration and the furnishings, which included a set of priceless Gobelin tapestries. She was also presented with estates in her beloved island which she and her brother the Cardinal, now Grand Almoner of the Empire, controlled closely if from afar. It was practically impossible to obtain any official appointment in Corsica without their approval. She became 'Patroness-in-Chief of the Charitable Institutions of the Empire' – although edifyingly pious, her reluctance to give even the smallest donation made her a not entirely satisfactory patroness. Her recreations were sewing, cards and snuff. 'Madame Mère', as Letizia was now universally known, was sufficiently softened by all these gifts to join in the campaign to force Lucien to disown his wife, dictating honeyed letters to this erring son – to no avail. Whenever possible, she still attempted to rule her family with an iron hand, though it was no longer so easy. She remained implacably hostile to 'that widow' and the Beauharnais brood. Nevertheless, her first public reappearance was at Saint-Cloud in March 1805 when, in the presence of the Pope, her brother Fesch christened Hortense's second son Napoléon-Louis with all the new imperial pomp (the ceremony being that once used to christen a Dauphin). A formal announcement of her grandson's birth had been sent to all the reigning sovereigns of Europe. It was indeed a long time since she had done her own washing in a stream at the bottom of the garden.

The marriage of Louis and Hortense had grown no happier. Mme de Rémusat tells a disgusting story which gives some idea of what the unfortunate girl suffered. His disease made her husband stiff in every joint so as a last resort his doctors suggested an 'eruption of the skin', to be induced by procuring from a hospital the nightshirt of a patient afflicted with boils. To make sure that this treatment should not become public knowledge, Louis insisted on Hortense's sleeping next to him – though in a separate bed – while he was wearing the shirt. When he was away, however, she enjoyed herself thoroughly with old school friends and other young married ladies, playing girlish games such as blind man's buff. She was a talented musician and composed stirring songs in praise of her stepfather which were sung all over France, the best known being *Partant pour la Syrie*. Her only fault was 'not maintaining at her house that ceremonious demeanour demanded by the rank to which she had been elevated'. Her husband refused to let her go to her brother's wedding in January 1806, from sheer tyranny.

In contrast Eugène made a very happy if also very grand match with the King of Bavaria's daughter. Pretty, tough and clever, the eighteen-year-old Augusta Amelia of Wittelsbach was to make him a charming wife and a most suitable Vicereine at Milan. Napoleon adopted Eugène formally as his son, gave him the rank of Imperial Highness and made him heir presumptive to the throne of Italy; later he created him Prince of Venice. He wrote amiable letters to them both. 'My son, you are working too hard, your life is too monotonous,' he told Eugène the following April. 'It's all right for you since you enjoy your work, but you have a young wife who is pregnant. I think you should try to spend your evenings with her and have a circle of friends around you.' When Augusta Amelia had a miscarriage he told her, 'I understand how lonely you must feel, alone in the middle of Lombardy. But Eugène will soon be back and you only realize how much you love someone when you see him again.' During the wedding celebrations at Munich the Emperor's too open admiration of the bride's stepmother, the agreeably shaped young Bavarian Queen, upset Joséphine who thought her 'more flirtatious than was desirable'. Nevertheless, it did not alter the fact that she had triumphed over the Bonapartes.

In her kind-hearted way the Empress did her best for all her relations, arranging another ambitious marriage between her first husband's little kinswoman Stéphanie de Beauharnais – a pert and high-spirited seventeen-year-old, who had attended Mme Campan's famous academy – and the girl's adoring admirer, Charles Louis of Zahringen, who would one day be Grand Duke of Baden and whose sister was the Russian Tsarina. (He had been forced to break off his previous engagement to Augusta Amelia to make way for Eugène.) Since his parents were inclined to look down their noses at the match, Napoleon adopted her too, giving her the remarkable name of Stéphanie-Napoléone and precedence over his mother and sisters, much to their fury. Caroline, who had already retired to bed when she heard she would have to give place to Augusta Amelia, had yet another fainting fit when Stéphanie-Napoléone was ushered into an imperial reception before her while Madame Mère used the 'affront' to extort a further 180,000 francs a year from her son. (Two months later Letizia tried to extract still more, complaining she did not have enough money 'to provide me with sufficient china, linen and furniture'.) These alliances with the old ruling families of *ancien régime* Europe delighted the Emperor. As Stendhal discerned, he 'had the defect of all parvenus, that of having too great an opinion of the class into which he had risen.'

At the time of Eugène's wedding Murat rebuked Napoleon for such social climbing.

When France raised you to the throne it was because she expected you would be a people's chief, a plebeian given a title placing you above every other European sovereign, not because she wanted to recreate Louis xiv's monarchy with all its abuses and the old court's pretensions. Yet you surround yourself with old nobility and fill the Tuileries drawing-rooms with them so that they think they've recovered all their former privileges – they feel much more at home there than they suspect you do. The old nobility regards every one of your soldier comrades, and possibly you too, as mere parvenus, intruders and usurpers. Now you intend to ally yourself with the Bavarian royal house through this marriage of Eugène's, while all you're doing is show Europe how much you value what each one of us lacks – blue blood! You pay homage to great titles which weren't created by you, which make nonsense of ours, and you're demonstrating only too plainly to France and to these sovereigns that you simply want to carry on the *ancien régime*, although you're reigning just because France doesn't want an *ancien régime* dynasty. Well, I can tell you that your dynasty is always going to seem new to other monarchs.

His brother-in-law haughtily answered 'Monsieur le Prince Murat' that it was a political manoeuvre. 'So this marriage doesn't please you? Well, it pleases me and I consider it a great success.'

The Emperor was still very fond of his own wife, though there were frequent quarrels – during which he smashed the bedroom furniture and she cried – and though they had nothing in common. Joséphine's life continued to be a simple routine of frivolity and extravagance. Her friend and lady-in-waiting Claire de Rémusat admits 'she never opened a book, she never took up a pen, she worked scarcely at all but never seemed bored'. Her consuming interest was still clothes and she spent astronomical sums on her wardrobe. Yet she had another passion which commands genuine respect. After roses her chief love was camellias, but she was interested in every beautiful plant from magnolias to eucalyptus, from lianas to heathers, from the Japanese lily to the blue lotus of Egypt. Alexander Humboldt sent her cacti which were gratefully received. She systematically acquired thousands of rare blooms, shrubs and trees from all over the world – including Kew – many of them flowering in France for the first time in her gardens. When in 1803–4 the famous botanist Ventenat brought out the two magnificent volumes she had commissioned, *Jardin de la Malmaison*, they were illustrated by her other protégé, Redouté – formerly the protégé of Marie Antoinette. She also spent a lot of money helping her needy Beauharnais and Tascher relations. She obtained official appointments for them or arranged rich marriages – though none so grand as that of Stéphanie-Napoléone.

Joséphine's constant fear was that her husband might father a child on one of his mistresses, despite her repeated insistence to her friends that he was sterile. In consequence she was always desperately jealous of his infidelities – which he himself described as 'these innocuous diversions of mine which in no way involve my affections'. He was infuriated by her tears. Hoping the Emperor would beget a bastard, and have to admit to himself that a divorce was necessary for dynastic reasons, the Murats deliberately placed personable young women in his way, such as Mme Duchâtel. Joachim even tried to persuade the actress Mlle Georges to continue her affair with Napoleon when it showed signs of coming to an end. Early in 1806 they introduced him to Mme Eléonore Denuelle de la Plaigne, a tall, willowy, black-eyed brunette who was another product of Mme Campan's academy and one of Caroline's readers. Although only eighteen, she was already a grass widow since after a mere two months of married life her husband had gone to prison for forgery. Beautiful and ingenuous, not very intelligent, she appealed at once to Napoleon who was soon sleeping with her. Eléonore was to fulfil the Murats' wildest expectations.

The imperial court was an extraordinary mixture of ostentatious luxury, elaborate ceremony and considerable vulgarity, dominated by the brooding presence of its creator. No expense was spared on banquets, orchestral and theatrical entertainments, balls and receptions, every effort being made to impress visiting royalties. The imperial residences were decorated in the most lavish and extravagant style, and staffed by hordes of chamberlains. But although the military parades and colourful uniforms were undeniably impressive, attempts by dug out old courtiers at reviving the etiquette of Versailles were not entirely successful even if the Emperor paid his customary meticulous attention to every detail. According to one spectator, Count Pelet de la Lozère, he went as far as 'deciding himself what the Empress should wear and actually seeing it tried on first'. He introduced pompous new rituals copied from what he had seen at German courts: every one of his courtiers had to file past his throne, bowing or curtsying. He took up hunting and shooting, despite being bored by the former and an almost comically bad shot, since these were suitably regal pastimes. (Rather as Mussolini had tea in a dinner jacket, in the fond belief that this was the custom of the English nobility.) An imperial hunt was established in imitation of that of the Bourbons, with elaborate green and gold uniforms. Sometimes he would shoot at the unfortunate swans at Malmaison just to tease Joséphine. The courtiers were an oddly assorted mixture of returned émigré nobles who remembered Versailles in the old days and of gallant but uncouth officers who had all too obviously risen from the ranks, their only common characteristic being a terrified obsequiousness towards their master. Countess Potocka, a niece of the last King of Poland and well used to royal courts, passes a merciless verdict on what she saw with her own eyes.

> However splendid it may have looked from a distance, the court [of Napoleon] simply did not stand up to close examination. There was a noticeable combination of muddle and discord which destroyed the aura of majesty and brilliance which people expected. It really was the most absurd scene. One might have thought one was at a rehearsal in some theatre with the actors trying on costumes and practising their parts.

The theatricality was beyond question. For some years the Emperor deliberately dressed with studied plainness in a drab military uniform while ordering his courtiers to glitter. He personally rebuked ladies whose clothes were dowdy or too simple, lining them up at his soirées and inspecting them as though they were troops. (By now it was good form to wear stiff, high-necked, dresses and even to wear a rosary as a necklace.) Mme de Rémusat confesses that the strict etiquette which he imposed made life at his court 'a daily misery'. He does not seem to have enjoyed it very much himself.

Metternich, who frequently witnessed his performance, says,

> It is difficult to imagine anything more awkward than Napoleon's manner in a drawing-room. The effort which he made to correct mistakes due to his background and education only served to make them more obvious. He simply did not know how to conduct a polite conversation. He never ceased trying to impress and, aware of his undignified lack of inches, walked by preference on tiptoe.

Metternich, who privately considered him a complete parvenu, adds that 'his appearance grew even more common as he put on weight'.

Needless to say, the Emperor had other matters to ponder besides court etiquette and polite conversation. For a long time he hoped to invade Britain. But in the summer of 1805 British subsidies enabled Austria to re-arm and a fresh coalition joined Britain in waging war on the French: Austria, Russia, Sweden and the Two Sicilies. Postponing his promenade across the Channel, Napoleon invaded Germany in September. On 20 October the *Grande Armée* (as it was now known) forced over 40,000 Austrians to surrender at Ulm. Three weeks later it marched into Vienna. The French may be forgiven for shrugging off their navy's destruction at Trafalgar the day after Ulm, though it ended any hope of invading Britain. This did not seem to be of crucial importance, especially in the ensuing light of the most brilliant of all Napoleon's victories on 2 December at Austerlitz, when he smashed the combined forces of Austria and Russia, destroying over a third of their army and capturing 45 colours and 180 cannon. The Austrians hastily made peace at Pressburg, abandoning their Venetian possessions and the Tyrol. The following year Francis II exchanged his title of Holy Roman Emperor for that of Emperor of Austria, abolishing his ancient throne to stop Napoleon usurping it. The Russians withdrew. The Third Coalition collapsed. It is said that the news of Austerlitz hastened the death of France's most relentless enemy, the British Prime Minister William Pitt, early in 1806.

The French Emperor was now able to rearrange the map of Europe, and in particular of Germany and Italy. In place of 370 German states he set up the Confederation of the Rhine, consisting of sixteen kingdoms, grand duchies and principalities; the Electors of Bavaria and Württemberg assumed the title of King while Napoleon appointed himself its 'Protector.' Austria and Prussia were excluded. Austrian possessions in northern Italy were incorporated into Napoleon's Italian kingdom, while Naples was overrun and its Bourbon sovereign took refuge in Sicily under the protection of the British navy. The Emperor now ruled an area almost identical with that ruled by Charlemagne, whom he openly considered his predecessor.

Indeed Napoleon was always trying to convince himself that he was Charlemagne's heir and wearied Metternich by constantly harping on this theme in interminable discussions, 'with the feeblest of arguments'. The Austrian Ambassador clearly regarded these Carolingian aspirations as slightly comic. When explaining to Napoleon that the Austrian Emperor's style of 'Sacred and Imperial Majesty' derived from Holy Roman Empire usage, the Emperor commented 'in a grave tone' that it was a fine custom which he himself would adopt one day.

The Bonaparte clan had been of little significant military assistance to its chief during the campaigns which created his amazing dominance of Europe. Prince Joseph's principal contribution was to travel through Flanders and the Rhineland giving innumerable luncheon- and dinner-parties for garrison officers. Prince Louis, commanding the Army of Paris, somehow found time to inspect the garrisons of Antwerp and Amsterdam – as soon as the war was over he retired to his new country house of Saint-Leu on the usual grounds of ill health. Only Joachim Murat had been of real service, fighting with wild heroism if not much strategic sense. Time and again he spearheaded the advance into hostile territory, leading his cavalry at unbelievable speed to take the enemy by surprise, harrying, charging, pursuing. As the Emperor was to say to Count Roederer in 1809, 'Murat is a fool but he has dash and daring!'

On 15 March 1806 Joachim and Caroline were created Grand Duke and Grand Duchess of Berg and Cleves. These two ancient duchies of the former Holy Roman Empire, until now occupied by a Wittelsbach and a Hohenzollern respectively, were on the right bank of the Rhine and together stretched from the river Lippe in the north down through Hesse to the Westerwald. The new state was intended, under French rule, to counter the influence of Prussia along the Rhine. It contained some 320,000 inhabitants. On 25 March, wearing the blue velvet mantle of the Grand Admiral of France and seated on a throne beneath a golden canopy, Grand Duke Joachim I attended High Mass in his capital of Düsseldorf and took the oath as sovereign. Shortly after, he was made a knight of the Spanish Order of the Golden Fleece, one of the most coveted of *ancien régime* distinctions. A court was set up, recruited from the local nobility. The Grand Duchess Caroline – her son Achille now Duke of Cleves – had at last caught up with the Princess Elisa of Lucca, even if the latter was determined to acquire more territory as soon as possible.

Pauline too was elevated. She was delighted by her brother's decree of 30 March. 'The Duchy of Guastalla being at Our disposal, We do hereby dispose of it in favour of Our well-beloved sister Pauline to enjoy in full ownership and sovereignty under the titles of Princess and Duchess of Guastalla.' She was less enchanted when she learnt that this former fief of the Duchy of Parma was only 50 miles square, with a ruined hilltop town for a capital and no more than 5,000 inhabitants. In tears she complained to Napoleon that Caroline had been given a real state 'with ministers and regiments' while 'all I have to rule is a single miserable village with a few beastly pigs'. She went on, 'Dearest brother, I warn you that I'm going to scratch your eyes out if you don't give me a proper state to rule, a bit bigger than a pocket handkerchief and with subjects who don't have four feet and curly tails. I need it for myself and my husband.' The Emperor interrupted 'He's a fool!' 'No one knows that better than I', retorted Pauline. 'Though what on earth has that got to do with ruling a country?' In the end she kept the title but ceded the Duchy itself to the Kingdom of Italy in return for six million francs. The Duchess Pauline was not really interested in governing anything, not even men.

Little Madame Bernadotte, once Désirée Clary, was not forgotten. For her sake Napoleon had forgiven her husband's involvement in Moreau's conspiracy, to the point of buying Moreau's house in the rue d'Anjou and presenting it to Bernadotte. In 1806 Bernadotte was made Prince of Pontecorvo with an income of 300,000 francs and 200,000 in cash as an endowment. Pontecorvo was a tiny enclave within the Kingdom of the Two Sicilies, between Naples and Gaeta, but none the less a sovereign state. No doubt it made the new Prince still more aware of 'the precious worth of Liberty'.

However, another imperial decree fuelled the Bonaparte family's ambitions yet further. Prince Joseph had been sent with the French troops under Masséna who had occupied Naples in February 1806. His brother's decree of 31 March – and his brother's bayonets – created him King Joseph Napoleon I of the Two Sicilies. Now the entire clan would want nothing less than crowns.

6
Kings and Queens –
The Continental System

'After becoming an Emperor Napoleon no longer liked to see republics, especially on his own borders.'

TALLEYRAND

'I felt my isolation. And so, on all sides, I let go anchors of safety to the bottom of the sea.'

NAPOLEON.

The Emperor Napoleon's dominance alarmed Prussia and Russia. The former was infuriated on learning (from the British) that he had offered to return Hanover – currently occupied by the Prussians – to Britain in exchange for Sicily. Murat's plans to enlarge his Grand Duchy at Prussian expense also gave offence. Russia was still smarting from the humiliation of its army at Austerlitz. As usual Britain was ready with subsidies to encourage these two great powers to attack France. Sweden announced her intention of joining them.

The Prussians, under the impression that their troops were no less formidable than in Frederick the Great's day, were the first to take up arms and the first to suffer. Early in October 1806 Napoleon advanced through Saxony like a whirlwind. On 14 October at Jena in a mere few hours he inflicted 12,000 casualties on Prince Hohenlohe, capturing 15,000 men and 200 guns. The same day, only fifteen miles to the north, Marshal Davout routed another Prussian army at Auerstädt, killing all three of its generals. Bernadotte – later nearly court-martialled for failing to engage the enemy in either action – led a swift advance on Berlin, which the Emperor himself soon entered. By the beginning of November, save for a handful of troops in East Prussia, the Hohenzollern no longer had an army – largely because of Murat's merciless and untiring pursuit. Now it was the Russians' turn.

At the end of the month Joachim rode into Warsaw, in a white uniform and red boots, ablaze with gold and diamonds. There were rumours that his brother-in-law intended to re-establish the Polish monarchy, and Murat hoped to be King of Poland. However, Joachim's hopes were dashed when Napoleon and the imperial court arrived at Warsaw. The lesser males of the Bonaparte clan proceeded to make themselves a laughing-stock by their pretentious airs. Piqued at her failure to be impressed by him, Murat rebuked Countess Potocka in his – to her – ludicrous Gascon accent, 'Mme Anna, you aren't ambitious. You don't seem to be interested in princes!' She comments in her memoirs, 'How petty and absurd all those princelings of Napoleon's family looked to us next to the colossus who towered over them.'

On 8 February 1807 in the snow at Eylau the Russians gave the colossus one of the closest-run battles of his career, even if they withdrew after losing 25,000 men compared with French losses of 10,000. Undoubtedly he was saved by Joachim's magnificent charge at the head of over 10,000 sabres, which broke the enemy squares and overwhelmed their guns. Then at Friedland in June the Emperor defeated the Russians decisively, going on to capture Königsberg, the last Prussian stronghold. The following month he met Alexander I of Russia at Tilsit on the famous raft on the river Niemen. They agreed to divide the world between them.

Napoleon had already introduced the 'Continental System' by the Decree of Berlin of November 1806. England, which had been blockading the French, Dutch and German coasts was herself to be blockaded in reverse, prevented from landing her exports in any European port. For the system to succeed, not only would Russia have to co-operate but other countries must be coerced. The logical inference was that all Europe should be ruled from Paris. The basis of this earlier *Festung Europa* was the French Empire, the Confederation of the Rhine, of which Napoleon was Protector and virtual ruler, and a group of vassal states under the Bonaparte clan. Inevitably Spain and Portugal would have to be brought into the system.

The Emperor's grand design of a Europe ruled by Bonapartes was to prove disastrous, not least because of the personal qualities – or lack of them – of the members of the 'dynasty'. Most spectators feel a sense of outrage when invaders evict neighbours from their homes, and Napoleon's family took over not just royal palaces but entire countries. Moreover, the Emperor expected his newly regal brothers and sisters to rule the lands which he had conquered as governors of puppet states. They were vassals who remained French subjects and continued to hold high office in France – Joseph as Grand Elector, Murat as Grand Admiral – and whose subordination was defined by the family statute which gave Napoleon special rights over all imperial princes and princesses. Since they were determined to reign as independent sovereigns, and since their subjects, apart from a few personal friends, never really accepted them, they were always in an impossible position. Yet with purblind fatuity they refused to admit to themselves that they were, at best, imitation royalty who owed everything to their brother's military genius and over-ambitious foreign policy – indeed some of them came to think that they could even survive his

military and political demise and would actually intrigue against him. In
the words of Pieter Geyl, most balanced and perceptive of all the
Emperor's historians,

> The whole system of the vassal kings was a mistake. There was an insoluble
> antinomy between the investing of a man with the old historic majesty of
> kingship, calculated to awaken expectations in his people and ambitions in
> himself, and the insistence that he remain a Frenchman, act upon Napoleon's
> slightest hints, and accept the offensive remarks to which the great man's
> impatience so easily led him.

King 'Giuseppe Napoleone I' had been in residence at Naples since
February 1806, even before being proclaimed sovereign of the Two Sicilies
in March. Prince Louis was proclaimed King of Holland in Paris on 5 June
the same year, entering The Hague three weeks later accompanied by
Queen Hortense.

The Jacobins of a dozen years before accepted the existing social
hierarchies of their new realms without demur. Some feudal privileges
were abolished while the property of hard-line supporters of the former
rulers was confiscated. On the whole the old nobility kept its lands and
position, continuing to hold the higher ranks in the army and administration, and staffing the usurpers' courts. At Naples, as Frédéric Masson
says, 'Joseph claimed he was purely and simply substituting his House for
the House of Bourbon, his person for that of Ferdinand [IV], in order to
govern better through and for Neapolitans, taking the former's place as the
nation's King and putting his own Italo-French dynasty in place of a
Spanish-French dynasty.' He totally rejected Napoleon's advice that he
should treat Naples as a conquered country, confiscate the native nobility's
estates and impose a new French nobility. Nowadays Joseph had no
quarrel with the *ancien régime* – he was at the top of it. When they had their
own Kingdoms Louis and Jérôme would take a similar attitude towards
what remained of it. Not one of the three was a man of a new order.

Joseph Napoleon at once assumed what he considered to be approp-
riately regal airs. He has often been described – notably by his imperial
brother – as a man without ambition, but his behaviour shows the
opposite, even if he vacillated and let himself be swept along by the tide of
events. He thoroughly enjoyed grandeur, deference and luxurious idleness
on a regal scale. Masson calls him the Emperor's 'most level-headed
brother', yet his conduct in the countries in which he was set up as a
monarch scarcely bears this out. In Naples, and later in Spain, he appears
to have been quite out of touch with reality. Intoxicated by his delectable
capital, convinced that he was welcomed by the Neapolitans, he took very
quickly to being a king. He established a royal household and a court,
spending vast sums on royal entertainments and royal amusements – his

hunt rivalled that of the Bourbons and killed a hundred wild boar on a single day at Venafro. Each evening all the ladies of the court would line up to kiss his hand. He even founded a new order of chivalry, the 'Order of the Two Sicilies' – his brother had to stop him from reviving the fifteenth-century 'Order of the Crescent' – besides inventing a new and elaborate coat of arms for himself. He lavished patronage on men of letters and the theatre. He allowed the former regime's officials to keep their posts, began to rebuild the Neapolitan army – recruiting a bodyguard from the Neapolitan nobility in direct opposition to Napoléon's wishes – let the nobles keep their privileges, left the great monasteries alone and declined to introduce the Code Napoléon or a decimal currency on the French model. He attended the liquefaction of San Gennaro's blood at the duomo. (Napoleon enquired sarcastically, 'Congratulations on making peace with San Gennaro, but am I to understand that you have repaired your fortifications as well?')

All this, together with the money he spent, earned Joseph a modest popularity among the cheerful and naturally tolerant inhabitants of Naples, though hardly so much as he fondly imagined. He was certainly very different from the jackbooted, mail-fisted conqueror that they had expected and unquestionably *simpatico*. The volatile *lazzaroni* were ready enough to cheer his coach in the streets out of love of a spectacle, even if their real cheers were reserved for the exiled Bourbons. Joseph was speedily infatuated with his new country, the most beautiful in Europe. He informed the Emperor that everyone of his subjects supported him, from the notorious bandit Fra Diavolo to the haughtiest duke. He told visiting French senators that the Neapolitans thought of him in the same way as the French thought of Napoleon. It made no difference when the latter asked him brutally, 'What sort of love can a people feel for you, do you suppose, when you've done nothing to deserve it?' Joseph did not agree that he was 'among them only by right of conquest', that he was no more than a viceroy of a mere extension of the French Empire. Nor was he prepared to impose a levy of 30 million francs as his brother demanded. Queen Julie had not accompanied him, staying behind at Mortefontaine to bring up their daughters, so he was able to acquire an aristocratic Neapolitan mistress whose embraces made him still more confident of his popularity. (This was the beautiful Maria-Giulia Colonna, the twenty-one-year-old Duchess of Atri, on whom he was to father two children.) The circle of flatterers who had accompanied him from France all added to his illusions. For once he nearly made himself ill from overwork, toiling over state papers, convinced that his efforts would make the Neapolitans love him still more. He wrote an account of his labours to Mortefontaine: 'Read this, my good Julie, to Mama and Caroline. . . . Tell them that one doesn't change at my age. Remind Mama that at every period of my life, whether as obscure citizen, landowner or magistrate, I have always been ready to give all my time to my duties.'

In reality, just as Napoleon had warned him, King Joseph's throne was of course entirely dependent on the bayonets of the army of occupation commanded by Marshal Jourdan. In July 1806 a British expedition landed in Calabria and inflicted a humiliating defeat on a far larger French force at Maida. Although the British quickly withdrew to Sicily, southern Italy rose to wage a peculiarly vicious guerrilla war on the invaders. Astonished, panic-stricken, Joseph wrote to his brother begging for help and for money. 'The treasury is empty. Trade does not exist. The army lacks for everything and I have no means of equipping it. . . . Will Your Majesty send me six million [francs] as soon as possible? The enemy is all along the coast and our army is beginning to lose heart.' In the event, using the utmost cruelty, the French put down all opposition by the following February. The campaign was financed by forced loans and the sale of crown lands, while the nobility's feudal privileges were abolished to facilitate French administration – e.g., hanging the populations of entire towns – and martial law was imposed on Naples itself. Between forty and fifty thousand troops were needed to hold the country down. Joseph, who was more interested in patronizing the arts in his capital, gave them a free hand. He remained convinced of his popularity.

By now King Louis in the Netherlands could only write with a pen tied to his wrist and was fearful lest the Dutch climate damage his health still further. He had accepted his promotion after Napoleon had told him that it was better to die on a throne than live as a mere prince. Surprisingly, he proved to be a little too successful, attracting considerable support from the Dutch. In the view of the most knowledgeable of the Empire's recent historians, Jean Tulard, 'An excellent sovereign, he took to heart the interests of his state, stricken as it was by the Continental Blockade; from thence onwards a conflict with his brother was inevitable.' The Dutch had been ruled from Paris for over a decade and were flattered at having a king, a king moreover who took lessons in their language from the dramatist Bilderdijk as soon as he arrived. Just as Joseph had done at Naples, Louis set up a lavish and costly court, recruiting a royal bodyguard and founding not one but two new orders of chivalry. He also introduced the rank of marshal into the Dutch navy as well as the Dutch army. However, his bodyguard was composed exclusively of Dutchmen and he brought almost no French advisers or hangers-on with him, identifying himself entirely with the Dutch people, who began to refer to him as 'Good King Louis', much to the Emperor's irritation. It was soon clear that he was not prepared to be just an instrument of Napoleon's policies. He was not allowed to create a new Dutch nobility – a *folie de grandeur* typical of the clan – but he succeeded in persuading the Emperor to withdraw a number of French garrisons, to the joy of those on whom they had been billeted, while he was to win genuine popularity by commuting death sentences. Even so it was some time before he made himself felt as a ruler.

Indeed, initially Louis seemed the merest cipher of a sovereign, at home and abroad. Like Joseph he asked for money and was told to find it from his own resources. Queen Hortense – who had wept at the prospect of becoming a queen – made the happiest of impressions, especially on the diamond merchants of Amsterdam where she spent 20,000 francs on stones in one afternoon alone. Alas, the King speedily succumbed to melancholia and within a month had left Holland for his favourite health resort. His dislike of his wife was growing worse than ever. He returned in September and, after his brother's triumph at Jena, belatedly began a very leisurely invasion of Hesse and East Friesland. Everywhere he went he hoisted the Dutch flag instead of the French. The only action throughout his 'campaign' was a single insignificant cavalry skirmish between his men and some Prussian stragglers. Napoleon sent him furious dispatches, complaining of his negotiating independently with the enemy, of taking possession of territories on the right bank of the Rhine in his own name, of disobeying orders. Told to occupy Hanover – and gain some ill-deserved credit – Louis replied he dare not advance without reinforcements. All that stood between him and defenceless Hanover was an antiquated fort with a tiny garrison. The disgusted Emperor ordered him to hand over his command to Marshal Mortier and go home. Nevertheless Napoleon did what he could for Louis's name by announcing that only ill health had made his brother return to his kingdom and that East Friesland would be added to it as a reward for his heroic services.

In August 1807 Jérôme – a Prince of the Empire since the end of 1806 – was made King of Westphalia, a newly created state. It was an entirely artificial country, a mosaic of territories including the former states of Hesse, Brunswick and Nassau together with the Prussian lands west of the Elbe and part of Hanover. The new King had not done a great deal to deserve his crown. After a long stint at sea, during which he again visited the Caribbean though *not* Baltimore – despite bland letters to 'Elisa' – he had served nominally and ineffectually as a corps commander against the Prussians and the Russians. (The roads behind him were blocked by his luxurious personal baggage train and carriages containing his hangers-on.) He did not go to his capital of Cassel to take possession of his realm for several months after his 'accession', remaining in France for the long-drawn-out festivities which accompanied his second wedding. A sycophantic French ecclesiastical court having declared his first marriage

Napoleon at the zenith of his career, during the first consulate, painted by Gérard

The Casa Buonaparte at Ajaccio, where Napoleon was born in 1769

Carlo Buonaparte, Napoleon's father, as he
was before his posthumous transformation
by court painters

Madame Mère, Napoleon's mother

Joseph, King of Spain, Napoleon's brother. He resembled Napoleon physically but in no other way.

Elisa, Napoleon's sister, Grand Duchess of Tuscany and Princess of Piombino. After Napoleon she was the most able of the clan.

Lucien, Napoleon's brother and Prince of Canino. The one member of the family to refuse to obey his brother.

Marshal Bernadotte, who married Napoleon's former mistress, Désirée Clary. They were both to betray the Emperor. A portrait dated 1805 by de Lose.

Pauline, Princess Borghese,
Napoleon's sister. She was the most
promiscuous and the best natured
member of the family.

Jérôme, Napoleon's brother and King
of Westphalia, known as 'Fifi' for
his love of pleasure

Caroline Murat, Queen of Naples – the sister who intrigued against the Emperor

Marshal Murat, Caroline's husband and King of Naples, as he liked to see himself

Napoleon's stepson, Eugène de Beauharnais, Viceroy of Italy and the most loyal of the clan

Hortense de Beauharnais, Queen of Holland, Napoleon's stepdaughter and sister-in-law

A portrait by Gérard of Louis, King of Holland, Napoleon's brother – a paranoic whom Hortense was forced to marry

Joséphine de Beauharnais, Napoleon's first wife. One of the few likenesses, this one by the artist Isabey, to convey her real charm.

Marie Louise, ex-Empress of France and Duchess of Parma, Napoleon's second wife. A daguerrotype taken shortly before her death in 1847.

Adam, Count von Neipperg, Marie Louise's dashing lover, second husband and Prime Minister; his official court title was Cavaliere d'Onore to the Duchess

invalid, in the month that he became monarch he married a Protestant princess of Württemberg. Catherine of Württemberg was the blonde daughter of the monstrous King Frederick, a highly intelligent, sweet-faced but excessively plump girl who blushed when anyone spoke to her. She had not wanted to marry him, but fell hopelessly in love as soon as she did, learning to call him Fifi like the rest of the clan. From the beginning he behaved badly to her. An eye-witness, Mme de Rémusat, tells us that he flirted outrageously with the attractive young Princess Stéphanie-Napoléone of Baden (formerly Beauharnais). At Fontainebleau, 'Princess Catherine, already a little too plump, did not dance and stayed sitting down watching sadly the gaiety of the two young persons who glided to and fro before her regardless of her feelings. Finally, in the middle of a ball one evening, we suddenly saw the new Queen of Westphalia go white, burst into tears, collapse in her chair and finish by fainting away.' The angry Emperor sent his brother off to Boulogne to cool his heels for a few days.

Jérôme was glad to leave Paris at the end of 1807, for more reasons than one. Before his departure he had to ask the Emperor to pay his debts, amounting to nearly two million francs in France alone. As the nucleus of his royal household in Westphalia he took various old cronies who had served with him in the French navy, Lieutenant Meyronnet being appointed grand chamberlain. In December the twenty-year-old King was welcomed to his capital of Cassel by cheering crowds who had not yet taken his measure. An unending succession of wild parties began at his royal palace of Napoleonshöhe – formerly Wilhelmshöhe, a feeble imitation of Versailles built by the Electors of Cassel – ball after ball and banquet after banquet. 'Hieronymus Napoleo' (as he now styled himself on his coinage) was soon in financial difficulties and within three weeks of his arrival was writing to his brother to borrow more money, explaining that it was 'painful' to have to turn away needy creditors. Napoleon was unsympathetic. Luckily a kindly banker in Cassel, a certain Herr Jacobsohn, understood just what was wanted and advanced the necessary funds at enormous interest. In complete disregard of his brother's instructions Jérôme recruited an entirely German bodyguard. However, for his Secretary of State he chose a young Frenchman, his boon companion Alexandre Le Camus, whom he created Count von Fürstenstein – no doubt to soothe German susceptibilities. King Jérôme soon began to cause scandal. He installed notorious 'actresses' at Napoleonshöhe besides having affairs with the ladies of his court. In any case he had two wives. He dispatched his Secretary of State to Baltimore to beg the Pattersons to entrust his son to him so that he could be brought up in Europe 'in a manner befitting his rank'. Le Camus came back with a letter from Betsy and another purporting to be from the three-year-old Jerome Napoleon.

His first wife wrote that she had been negotiating directly with the Emperor, asking him to allow her to come to France and to recompense her with a title and funds to educate their child. Little Jerome Napoleon's letter – presumably written for him – said he would never leave and 'break Mama's heart'. The King wrote back claiming that 'his Elisa and his Jerome had a place in his heart which no power on earth, no political considerations, could ever take away', but that it was no use appealing to his brother. He had a better idea – she must come to Westphalia where he could make her a princess and her son a prince and endow them with large revenues. He assured her that the Emperor knew and approved of his scheme (a complete lie), signing himself 'Yours devotedly for life, Jérôme Napoleon'. Betsy was quite shrewd enough to recognize a ruse to take away her child. She replied with some dignity that 'the Kingdom of Westphalia is not big enough to have two Queens', and went on grimly with direct appeals to her brother-in-law from whom she obtained a not inconsiderable sum of money though nothing else. Her husband does not seem to have been unduly perturbed. He was enjoying himself far too much. His dumpy German Queen continued to love him to distraction despite his flagrant infidelity. To console her, he renamed their country schloss 'Catherineshöhe'.

Jérôme was proving an unmitigated disaster at Cassel. When creating the Westphalian Kingdom the Emperor had described it as an *école normale* for other German states, in the hope that its French balance between old and new would inspire them, and on his arrival the King had been welcomed with genuine enthusiasm by his subjects. In the event his regime was the very reverse of a good example, and soon became thoroughly unpopular – though the Westphalians always remained fond of Catherine. Napoleon had told him, 'I want your subjects to experience liberty, equality and prosperity on a scale hitherto undreamt of by Germans.' Jérôme's two principal ministers, both Frenchmen, did what they could, liberalizing customs duties, emancipating Jews and introducing free vaccination for those brave enough to try it. However, the Westphalians soon groaned under exorbitant taxes and the exactions of the French troops billeted on them, while the treasury was chronically in debt and unable to meet the ruinous demands of an inflated defence budget. The King squandered what money there was all too publicly: his palaces were thronged with chamberlains in scarlet and gold, and the royal mews housed 200 horses and nearly 100 coaches. Even courtiers on whom he lavished diamonds groaned at the cost of their uniforms and of costumes needed for an unending succession of masked balls. He himself was the most expensively dressed man in Europe. Vast sums were spent on the opera and the theatre, Jérôme personally treading the boards. In a ballet in

The Marriage of Figaro he danced the part of Figaro to the sound of castanets, supported by Mme de Boucheporne, both of them scattering flowers on the audience. There was also an *opera buffa, The Comic Shipwreck*, which the cast sang in the nude, though in this instance the monarch did not himself perform. He claimed that such extravaganzas were to encourage the arts, and admittedly in 1808 he invited Beethoven to become *Kapellmeister* at Cassel but the invitation was declined. The extent of his artistic interests may be gauged by the fact that his librarian at Napoleonshöhe, Jacob Grimm, one day to be famed for fairy-tales, was required to supply him with one book during his entire reign. (Fittingly, it was a life of Mme du Barry.) To be fair, he did produce a book of his own, his reign's most positive achievement, entitled *Etiquette at the Royal Westphalian Court*. His real interest was women, the greedy adventuresses with whom he slept, such as the Genoese Blanche Carrega and the French Jenny La Flèche – whose husband was created Baron Kudelstein – being given court appointments and extracting huge sums in cash. Dreadful letters arrived from his brother at Paris, telling him, 'Sell your furniture, your horses, your jewels', to no avail.

Yet Napoleon forgave Jérôme for faults which he would have found inexcusable in anyone else, so strong were family ties. At the end of one letter of furious remonstrance he added in a postcript, 'My dear boy, I do love you, but you are still very, very young.' Ironically, Jérôme's fecklessness was not entirely unacceptable to him. The boy had all the clan's vainglory and like Joseph and Louis wanted to show the world that he was no mere puppet, believing in more manic moods that he was adored by 'his people'. However, he was too busy being *der lustige König* – 'The Merry King' as the Westphalians called him with increasing sourness – to spend much time bothering about political independence. In consequence French troops and officials were able to carry out orders from Paris without hindrance. He acquiesced supinely in the press-ganging of an excessively large proportion of his male subjects into the imperial army.

Since the Emperor Napoleon was most often to be found at Paris the family visited it frequently. The Murats went there as much as possible, both indulging in more or less public love affairs. Laure d'Abrantès informs us that Joachim 'had adopted habits of gallantry which he thought *bon ton* and were nothing more or less than trivial *amours*, which might have passed unnoticed but became ridiculous with his unfortunate accent, his curls which became uncurled in the rain, his polonaises and his itinerant comedian's wardrobe. A great many women nevertheless allowed themselves to be caught by this bird lime.' He had far too keen an eye for the main chance ever to have a really serious liaison which might alienate his formidable wife.

Despite bearing her fourth child early in 1805 and despite the strict etiquette which prevailed at her palace of the Elysée, Caroline amused herself with much more abandon than her husband. If Hortense is to be believed, the Grand Duchess had briefly taken Murat's ADC the Comte de Flahaut as a lover, but generally her affairs were with men of power and influence – and tempestuous. She had an impassioned romance with Laure's husband General Junot in the winter of 1806–7. Vain, insolent and arrogant, he had a name as a lady's man and while his wife was pregnant constantly accompanied Caroline to the Opéra, where she shared his box, and escorted her to ball after ball. (As Governor of Paris he would be a useful friend in the event of Napoleon's death.) On his return from fighting the Russians the Emperor rebuked Junot for having an affair with 'that little fool of a Mme Murat' and stopped a duel which he intended to fight with Joachim. The romance caused much misery and ill feeling, but eventually the Grand Duchess passed on. Junot called her a Messalina, warning his wife to be on guard against her.

Caroline's next sleeping companion was a tall Westphalian nobleman in his mid-thirties with wavy blond hair, the features of a falcon and an irresistibly cheerful manner, a striking figure in a Knight of Malta's red uniform which he always wore to receptions. He was the Austrian Ambassador Count Clemens von Metternich-Winneburg. The Grand Duchess had never before had a lover interested in science, philosophy and music – especially Italian *bel canto* – and who danced beautifully. His easy manners were in pleasing contrast to the airs and graces of Joachim and Junot. He was also an experienced womanizer. She speedily became infatuated. For his part Metternich, while only too well aware of the value of Napoleon's sister as a mistress, seems to have been surprisingly fond of her, wearing a bracelet plaited from her hair. She pretended to give him information, though it was never of much worth. Later he would try to save her from sharing her brother's ruin. Metternich's undoubted affection for her was all the more curious since he regarded the Revolution as a 'monstrous social catastrophe', privately despising the new French society and its leaders who had no more dangerous an enemy than this suave, brilliant, pragmatic champion of the *ancien régime*. Murat grew furiously jealous of the aristocratic ambassador and had some violent quarrels with Caroline, from which she always emerged victorious – both husband and wife knew that without her Joachim was no more than a useful cavalry general.

Hortense, who had a species of love-hate relationship with the Grand Duchess, tells us in her memoirs that no one but Caroline had such 'an art of attracting and charming, with a grace which had something of an Eastern slave girl's seduction in it. Admittedly a small claw sometimes showed itself. . . . Courageous, determined, emotional, the charm which made one long to serve her could not hide her lust for total domination and her envy of anyone else's success.' Talleyrand says that the Grand Duchess 'had the mind of a Cromwell in the body of a pretty woman. Born with a forceful character, graceful, charming, inexpressibly attractive, she lacked only the gift of knowing how to conceal her love of power.'

Metternich's predilection for Caroline did not prevent him from seducing the flirtatious Mme Junot during his embassy at Paris. Laure describes him in those days as 'truly the grand gentleman at his most elegant'. Their affair dragged on for over two years until the Grand Duchess put an end to it in her own inimitable way after he had gone back to Vienna. Masked, she accosted Junot at a ball and told him that he would find in his wife's boudoir a casket which contained love letters from Metternich to Laure – she had discovered their location by bribing Mme Junot's personal maid. The General, whose insanely violent temper was notorious, went home and found the letters. He then attacked Laure, half strangling her and stabbing her repeatedly with a pair of gold scissors, leaving (in her words) 'a blood drenched wife, half dead and cut to pieces by his own hand'. He wanted to challenge Metternich to a duel, but was reconciled to Laure. By the time she wrote down this lurid tale Laure had become an opium addict and was not invariably reliable. Nevertheless it rings true and reveals something of the vindictive savagery of Caroline's nature.

Meanwhile in Paris the beleaguered Joséphine had received ultimately mortal wounds. For years she had said it was impossible for the Emperor to beget a child, putting round her little *mot*, 'Bon-a-parte est bon-à-rien' and joking that in bed her husband could only produce 'piss'. But at the end of December 1806 Eléonore Denuelle gave birth to a son, and there could be no doubt that Napoleon was the father. Caroline Murat at once sent the glad tidings to him in Poland and, presumably to make certain of the evidence, took the child into her own household to be brought up by her own nurses. Eléonore disappeared into obscurity, being married off to an amenable junior officer; her son – Count Léon as he was to be styled – was provided for by his delighted sire.

The Emperor was to beget other bastards. When he had entered Warsaw in December 1806 he had established his headquarters at the Wawel, the former royal palace. Here, during a ball which he gave for the Polish nobility, his sharp eye was caught by a young lady in a plain white dress who, in contrast to almost every woman present, was not wearing jewellery. She was Maria Laczynska, Countess Walewska, then about eighteen, an enchanting, slightly-built blonde with a retroussé nose and a husky voice. She rejected all Napoleon's advances, refusing to answer his notes. However, not only was her husband fifty-five years older, but she was a fanatical patriot. After a week of frenzied persuasion by other patriots led by the Emperor's protégé Prince Joseph Poniatowski, a leading figure in the struggle to restore Poland's nationhood and a nephew of the last Polish king, she abandoned her religious scruples and became Napoleon's mistress. After Eylau he installed her at the vast castle of Finckenstein in East Prussia to where he had moved his base, giving her a room next to his study. Here they spent ten weeks together, until he and his army marched off to fight the Russians at Friedland. At the end of 1807 she followed him to Paris where he found her a house in the rue de la Victoire – near that in which he had first lived with Joséphine – and she was to spend much time in secret there for the rest of his reign.

Nevertheless, after Tilsit in 1807 the Emperor began to contemplate marriage with one of the Tsar's sisters. Headed by the Grand Duchess of Berg, the entire clan set to work to urge a dynastic alliance on its leader. Caroline succeeded in persuading Fouché – who finally severed his last links with the Beauharnais – to tell Napoleon that the French people were so eager for him to have an heir that demonstrations might be expected beneath the windows of the Tuileries. Talleyrand, still eager to thwart such a rival whenever possible, convinced the Emperor that his police chief was organizing entirely spurious demonstrations for his own ends. Moreover, the dowager Tsarina did not want to part with her daughter. Even so, Joséphine now had little hope of escaping a divorce.

The position of the Empress's children was also threatened. During the Russian campaign, discussing the future of France should Napoleon be killed in battle, she had told Junot that Eugène de Beauharnais was the man most likely to succeed to the imperial throne. When the Marshal pointed out that Joseph and then Louis, then her own grandchildren by Louis, were the heirs to the throne, she brushed this aside arguing not implausibly that while they would all be opposed, 'No one would be against my son Eugène.' Now, however, should Napoleon remarry and beget an heir, it would mean the end of her fine hopes for Eugène – quite apart from her own humiliation.

Eugène continued to be a most satisfactory Viceroy of Italy, firm and efficient yet popular. The Vicereine was no less charming and no less admired. They genuinely liked Italians and not simply because Eugène was heir presumptive to the Iron Crown. They lived at Milan in the elegant neo-classical Villa Bonaparte off the Corso, which they preferred as their official residence, instead of in the gloomy ducal palace opposite the cathedral. Their favourite house for the summer was the palace of Monza, a few miles outside the city, with its park of Mirabello, while they had another summer palace in former Venetian territory at Stra on the Brenta, together with official residences at Venice itself and at Verona, Vicenza and Mantua. The Viceroy's duties were demanding, in particular the building of fortifications against possible Austrian aggression and conscripting and training a large army. He none the less found time to be an enthusiastic patron of the arts. At Milan he established a palace of arts and sciences and a new conservatoire, besides being a keen supporter with his wife of the opera at La Scala, while at Venice he re-established the Accademia gallery. The couple spoke excellent Italian and did their best to please their subjects, making many friends among the nobility, wooing the populace with festas and lavish public celebrations. Eugène's dependability made him a favourite with his stepfather and strengthened his mother's standing in the Emperor's eyes.

Joséphine lived in dread of Caroline Murat's machinations despite the Grand Duchess's pretended amiability. In March 1807 Caroline and Pauline entertained the Empress on her feast-day with amateur theatricals at Malmaison, both sisters sang out of tune, each laughing spitefully at the other's performance. In May she had further reason to feel insecure when news came from Holland that her grandson, regarded as Napoleon's ultimate heir, had died in convulsions from croup. The mother Hortense, already unbalanced because of Louis's ill-treatment, was so grief-stricken that doctors feared for her mind. Her husband made her worse by visiting her bedside and telling her to confess her 'guilt' to him. For once Caroline showed herself good-natured, going to Holland and taking her old schoolfriend away to Laeken outside Brussels, then to Paris. On medical advice Hortense went off to the Pyrenees to recover in the mountain air. King Louis followed her there, to accuse her of having an affair with his agent in Paris, Decazes. Eventually she returned to Holland. Her child's death put the question of the succession – and of Joséphine – into everyone's mind again. Her surviving son was delicate (he would die prematurely as a young man) and the Emperor was so concerned that he ordered his doctors to find a cure for croup. Amazingly, in view of their relationship, Louis and Hortense began to sleep together again. In 1808 a third son was born to them, Louis Napoleon – the future Napoleon III. Nobody can have been more relieved at the baby's birth than the Empress.

Unlike Joseph, Louis and Jérôme, Elisa was proving an outstanding success as a sovereign and had become respected if scarcely loved by the Lucchesi. Her supreme achievement at home was to revive the moribund quarries of marble at Carrara, which she financed with a special state bank and staffed with artists and sculptors. Soon the quarries were supplying all official busts of dignitaries throughout the Empire, including 500 of Napoleon in the single month of September 1808. They also exported funeral monuments, fireplaces, clocks, columns and altar pieces, besides an entire mosque for the Bey of Tunis. She drained marshes, imposed a state monopoly on tunny fishing, developed the alum deposits of Piombino, encouraged and improved the manufacture of silks and velvets by engaging experts from Lyons and Genoa, improved tanneries and soap factories, and established libraries, university chairs, a medical college and a Napoleonic Institute modelled on the Institut Français. There was also an Institut Elisa for the education of girls of noble birth – no doubt inspired by her days at Saint-Cyr. Lucca's budget was more than balanced, its treasury replenished by the confiscation of church lands. A state gaming-house also brought in useful revenues. She took pains to beautify her little capital, especially its palace and its theatre, and her influence on Lucca may be seen even today. For relaxation she had a number of country retreats, notably at Bagni di Lucca, at Viareggio by the sea and, above all, at Massa near Lucca which she adorned with superb gardens and an *al fresco* playhouse in which she took an enthusiastic part in amateur theatricals (Racine's *Phèdre* being her favoured role). Abroad the Princess slyly found pretexts for quarrelling with her neighbour, the neurotic Queen Maria Louisa of bankrupt and ramshackle Etruria, forcing her to cede territory – ultimately Elisa intended to take over all Tuscany. When she reviewed her tiny army of Corsican mercenaries on horseback, in a fur-trimmed green uniform and toque, they did not laugh. Her realism was symbolized by her use of the old Buonaparte family coat of arms, instead of some pretentious new imperial creation. She knew just how to handle Napoleon even if he did not like her. His birthday on 15 August was always celebrated with carefully staged public rejoicings and the *Te Deum* sung when news came of an imperial victory. She governed her little state like an eighteenth-century benign despot, and treated lovers just as her brother did his mistresses. There was always a hint of scandal about her court: it was typical that her reader should be an adventuress, Ida Saint-Elme, who had been kept by Marshal Ney.

Elisa's most intriguing affair was with that sinister violinist Paganini – later said to have sold his soul to the devil – whom she appointed *virtuoso di corte* (or court musician) and captain of her bodyguard. During his time at Lucca he composed a sonata for violin in her honour, a sonata for violin and orchestra in the Emperor's honour known as the 'Napoleon' and a peculiarly haunting sonata for violin and guitar. It was not just that her husband Prince Felix had given her a taste for the violin – she genuinely loved music. That renegade Neapolitan Paisiello dedicated his opera *Proserpina* to her, being rewarded with a gold medal, as did the long-forgotten Spontini his *La Vestale*, while she chose the gifted Maestro Puccini (Giacomo's grandfather) for her *maestro di cappella*.

Alone of the family Lucien remained without a crown. He at least acquired a feudal domain, though not from Napoleon. In 1806, hearing that the Papal treasury was short of funds, he offered it a large loan. The amiable Pius VII accepted gratefully and in return insisted on giving him the Roman fief of Canino. Lucien administered Canino with zest, restoring its spa, improving agriculture and vines, refurbishing the local ironworks and excavating a Roman villa which produced some fine statues. In Rome, where he always spent the winter, his luxurious palace, the Palazzo Nuñez, was famous for its pictures and for a theatre in which operas, concerts and plays were performed by the best musicians and actors available. Lucien was visited here by men of letters such as Humboldt and by artists like the sculptor Canova. The Cardinals and the Black, or Papal, aristocracy received him despite his unimpressive appearance – his voice had grown squeaky and he wore spectacles which did little for his short sight. In the hottest weather he would escape to a delightful villa at Frascati. His wife Alexandrine was a sympathetic companion and joined in his activities, including amateur theatricals at their palace in Rome. He met Napoleon at Mantua at the end of 1807 to discuss his position, a discussion which began in the evening and continued until dawn. Although almost certainly offered a crown if he would do so, Lucien still stubbornly refused to give up Mme Alexandrine and deprive his sons of their 'dynastic rights'. He none the less asked for the *cordon* of the Legion of Honour 'as a gesture of good will'. He did not get it.

The Murats were dissatisfied. Instead of making Joachim King of Poland, the Emperor had created a Grand Duchy of Warsaw and presented it to his ally the King of Saxony. For the time being the Murats concentrated on extending their own Grand Duchy, even if they rarely visited it. Joachim refused melodramatically to hand over his single fortress of Wesel to his brother-in-law when requested. 'We are going to see if the Emperor will dare to besiege me there in front of all Europe,' he declaimed. 'If he does, I shall hold out to the very last!' Napoleon showed surprising patience with his sister's idiotic husband – whom he had had to rebuke on the recent campaign in Poland for dressing 'like Fanfani' [a circus rider] – and in January 1808 increased Berg's territory by 150 square miles. Grand Duke Joachim now had almost a million and a quarter subjects. It was not enough. He remained resentful that Berg had not been made a kingdom, that he was not received at the Tuileries with the honours due to a visiting sovereign. The Emperor told him firmly, 'Your rank in my palaces is fixed by the rank you hold in my family, and your rank is fixed by that of my sister.' Joachim had to yield precedence to the despised Camillo Borghese. In the autumn of 1807 the Grand Duke had insured his dignity against outrage by giving a suitably regal reception in Paris at the Elysée. It was for the wedding of his niece Antoinette Bonafoux, who had changed her name to Murat, to Charles of Hohenzollern, son of the Prince of Sigmaringen, who was head of the Catholic, South German Hohenzollerns. The marriage turned out a very happy one, and the couple's grandson became the first King of Roumania. Antoinette received a magnificent dowry, as befitted her uncle's rank. Unflaggingly, Joachim and Caroline continued trying to ingratiate themselves with Napoleon and giving glittering entertainments at the Elysée, which was their real home at this period. Despite frequent infidelity to each other, ambition was forging an increasingly strong bond between husband and wife. Suddenly they saw dazzling prospects.

The Continental System was not working well, English goods entering Europe through Portuguese, Spanish and Papal ports. At the end of 1807, with Spain's agreement, a French army invaded Portugal whose Prince Regent fled to Brazil, and Laure Permon's husband Junot, created Duc d'Abrantès, was appointed Governor-General of Portugal. The invasion enabled the French to concentrate large forces in northern Spain, forces which rapidly turned into an army of occupation. The Emperor was planning to take over the entire country. In February 1808 Murat was made Lieutenant-General in Spain (in France Lieutenant-General meant Viceroy), receiving secret orders. He began to occupy Spain's northern strongholds and then marched south to enter Madrid. The Spanish were already angry, and a rising had broken out which forced King Charles IV to abdicate in favour of his son Ferdinand on 19 March, four days before Joachim's entry into the capital. The latter refused to recognize the abdication, persuading father and son to go to Bayonne where Napoleon would 'arbitrate' between them. The Emperor instructed Murat to 'treat the King well and the Prince of the Asturias and everybody else. Tell them you know nothing and are waiting for my orders.' That very same day Napoleon wrote to offer Louis Bonaparte the crown of Spain instead of Holland. When Charles and Ferdinand arrived at Bayonne they were both bullied into abdicating – there were veiled allusions to Enghien's fate – and taken off to semi-captivity in France.

However, although Joachim had nearly 50,000 troops outside Madrid and although most of the Spanish garrison remained in its barracks, on 2 May the people of the capital attacked the invaders with knives and sticks. Murat later estimated the number of insurgents at 20,000. They took him by surprise and, breaking into the arsenal, obtained guns and ammunition. The fighting began in the morning – precipitated by the enforced departure of some members of the royal family – and lasted until evening. Joachim mowed down his extremely gallant attackers in the streets with grapeshot, then sent his men into their houses after them with the bayonet. He reported to his master that he had killed 1,200 and shot 200 more out of hand, referring to them as *canaille* and claiming that 'better-class' Spaniards were horrified by the rising. He told the Emperor smugly, 'The outcome of 2 May guarantees Your Majesty decisive success. . . . Your Majesty can dispose of the crown of Spain without any risk of disturbing the peace. Everyone accepts the situation and is only waiting for the new king whom Your Majesty is about to give Spain.' Murat was quite certain that he would be the king.

In the mean time, although Louis had declined the Spanish throne, it had been accepted with alacrity by Joseph, who hoped to keep Naples as well. (Not even the Bourbons had aspired to that, dividing the two crowns.) Joachim received a letter from Napoleon, written on the same day as the rising. 'I intend that the King of Naples shall reign at Madrid. I will give you the Kingdom of Naples or that of Portugal.' The Emperor added a comment which showed his opinion of Caroline's abilities. 'With a wife like yours, you can always leave should war summon you back to my side; she is perfectly capable of being regent.'

Murat was bitterly disappointed. He replied, not uncharacteristically, 'Sire, I have received your letter of 2 May and floods of tears flow from my eyes as I answer you. . . . I prefer Naples, and have to inform Your Majesty that at no price would I accept the Portuguese crown.' His dislike of Portugal was probably due to the realization that at Lisbon he would have to play second fiddle to Joseph at Madrid. Some very tough bargaining then ensued, conducted by Caroline. Even that shrewd lady was no match for her imperial brother, who forced the Murats to cede Berg and all their French estates and palaces (valued at 16 million francs) to him. In return, on 1 August 1808 Joachim was proclaimed King Joachim Napoleon of the Two Sicilies at Naples, although still in France to which he had returned after a physical breakdown. The Emperor had told him he need not be in any hurry to leave for his kingdom. However, Napoleon suddenly ordered Murat to set out for Naples as soon as possible.

It is likely that the Emperor's order was provoked by plaintive appeals from 'Don José Primero' to be allowed to return to his beautiful Italian realm which he regretted ever having left. Blissfully happy at the prospect of becoming The Most Catholic King of the Spains and of the Indies, he had crossed the Bidassoa in July to find his new realm convulsed by a full-scale war. Murat's glowing reports had given a totally erroneous impression that the Spaniards were cowed and docile. In the event, Joseph could not even reach his capital before an army of 40,000 of his 'subjects' had been beaten. He wrote wistfully to his mistress at Naples, the Duchess of Atri, 'I find myself crowned king of a people who seem to reject me', but admitted that as usual he was being swept along 'by force of circumstances'. When he entered Madrid the streets were empty and the houses were shuttered, while the nobility had left *en masse* save for a few rare exceptions. The pro-French party, mainly liberals and free-thinkers, was tiny and its members – the 'Josefinos' – were regarded as traitors and collaborators by the vast majority of Spaniards. On 9 August he told his imperial brother, in what was obviously a heartfelt letter, that he wanted to issue a decree 'to the effect that I decline to reign over a people whom I have to subdue by force of arms and, being free to choose such a people and that of Naples which can appreciate my rule and respect my character, I prefer the people who know me and will go back to Naples, expressing my best wishes for the welfare of Spain but devoting myself to working for that of the Two Sicilies.' It was too late.

The Spaniards continued to wage ferocious war on the hated French invaders. As Talleyrand comments in his memoirs, Napoleon had 'attacked Spain shamelessly, without the slightest pretext; no nation could accept such dishonour'. An extremely able French commander, General Count Dupont, was forced to surrender at Baylen with 18,000 men only a week after King Joseph's arrival in Madrid. Joseph had to flee headlong from his capital, accompanied by mutinous and drunken troops who looted his own baggage train, and eventually took refuge at Vitoria within easy reach of the French frontier. The English landed in Portugal, General Wellesley (the future Duke of Wellington) defeating the Marshal Duke of Abrantès (Junot) at Vimeiro on 21 August and occupying Lisbon. By the end of August 1808 Portugal was lost and in Spain the unhappy Joseph retained only a few provinces north of the Ebro. The Emperor had to come down in person to save him, destroying the Spanish armies in a short and bloody campaign, while Marshal Soult chased the little English expeditionary force out of the peninsula. Joseph was able to re-enter Madrid in January 1809, shortly after his brother returned to Paris. But as soon as Napoleon departed, and although he left 270,000 troops behind him, the situation began to deteriorate again. There was a national uprising which took the form of pitiless and unrelenting guerrilla warfare to the death with countless small engagements rather than decisive battles, a blood feud between Spanish and French which found expression in horrible atrocities by both sides. The English would quickly reappear. The French marshals bickered among themselves as to what was to be done about this impossible situation, something quite new in their experience. King Joseph had good reason to lament his two, all too short, years at Naples. Yet with fatuous over-confidence he none the less continued to aspire to be an independent ruler. In a pathetic letter of December 1808 he had complained to his brother that, because of his lack of power, 'I blush with shame before my subjects.' To save Joseph's face the Emperor gave him just a little more authority and to display it 'His Most Catholic Majesty' announced unconvincingly that among other duties he accepted that of maintaining 'the unity of our holy religion'. After his return to Madrid he boasted to Napoleon, 'Give me a million men and a million francs and I will give back peace to this country'. The following month, February, he asked to be allowed to abdicate – an offer to be repeated on many occasions – if he was not allowed to govern the Spanish people 'in my own way'. Many of his letters went unanswered. He was no more than an irrelevance, whose sole justification was that he was a Bonaparte, a cipher in the hands of baffled military advisers who snubbed him and laughed at his 'plans'. He consoled himself in his usual way, with the Condesa Jarnuco, the widow of a Governor-General of Cuba, and with the Marquesa del Montehermoso, a mature, ripe-figured lady of twenty-five, whose husband he rewarded by creating him a grandee of Spain – a number of actresses also served, notably the beautiful Italian La Fineschi. The 'Spanish ulcer' (Napoleon's own description) in the flank of the French Empire and of the Continental System was to prove a mortal wound.

The Emperor was committing another costly error, not quite so obvious yet just as deadly in its consequences as his invasion of Spain. He made the fatal mistake of quarrelling with the Catholic Church. Pope Pius VII was by nature a timid, even an accommodating, man who had travelled to Paris and to Milan and meekly crowned Napoleon, accepting his accompanying humiliations. But while the old pontiff – he had been born in 1740 – showed the meekness of the Benedictine monk that he was, he also possessed the dedication of a monk. Inevitably he enraged the Emperor who expected him to be blindly obedient out of gratitude for the concordat. Among his offences there were three in particular: first, the Pope refused to annul King Jérôme's American marriage; second, he declined to recognize Joseph as King of Naples; and third, he insisted on remaining neutral, refusing to close the ports of the Papal States to English ships. Moreover, he would tolerate no further interference in the affairs of the Church. In April 1808 Napoleon's troops occupied Rome. In 1809 the Patrimony of Peter would be absorbed into the swollen French Empire, and Pius would then excommunicate the invaders and be imprisoned at Savona in the Apennines. Catholics everywhere, including Uncle Fesch – a political prelate if ever there was one – were to be outraged. In France the Church, purified and rejuvenated by years of persecution, was going to revert to royalism and counter-revolution and mount a discreetly formidable campaign against the imperial regime. Napoleon would find that he had done incalculable damage to his popularity among many who had hitherto been his warmest supporters.

The Spanish war and the emerging conflict with the Papacy were unmistakable danger signals. Indeed Talleyrand, that supreme realist, had ceased to be Foreign Minister as early as August 1807. He was already convinced that his master was overreaching himself. He tells us, 'At that crucial period in his career one is almost led to believe that he was swept on by some irresistible force blinding his powers of reason. His Spanish enterprise was sheer madness.' Both Talleyrand and Fouché saw ultimate disaster and began to conspire against him. Others noticed the deterioration, even in his personal appearance, the signs of decay. The Duc de Broglie, who saw Napoleon in the spring of 1808 on his way to Bayonne to browbeat the Spanish royal family into abdicating, records,

> Already that young First Consul, whom I had first seen striding briskly through the Tuileries, arm in arm with Bourrienne and a light Turkish sabre under his other arm, slim and quick, with olive skin and bright eyes, had completely vanished. His looks had changed entirely. His figure had grown stocky and thickset, his short legs had put on flesh, his complexion was livid, his forehead was balding and his face was like something on a Roman medal. . . . As one of the crowd who had gathered to watch him go in and out, I really did think that everything about him savoured of a [Roman] Emperor and of such an Emperor at his worst.

By now Napoleon not merely accepted but drank in flattery. He was starting to alarm the notables.

The Emperor was not the only member of the clan whose appearance was deteriorating. Joséphine's 'slender and elegant figure which had been one of her principal attractions had entirely disappeared', reports Mme d'Abrantès, 'and assumed that maturity which we find in the statues of Agrippina' – a disaster for the poor woman in her particular circumstances. Joseph too was thickening, while Elisa was beginning to look like Napoleon in skirts. Joachim now sported a villainous moustache, which did not suit him. (Seeing a portrait of Murat painted at this time, Lady Blessington would say that it gave her 'the impression of a bold captain of banditti, dressed in the rich spoils he had plundered', a fair enough description.) However, Pauline still kept all her ravishing and widely acclaimed allure, and Madame Mère remained as astonishingly youthful as ever.

Needless to say, none of the Bonaparte clan was as yet aware of any cause for alarm, not even hard-headed Elisa. There was one exception, Letizia. Her son was essentially a compulsive professional gambler on a gigantic scale, just as her husband Carlo had once been one on a very small scale. The Emperor's entire position always depended on taking more and more desperate risks with ever-dwindling resources; in consequence, while his family rose with him, at the same time all of them lived with him on the brink of total ruin. Madame Mère seems to have sensed this from the very beginning. As she put it in her vile French, '*Pourvou que ça doure*'

(Provided it lasts). This was undoubtedly the reason why this shrewdest of matriarchs never flagged for a moment in her attempts to extort as much money as possible from him. She was preparing for a very rainy day indeed. 'My son has a fine position,' said Letizia, 'but it may not continue for ever. Who knows whether all these kings won't some day come to me begging for bread?'

7

Imperial Summer

'Not one of us.'

LETIZIA BONAPARTE ON THE ARCHDUCHESS MARIE LOUISE

'I did not have Genghis Khan's good fortune in possessing four
sons whose sole rivalry consists in trying to serve him. In my case
I only had to nominate someone a King and he would at once
believe that he was a King "By the Grace of God". Instead of
having a lieutenant on whom I might rely I merely acquired yet
another enemy to worry about.'

NAPOLEON TO LAS CASES, *The Memorial of St Helena*

The chief of the Bonaparte clan was to succumb to its greatest weakness, its
passion for blue blood. By divorcing Joséphine and marrying the daughter
of the Austrian Emperor – Marie Antoinette's niece – he hoped to bury his
reputation as a Jacobean and legitimize his dynasty. After 1808 he no
longer styled himself Emperor of the French Republic but Emperor of the
French. He also created a new aristocracy. Secretly he retained a deep
respect for the nobles of the *ancien régime* but he none the less wished to
humiliate them, while he had followers who were avid for titles of their
own. Outside France he erected duchies and principalities in Italy and
Germany which he endowed with immense estates. Inside France he
created counts and barons. Among the marshals who received titles
Augereau, the former footman, became Duke of Castiglione, Masséna the
ex-pedlar Duke of Rivoli, Lannes, once a dyer's apprentice, Duke of
Montebello and Ney, who had begun life as a cooper, Duke of Elchingen.
Lefebvre, a former hussar trooper whose father had been a miller and who
had married a washerwoman, was created Duke of Danzig; when
addressed as 'Duchess' at the Tuileries by the Empress, his wife winked at
the footman and said, 'What do you think of that, old boy?' The Emperor
was painfully aware that his new nobles and their titles were the laughing-
stock of the Faubourg Saint-Germain, the aristocratic quarter of Paris.

Throughout his reign Napoleon suffered from an acute sense of not
really belonging on the throne. Metternich realized that the Emperor
'deeply regretted not being able to claim that his power was based on the
principle of legitimacy'. Yet might not legitimacy be acquired through
marriage? An Austrian wife was very far from Napoleon's mind, however,

when he left Spain at the beginning of 1809. Encouraged by his involvement in the Iberian Peninsula, the Austrians had declared war on France. Their main army was commanded by the Grand Master of the Teutonic Knights, the Habsburg Archduke Karl 'der Feldherr', who during the two battles of Aspern-Essling on 21-2 May forced the Emperor to retreat for the first time in his career. He retrieved the situation at Wagram on 6 July, where he routed Karl's army, and Austria was forced to cede so much territory that the Emperor Francis lost three and a half million subjects. Yet those close to Napoleon noticed that he was unusually preoccupied despite this latest triumph.

Even the Emperor Napoleon was himself starting to feel the strain of the constant campaigning and blood-letting which, slowly but inexorably, was sapping France's strength. The dynamism engendered by revolutionary ideals had long since vanished. He wanted peace, to settle down, to establish his Empire on a lasting basis. As early as October 1807 he had not disagreed with Fouché when the latter had pointed out to him that the English persevered in their struggle against France only because they were encouraged 'by the single-minded reflection that since he was childless and consequently had no real heir the Emperor, in the event of his death which could happen at any moment, would destroy his own government'. And while Napoleon had by no means lost faith in his star, he nevertheless wanted his Empire – and his family – to survive him. Fouché and the entire Bonaparte clan continued relentlessly to remind him that everything depended on his having a son. But there was the problem of the Empress, for whom he still retained a deep affection.

As early as the autumn of 1807 Joséphine too had admitted to her son that she lived in fear of a divorce, writing to Eugène in Italy in September about the machinations of the Murats after the birth of Eléonore Denuelle's child. The Viceroy answered that he himself had heard rumours at Munich of an impending divorce, calmly telling his mother not to worry. 'If His Majesty continues harassing you about the need to have children, tell him that it is simply not fair of him to persist in chiding you about it. If he really does believe that his own personal happiness, and that of France, depends on his producing heirs, then he will have to act accordingly. But he must treat you properly, give you enough money, and let you live in Italy with your children.' The Empress was still sufficiently light-hearted and frivolous to enjoy the company of a young male admirer, the Duke Frederick Louis of Mecklenburg–Schwerin, who was extremely good-looking and not yet thirty, although she must have known that her foolish flirtation would irritate the most intolerant of husbands. But she cannot have been exactly reassured when a remark of Fouché was repeated

105

to her, that her death would be very convenient: 'It would remove so many difficulties.' The Minister of Police actually approached her directly just before Mass one Sunday in 1807, to ask her to allow her marriage to be dissolved 'in the national interest'. Thenceforward she lived in fear of being poisoned. Napoleon told Lucien that she 'cries whenever she has indigestion, suspecting that she has been poisoned by the people who want me to remarry'. In 1808 she was silly enough to let herself be caught visiting a slightly disreputable theatre incognito with Frederick Louis. The Emperor was furious and banished the Duke from France. She moaned to Eugène, 'I can't go out any more, I have no enjoyments.' That spring Napoleon informed Talleyrand that he wanted a divorce, but then spent the night with the Empress telling her again and again, 'My poor Joséphine, I can never leave you.' She lived a wretched life, devoured alternately by apprehension or hope. Yet later that year she was able to write, 'For the past six months he has been nothing less than perfect in his behaviour towards me.' It was, however, her swan-song.

The Countess Maria Walewska joined the Emperor on his Austrian campaign of 1809. After he had captured Vienna in the summer and had installed himself in the Habsburgs' palace of Schönbrunn, she found a discreet house conveniently close and apparently saw a good deal of him during some of the hardest-fought battles of his career. Early in the spring of 1810 she would return to Poland, to her aged husband's country house of Walewice, to give birth to a son, Alexander Walewski; before that year was over she would be back in Paris showing him to his father, but by then Napoleon would long since have decided Joséphine's fate.

On his return to France from the wars in October 1809, the Emperor summoned his consort to Fontainebleau and began to hint that he wanted a divorce. His Secretary, Baron Méneval, tells us that he did so 'without explaining himself clearly, and more by innuendoes. . . . It was a state of affairs too painful to last for very long, since it brought into their daily intercourse constraints which were a torture to both of them.' This agony of suspense came at last to an end on 30 November 1809 at the Tuileries. The Prefect of the Palace, Baron de Bausset, records in his 'anecdotal memoirs' how on the evening of that day Joséphine 'gave me an impression of suffering and despair'. Later, after hearing piercing screams from the Emperor's salon he was summoned and found 'the Empress stretched on the carpet uttering heart-rending shrieks and moans. "No, I can never survive it", the unhappy woman was crying.' Napoleon asked Bausset to carry her along the private staircase which led to her apartments. The Baron thought that she had genuinely swooned, but then Joséphine hissed, 'You're holding me too tight.' Her husband complained, with some justice, to Bausset, 'I am all the more upset by the scene which Joséphine has just been making since she must have heard from Hortense at least three days ago of the sad necessity which has forced me to leave her.' An adventuress to the end, she was determined to extract both as much sympathy and as much money as she could from her difficult situation.

On 15 December the Bonaparte clan, including the Beauharnais, met at the Tuileries in a family council. Naturally the Murats made a point of being there as did Madame Mère and Pauline, though King Joseph had to miss the occasion. Eugène and his sister were there to support their mother – even if Hortense sobbed and cried throughout. With consummate hypocrisy Pauline and the Queen of Naples also shed a few decorous tears. The Empress rose to read a speech dictated by Napoleon in which she agreed to a divorce. 'With the permission of my august and dear husband, I must now declare that since I no longer have any hope of bearing the children who could satisfy the needs of his policies and the interests of France, it has pleased me to give him the greatest testimony of affection and devotion that has ever been offered. . . .' Before she had finished she broke down and burst into tears, to maximum effect. The gallant Eugène fainted after leaving the room. A clerical tribunal – though without the Pope's approval – subserviently annulled the marriage that had been privately solemnized just before the imperial coronation, on the very technical grounds that there had been no proper witnesses and that the priest (none other than Cardinal Fesch) had not been properly authorized. Reporting the divorce the official journal, the *Moniteur*, says, presumably with imperial approval: 'The Emperor wept.' Two days later, after fainting when Napoleon said goodbye to her, she left the Tuileries and drove off through the rain to find refuge at Malmaison. The 'old lady', as her former husband's troops called her, was still only forty-six. She retained the title of Empress, her numerous châteaux, all her jewels and an annual income of three million francs in gold. She also received the additional title of Duchess of Navarre (which was a far from modest one, considering that the Bourbons had been styled 'Kings of France and Navarre'). Moreover, her affecting performance had won her the sympathy of the public, not merely in France but all over the world. The Bonaparte clan would one day discover that they had won a truly Pyrrhic victory, one which had been their own ruin. 'No one in the palace will fail to rue the day she leaves', Talleyrand had prophesied to Mme de Rémusat. 'When some foreign princess arrives to fill her place, you are going to see ill feeling between the Emperor and his courtiers. We shall all be the losers by it.'

The reason why Napoleon had taken so long to rid himself of his barren wife is that he wanted a Russian bride and that the Russians would not give him one. A dynastic alliance with the Tsar might well have created a Europe with only two capitals, Paris and St Petersburg. Alexander I had

had a sister of just the right age, the Grand Duchess Catherine, but she had been married with suspicious promptness to the Duke of Oldenburg. Another sister, Grand Duchess Anne, was still only a child and the French Emperor could not wait for her. In January 1810 he called another family council at the Tuileries to discuss the problem. Three candidates were suggested for the recently vacated post of Empress – the little Russian Grand Duchess, the King of Saxony's daughter and the Archduchess Maria Louisa of Austria. Napoleon had already decided on the latter. She was eighteen, by report both pretty and healthy, and not only was her father Emperor of Austria but her aunt Marie Antoinette had been Queen of France, a qualification which enchanted her suitor. He was deaf to Murat's objection that she might revive unhappy memories of the 'Austrian woman' – King Joachim was too obviously influenced by the consideration that another aunt was the exiled Queen of the Two Sicilies at Palermo, Maria Carolina. Less realistically, Napoleon ignored well-grounded warnings that he would finally alienate those men of the Revolution who still remained loyal to him, and that 'within two years France would be at war with one of the two [Imperial] Houses, the one whose daughter the Emperor does not marry'. He was blinded by royal snobbery, by the belief that such an alliance, especially if blessed by a son and heir, would at last admit him to the tiny, charmed circle of *ancien régime* sovereigns and that the *grands seigneurs* of pre-1789 France would accept him as their legitimate monarch. He was far from candid in stating with feigned bluntness, 'After all, it's only a womb I'm marrying'. He convinced himself that Austria would now have an interest in preserving his régime come what may, that Russia could be drawn into a triple alliance of three Emperors. This outstanding political realist let his judgement be overshadowed by what in crude terms may be described as mere social advancement. The Austrians proved gratifyingly accommodating, in pleasing contrast to the Tsar. Metternich, now their Foreign Minister, advised the Emperor Francis to sacrifice his daughter in order to secure a breathing space 'to enable us to recover our strength'.

Accordingly the Archduchess Maria Louisa Leopoldina Carolina Lucia of Habsburg, Archduchess of Austria and Princess of Hungary and Bohemia, was betrothed to the man whom she had always been brought up to think of as 'the Corsican Monster'. In February 1810 he sent her a letter. 'The brilliant qualities which make you so distinguished have filled Us with the desire of serving and honouring you and We have accordingly addressed Ourselves to the Emperor your father, beseeching him to entrust Us with the happiness of Your Imperial Highness.' He ended, 'We pray God may keep you, my cousin, always in His holy and well-deserved care,' signing himself, 'Your good cousin, Napoleon'.

Marie Louise – she was soon to Gallicize her name – was a tall, blond eighteen-year-old with a splendid bust and a peach-blossom complexion. Writing to his wife at the time of the betrothal Metternich, a keen observer of young women who had seen her often, says that 'Plain rather than handsome of face, she has a very fine figure and when made up and properly dressed will do very well.' However, for once he erred in predicting that 'the new Empress will please at Paris'. Contemporary portraits show a pretty enough face, high-coloured and a little coarse, with protuberant eyes and the famous and unsightly Habsburg lip. The lip may well have been over-emphasized by official artists for dynastic reasons, since it is much less obvious in a daguerreotype taken just before her death in 1847 (which preserves a countenance of unmistakable amiability). Most interpretations of Marie Louise's character are by admirers of Napoleon, who cannot forgive her for what they see as her betrayal of the Emperor. Undoubtedly the French did not care for her during her brief period as their Empress, but this was for the same reason as they had disliked her aunt Marie Antoinette – her nature was too Teutonic. For her part she was instinctively disinclined to like the French ruling classes, both the old and the new. Yet she had a much more interesting and agreeable personality than is generally appreciated. She seems to have been an uncomplicated, good-natured and straightforward person, neither very clever nor particularly stupid, desperately shy, to the point of awkwardness. She painted surprisingly well, in oils, both landscapes and portraits, read a good deal, including much of Chateaubriand, and was a talented musician – she sang and played the piano and the harp, all very well, and not only enjoyed Mozart but shared her family's love of Beethoven. Later her Parmesan subjects were to be devoted to her in a way that they were to few other rulers, yet history has not been kind to this unfortunate victim of dynastic politics. She had been brought up in almost nun-like seclusion by the strictest of governesses, had never been left alone with any man save her father and, to ensure that she would not be contaminated by even a hint of the mysteries of sex, had only been allowed female pets. Nor had she ever visited a theatre. Her sole jewellery was a coral necklace and some seed pearls, her entire pleasures consisting in her dog, her parrot, her flowers and her Viennese whipped cream – with the notable addition of her painting and her music. What now took place must have been a horrifying experience for her. It began in March 1810 with a proxy wedding in Vienna at which her future husband was represented by her uncle the Archduke Karl (the hero of Aspern-Essling). Then there was a slow and stately progress to France. She was met *en route* at Munich by Caroline Murat, who had been sent to escort her – not a tactful choice. Next day she wrote with surprising shrewdness in a letter to her father, 'The Queen of Naples kissed me and behaved in a very friendly way, but I don't trust her.' Less shrewdly, Caroline reported to Murat that they would not have any trouble with Marie Louise. In reality she had made an enemy of her from the very beginning. Determined to assert herself over a Habsburg Archduchess, during the journey the upstart Queen – only too well aware that her charge's aunt at Palermo was the rightful Queen of Naples – arrogantly dismissed her former governess and one remaining Austrian lady-in-waiting, Countess Lazanski, sending her back to Vienna without even allowing her to say goodbye. Later the Emperor apologized for his sister's presumption.

The 'august brood-mare', terrified by the prospect of even seeing the Corsican ogre, reached France at the end of March. Napoleon met her at Saint-Cloud and, having first ascertained from Cardinal Fesch that the proxy marriage was valid, insisted on sleeping with her there and then, before the civil marriage took place, let alone the religious ceremony. This was no way to treat a nervous young Archduchess, disaffected noblemen observed, but one could only expect such manners from a parvenu monarch. The civil wedding took place at Saint-Cloud – spectators noted with amusement that the bride was half a head taller than the groom. With almost unbelievable lack of tact the celebrations that night, slavishly following those for Marie Antoinette's marriage, included a performance of *Iphigenia in Aulis*. The religious ceremony took place the following day at the Louvre, in the Salon Carré which had been converted into a chapel for the occasion, with every pompous extravagance of imperial display. It was conducted by Fesch. Marie Louise was in white tulle embroidered with silver, Napoleon – who, it must be remembered, was over forty by now – in white satin from head to foot. Four ladies placed the crown made for Joséphine's coronation on the head of the new Empress. Queen Caroline of Naples, Grand Duchess Stéphanie-Napoléone of Baden and the Vicereine Augusta Amelia of Italy walked in front of her bearing lighted tapers and insignia on tasselled cushions, while her train was carried by the Queens of Spain, Holland and Westphalia, Grand Duchess Elisa of Tuscany (recently promoted) and the Duchess Pauline of Guastalla. The last two ladies had complained that so menial a duty was beneath their dignity, but to no avail; even Pauline's pathetic plea that the train was far too heavy for someone in her frail state of health was rejected by the Emperor.

The Bonaparte clan, brothers as well as sisters, disliked Marie Louise from the start. Their aversion was heartily reciprocated, though she wrote carefully and insincerely to her father in Vienna, 'My mother-in-law is a very amiable and respected princess, my sisters-in-law are extremely agreeable and the Vicereine is very pretty.' (Plainly she guessed, with reason, that her letter would be intercepted *en route*.) Her relationship with the clan was defined by Letizia very early on, with typical bluntness and grimness: 'She is not one of us.' If the Bonapartes had once hated Joséphine for her superior airs, they now united in loathing an Archduchess who was infinitely higher in the social scale than a Viscountess of dubious reputation.

The marriage caused a good deal of cynical amusement throughout Europe. Across the Channel Lord Castlereagh joked that he supposed it was necessary to sacrifice a virgin to the Minotaur from time to time. However the Tsar was far from amused, grumbling that 'the next thing will be to drive us back into our forests'. Perhaps ironically, the wedding took place on 1 April. Marie Louise had been accompanied to Paris by Metternich in person, on a 'special mission' to the Emperor Napoleon. During the spectacular state banquet at the Tuileries which followed, that wily diplomat went to a window and, raising his glass before the crowd outside, shouted 'To the King of Rome!' He was deliberately giving the impression that the Austrian Emperor had recognized Napoleon as a full member of his own family and presented him with the gift of the title once born by the heirs of the Holy Roman Emperors.

'For the first three months of his marriage Napoleon was at the Empress's side day and night', we are told by his secretary Baron Agathon Fain. 'The most urgent affairs could barely drag him away for even a few moments.' He was always in her apartments, chatting with her, examining her books, listening to her singing at the piano. He tried to learn to dance, played billiards with her and gave her riding lessons. Beyond question Marie Louise returned his affection. Like her father, the much-married Emperor of Austria, her impeccably correct exterior concealed a demanding streak of sensuality. Physical love quickly became necessary for her well-being, to the point that she could not do without it. While this need ensured the success of her marriage to so virile a husband as Napoleon, it also made the marriage vulnerable, however faithful, however much of a one-man woman, she may have been by nature.

King 'José Primero' had not come to the wedding, being too busy with Spanish affairs of state. His brother had considered returning to Spain, where he might well have established French domination on a much more solid basis, but was prevented by his marriage. Instead Marshals Soult and Masséna directed military operations, the former as chief-of-staff frequently referring to Napoleon in Paris. The situation deteriorated steadily. At Talavera in July 1809 Wellesley had defeated a French army much larger than his own and, though he had had to withdraw, remained a major threat. Everything depended on driving the British expeditionary forces out of the peninsula. But the French divided their strength. Masséna had to sit outside Wellesley's lines at Torres Vedras unable to batter his way in because Soult had been forced to adopt Joseph's plan to conquer southern Spain, diverting 60,000 indispensable troops. As soon as Soult occupied Seville in 1810 a totally unsuspected army of Spanish patriots entered Cadiz – a natural fortress – and installed their Central Junta (the opposing government). Although Saragossa surrendered after a heroic resistance of eight months the city was of little strategic value. The Emperor himself began to despair of conquering this impossible country, once an almost slavishly obedient ally but now holding down immense numbers of irreplaceable veteran troops. In the end he would even contemplate trying to reach a compromise with the English. From time to time Joseph threatened to abdicate, though he had no intention of doing so. On one occasion he wrote to Julie telling her to leave Mortefontaine and come to him with as much money as she could lay her hands on. Apart from local taxes from Madrid and a few other cities, and some confiscated church property, he was virtually penniless. Although he might walk candle in hand in all the Holy Week ceremonies at Seville, he and his regime were despised. Despite being a modest drinker, he was popularly known as 'Don Pepe the Bottle' after a slanderous play of that name. (Oddly enough, his weakness for Spanish mistresses went uncensured.) His troops murdered and looted quite unchecked, Soult specializing in works of art. Joseph himself repudiated 'the horrible treatment of the people at the hands of the military governors' in a letter to his wife. Yet with smug fatuity he none the less remained convinced that if the Emperor would give him more independence the Spaniards would rally to him. In preparation for this he issued edicts in April 1810, dividing the country into thirty-eight departments on the French model and replacing the army of occupation by a civilian militia. He had lost all contact with reality.

Even Joseph must have become uneasy about his position when King Louis was forced to abdicate. The latter had proved incapable of understanding that his kingdom's purpose was to stop British goods from reaching Europe through its ports. Instead, Louis encouraged smuggling and allowed American ships to bring in British cargoes. The Emperor ordered him to employ French customs officials. According to Count Molé, he told Louis to remember, 'You are first of all, indeed above all, a French prince,' whereupon King 'Lodewijk' (as he signed himself) retorted, 'you should have said that before giving me my crown. . . . What you now demand spells ruin and disaster for a nation whose fate you have entrusted to me, and whose welfare is my supreme duty.' There were clashes between French and Dutch in Holland, the King invariably responding with ludicrous arrogance to complaints by his brother. At his little court at The Hague Louis was always surrounded by Dutchmen or by those who sympathized with the Dutch. On the other hand Queen

Hortense, devoted to her stepfather, still saw herself as a Frenchwoman and led a pro-French opposition party, which did not sweeten relations between the unhappy couple. In December 1809, when the King had come to Paris for the family council about Joséphine's divorce, the Emperor threatened to annex Holland, claiming it was 'nothing short of an English colony'. Napoleon then started to install French garrisons in the Dutch ports, at which his brother ordered the Governors of Breda and of Bergen-op-Zoom to resist the imperial troops – with little effect. By May 1810 Louis's entire realm south of the Rhine had been incorporated into France, while Utrecht and The Hague were occupied as well. Seemingly only Amsterdam would be left to the King. It was too much for his pride. On 3 July 1810 he abdicated secretly in favour of his son Napoléon-Louis. He had already sold some of his Dutch estates and sent money and diamonds out of the country. That night, with only two trusted officers, he fled over the German border until he reached a spa in Bohemia where treatment for his disease was available. It was a fortnight before the Emperor learnt where he had gone. He immediately incorporated the rest of Holland into the French Empire.

Jérôme was on better terms with his imperial brother, if only because he was far more interested in pleasure than in power – albeit pleasure on the grand scale. Life at his flashy imitation Versailles of Napoleonshöhe continued to be a spendthrift succession of lavish balls, banquets, sledge parties and theatrical entertainments, thronged by 'actresses' with whom he was still having countless affairs. Even his affectionate little Württemberger Queen began to lose patience with him. He spent yet more money when they went on shopping sprees to Paris during visits in the winter of 1809–10, squandering a million and a half francs – he purchased a crown and some unusually ornate coaches besides ordering a statue and fifty-four busts of himself, a statue and twelve busts of Queen Catherine, and twenty-six busts of other members of the clan (all to be supplied from Elisa's marble quarries at Carrara). He was mildly concerned when news of impending state bankruptcy arrived from Cassel and again tried to borrow from the Emperor, without success. When the latter insisted on revising his kingdom's boundaries, he blustered, 'Surely Your Majesty does not wish to humiliate me before all Europe?' but quickly gave way. Like Murat, he had hopes of Poland. In the mean time he diverted himself by designing extremely expensive uniforms for his Westphalian soldiers and obtaining the collars of all the great orders of chivalry, new and old – the Italian Iron Crown of Lombardy, the Danish Elephant. He not only affected his brother's uniform and hat but such mannerisms as placing his hand inside his coat. Since he alternated between saturnine pomposity and feverish gaiety the imitation was not a success.

In Naples King Joachim Napoleon and Queen Caroline were not altogether happy. On 6 September 1808 Murat had ridden into the 'Most Faithful City', wearing an enormous cocked hat with white plumes and encrusted from head to foot in 'gold and the inevitable diamonds. Dramatically, he was escorted by only a single ADC, the dashing, impeccably noble Count de la Vauguyon. Queen Caroline arrived three weeks later. The royal couple were enchanted by their kingdom and its truly regal palaces: the Palazzo Reale on the seafront at Naples (with a wonderful terrace of lemon trees) was vast enough but the palace of Caserta a few miles from the capital was even larger than Versailles. The Queen introduced the pompous ceremonial of her brother's court while, so we are informed by the French Ambassador the Duc d'Aubusson la Feuillade (a fastidious survivor from pre-1789 days) 'King Gioacchino Napoleone I' immediately assumed a notably stiff and haughty manner for his public appearances. They began to give balls at Portici, the Neapolitan Fontaine-bleau, and at the little palace of La Favorita by the sea. A month after his arrival Murat enjoyed a minor triumph when his troops overran Capri and captured its British garrison's commander, Sir Hudson Lowe. Yet there were many problems for Joachim and Caroline in their new realm, such as a bankrupt treasury, a countryside swarming with guerrillas loyal to the Bourbons, the menace of the British navy and an expensive French army of occupation. For Naples remained – in the words of Frédéric Masson – 'a well down which French gold and French blood had to be poured'.

Indeed Murat felt so unsure of his subjects that when not philandering he sat up for most of the night reading police reports. To ingratiate himself he made splendid offerings at the shrine of San Gennaro, his realm's patron saint, and was promptly told off by his brother-in-law for 'aping' Neapolitans. Napoleon also intervened in domestic affairs, insisting on the imposition of the Code Napoléon. He was irritated by the way in which Joachim treated his extremely capable sister as a mere consort and tried to push her into the background. Laure d'Abrantès tells us that 'Joachim, like all henpecked husbands, declared loudly that he would not be controlled by his wife and was not going to be "a second Bacciochi"'. She adds that 'he and the Queen became implacable enemies and there was never-ending discord in the palace at Naples'. Caroline's letters to the Emperor, frequently critical of her husband, made the latter still more angry when they were intercepted by his police.

Moreover, when the couple visited Paris at the end of 1809 for Joséphine's divorce and to discuss the new imperial marriage, Murat was alone in opposing the Austrian match – lest it put an end to his hopes of adding Sicily to his domains. Napoleon none the less let him organize an invasion to conquer the island. In the event the invasion, in the autumn of

1810, failed miserably and King Joachim blamed his brother-in-law. He was already incensed at being rebuked, with considerable justification, for recruiting French deserters into the Neapolitan army on a large scale. By now the Emperor was engaged in an acrimonious dispute with him for allowing American ships to smuggle British goods into Naples. The reconciliation between Murat and Caroline which had taken place in March – and resulted in a pregnancy – was not sufficient to dispel Napoleon's displeasure. He even took exception to the Murats' employment of two English governesses, Miss Davies and Mrs Pulsford, who had been caught in France by the outbreak of hostilities and by the royal couple's refusal to dismiss them.

Elisa had achieved her ambition of adding Tuscany to her domains, if only – and most untypically for a Bonaparte – by the shrewdest tact and dipolomacy. Instead of giving Tuscany and Parma to his sister when their ruler had been deposed in 1808, Napoleon incorporated them into the French Empire. Elisa was careful to show no sign of disappointment. 'I have little ambition', she wrote to Lucien, 'and the climate here suits me.' Even so, she paid discreet visits to Florence (as 'Contessa de Mondioni') to see the city's art collections and salons and began to correspond with Tuscan officials, including the chief of police, who grumbled to her about the administration's shortcomings. She continued to be obsequiously co-operative, ruling Lucca in exactly the way the Emperor wanted, compounding her customs revenues for an annual indemnity and introducing French inspectors to ensure that no British goods entered her ports. She had her reward.

In May 1809 Elisa was made Governor-General of Tuscany, with the title Grand Duchess. Her husband Prince Félix did not receive the title of Grand Duke but was merely appointed local commanding general, being obliged to take orders from his wife. She was in practice viceroy if, officially, Tuscany was part of France. She established her residence at the Pitti Palace which she refurbished, and chose various delectable Tuscan villas for country retreats – in summer she moved her court to Pisa. Her dominion now stretched from the Apennines to the sea (extending as far as the Isle of Elba and with hopes of Corsica), and she recruited a semi-regal household and bodyguard from the Florentine nobility. Their pomp and ceremony were a little too pretentious even though she took lessons on etiquette from Mme de Genlis (once governess to the Duke of Orleans's children). She haughtily used the letter 'E' for her signature, in imitation of her brother's 'N', and ostentatiously read Bolingbroke's *Idea of a Patriot King* in translation. She imported a French troupe of actors at vast expense to play on alternate nights with a native Italian company. Yet she remained realistic enough to quarter the old Bonaparte arms on her new flag and to sign herself, 'Your most devoted and submissive sister' in letters to the Emperor. She could not avoid occasional disputes, and when she refused to deport Bonny Prince Charlie's troublesome German widow, the Countess of Albany, he wrote, 'You are a subject and obliged to obey my Ministers like every other French person', threatening to arrest her. Nevertheless she succeeded in asserting her authority, putting enemies of the state in irons, executing brigands and dissolving monasteries. She also revived the Accademia della Crusca, guardian of the Tuscan language. The lands ruled by the Grand Duchess soon became noticeably tranquil and prosperous. Talleyrand called her sardonically the 'Semiramis of Lucca' (in ironic comparison with Catherine the Great of Russia, the 'Semiramis of the North').

Elisa's private life remained as idiosyncratic as ever. Paganini fled in December 1809, refusing to come back despite her pleas. He had numerous successors, including Baron Capelle, Prefect of Livorno, a Signor Eynard who was a Genoese merchant whom she allowed to trade with England, and Baron de Cerami, an amusing intellectual with whom she went on wild gallops through the countryside; she would then sleep with him on the grass. Prince Félix had his own court and his mistresses – Elisa was rumoured to choose them for him – at the Palazzo Crocetta, where the atmosphere put Mme Saint-Elme in mind of Louis xv's private brothel at the Parc-aux-Cerfs. Sometimes the two would meet in the evenings and with their daughter Napoléone-Elisa attend the theatre in the Grand Ducal box, after which they usually said goodnight and departed to their respective palaces – and bedfellows – though occasionally they slept with each other. When Elisa went to Paris in 1810 for Marie Louise's wedding, she was accompanied by six ladies-in-waiting, five chamberlains and two pages, in seven carriages – the visit cost nearly a million francs. Marie-Louise reported to her father, 'The Grand Duchess of Tuscany is very intelligent. She is ugly but has a daughter who is the prettiest child I ever saw.' During her stay in Paris Elisa gave birth to a third child, a son called Jérôme-Charles, and she made a most useful new friend in Fouché, a friendship which would last for the rest of their lives. Perhaps surprisingly, when little Jérôme-Charles died of water on the brain the following spring his mother collapsed. Characteristically, Madame Mère wrote to her son-in-law Bacciochi, 'I am incapable of offering you the slightest consolation, since I myself need consolation, but nothing can give it to us in this world.'

The Duchess Pauline continued to behave as oddly and self-indulgently as ever. She seems to have suffered from an inflamed uterine tube (salpingitis) – possibly the consequence of gonorrhea – causing pain, exhaustion and depression of a sort at which a man can only guess. It is also a condition which makes women excessively amorous. Her relationship with an over-endowed lover like Forbin had had a disastrous effect. Her physician, Dr Peyre, diagnosed her complaint and warned that physical love could only aggravate it. Pauline ignored such unwelcome advice. In 1807 Camillo Borghese had returned from the war in suitably comic fashion. He had behaved so well at the battle of Friedland that his brother-in-law promoted him to general, giving him the signal honour of bringing to Paris dispatches which announced the news of peace between France and Russia. Sadly, the official imperial messenger, M. Moustache, was given a duplicate set. The fat little Borghese was overtaken before he reached the capital, Moustache declining an offer of 20,000 francs to delay, so that when Camillo arrived with the glad tidings they were already public knowledge. Although he and his wife had grown more friendly, they did not set up house together. She established herself in a beautiful villa at Nice on the Baie des Anges where the climate and unaccustomed chastity did marvels for her health. However, despite a personal postal service which fetched her the latest fashions from Paris, she succumbed to loneliness. She therefore summoned a humble member of her household in the capital, her handsome master of music who had been 'noticed' by Caroline. Maestro Felice Blangini, a young Piedmontese, was a year her junior and the composer of a modestly successful opera, *Naphtali*. When he arrived he was invited to her boudoir, where, astounded to the point of terror, he was privileged to see how his employer was carried stark naked to her bath by her negro servant. Pauline immediately conceived a violent passion for the musician. Together they sang his songs, day after day. He had to set her dreadful poems to music and they sang those too, interminably. He was promoted to resident lover and not allowed to leave the villa for more than two hours at a time; if he did, a footman was sent to fetch him back. Whenever his mistress went out driving, she took the trembling maestro with her in her carriage. The trembling was due to Blangini's constant dread that her brother would learn of their liaison – the Emperor posted another lover of Pauline, Achille de Septeuil, to the Spanish front where he lost a leg.

Pauline was then commanded to take up residence with her husband at Turin, where Napoleon had appointed Camillo Governor-General of the new 'Department-beyond-the-Alps'. She was furious but dared not disobey her *caro fratello*, though she brought the ever more fearful Blangini with her. She complained that they were trying to kill her by making her live at Turin. She simulated fits and convulsions until allowed to go to Aix-les-Bains for a 'cure'. She then refused to return to Turin ever again. Since the angry Borghese stopped her Civil List allowance for the moment, and as she had hopelessly overspent her substantial personal income, she had to

make her peace with the Emperor. Despite all the trouble and embarrassment she caused him, he none the less remained extremely fond of his 'little
sister' and proved surprisingly indulgent, increasing her official allowances, which by 1809 were over a million francs a year and enabled her to
go on living at her accustomed rate. She never stopped adding to her jewels
– a *parure* of coral and diamonds, a *parure* of Brazilian rubies and a *parure* of
amethysts were among those which she bought from one jeweller in a single
year alone. In gratitude she procured a new mistress for Napoleon, her
lady-in-waiting Cristina Ghilini. When this youthful Piedmontese, a
plump little creature with golden hair, proved unwilling, she bullied her
into submitting – brother and sister joked with each other about the poor
girl's distress.

Often she could be curiously insensitive towards her own sex. When her
beloved reader, Jenny Millo – 'Dear Jenny', whose real function was to
retail gossip to her mistress rather than read books – became engaged to a
gentleman who was impeccably noble but penniless, it never crossed
Pauline's mind to provide poor Jenny with a desperately needed dowry. It
was left to the Emperor to subsidize the wedding (in response to a reminder
that he had been billeted on the bride's father in 1796), which shamed
Pauline into paying for the trousseau.

Pauline grew steadily more eccentric, becoming one of the sights of
Paris. Because of her perpetual exhaustion, on journeys between her hôtel
and the Tuileries she had herself carried in an old-fashioned sedan chair –
less tiring than a jolting carriage – which was borne by two footmen in
green liveries. She took a full part in the marriage celebrations of 1810,
trying unsuccessfully to teach Napoleon to waltz. When Borghese came to
Paris for the wedding and attempted to move in with her at the Hôtel de
Charost (which, after all, was now known as the Hôtel Borghese), she
refused to house his staff in the vast mansion and charged Camillo for his
meals. At the end of 1810 she acquired a new resident lover – Maestro
Blangini had long since bolted – in the swarthy person of General
Berthier's ADC, the twenty-five-year-old Captain Armand-Jules-Elisa-
beth de Canouville. Endowed with tireless virility, he was genuinely
devoted to Pauline. Once, when she had been frightened by her dentist, he
made the man extract a perfectly good tooth of his – Canouville's – in front
of her, to show that there was not too much to fear. The promising romance
was interrupted when his charger bolted at a parade and collided with the
Emperor's. Napoleon suddenly saw that the young officer's dolman was
lined with magnificent sable and realized to his fury that it could only have
come from a priceless set of furs presented to him after Tilsit by the Tsar
(who had received them as tribute from a tribe of Samoyeds), one of which
he had given to Pauline. He ordered Canouville to leave for Spain the same

evening. The ardent lover managed to return three times, being sent back each time on the Emperor's express orders – the affair ended only when he went off to fight in the Russian campaign. Pauline's amorous excesses seriously harmed her health and increased her hypochondria. She had recourse to such exotic remedies as enemas induced by the boiled intestines of a calf and still more milk baths, churns of milk being poured over her through holes bored in the ceiling above her tub. Her curious habits gave rise to countless grotesque tales, which enhanced neither the prestige nor the popularity of the Bonapartes – there were even rumours that she slept with her august brother.

Lucien nevertheless contrived to cause Napoleon the greatest embarrassment of any member of the clan. For a long time the Emperor, always loath to cast off a kinsman, refused to despair of him. In February 1810, after being persuaded by Madame Mère, Uncle Fesch and Pauline, Lucien sent a discreet envoy to the Emperor in the quite unjustified belief that his brother had softened, but Napoleon remained obdurate, insisting that Lucien must divorce his wife. Even so, he invited his niece the fourteen-year-old Charlotte (Lucien's daughter by his first marriage) to stay in Paris with her grandmother. 'Lolotte's' visit was not a success, the girl showing herself thoroughly distrustful and joking about Letizia's meanness in her letters home. Madame Mère sent a final frantic plea to her wayward son, begging him to part from his wife, 'You can give me back life and happiness. Have you the heart to refuse me?' But nothing would make Lucien abandon his Alexandrine. To make certain that they would not be separated, they decided to escape to the New World, in ironical contrast to Jérôme. In August 1810 Lucien and his entire family – he would be presented with ten children by Alexandrine – set sail from Naples, with King Joachim's connivance, on board an American ship, the *Hercules* of Salem, which was bound for the United States. (Murat was already showing signs of serious disobedience, even of disloyalty, towards the Emperor.) The vessel put into a Sardinian port where it was intercepted by a British warship. Lucien was forced to surrender as a prisoner of war, although he had never been a belligerent, and was taken off with his entire party on board the frigate HMS *Pomona*. After three months of comfortable internment on Malta in the former villa of the Prince and Grand Master, they were shipped to England where they landed at Plymouth on 12 December. Here Lucien received a tumultuous welcome as a refugee from Napoleonic tyranny, Lord Powis placing his country seat in Shropshire at his disposal. However, the exile had placed money in London banks and soon purchased Thorngrove in Worcestershire where he lived the life of one of Jane Austen's country squires for the next four years, going to hunt balls at local assembly rooms and displaying to advantage the art treasures he had managed to transfer from the *Hercules*. He found himself alarmingly short of money when one of his London banks suddenly failed. Louis offered to help and then, characterically, changed his mind. Finally Lucien had recourse to his mother; she sent him funds through a smuggler, who paid them to General Lefèbvre-Desnouettes, a paroled French prisoner from Spain living in Worcester. The English press made the maximum propaganda out of Lucien's flight. Nothing could have caused Napoleon more vexation and he had his brother's name struck off the roll of senators, all but outlawing him. None the less, while knowing all about Madame Mère's secret financial aid from his secret police, he did nothing to stop it.

Eugène de Beauharnais, now losing his hair but with luxuriant cavalry moustaches, continued to give his adoptive father the utmost satisfaction. His service in the field was consistently excellent and his Italian troops, if not always exactly victorious, performed adequately against the Austrians in 1809, reinforcing the Emperor at a critical moment. In 1810 he was informed that he was to become an independent sovereign in his own right, Grand Duke of Frankfurt, though at some future date. This signified that his stepfather no longer regarded him as heir to the Kingdom of Italy. Nevertheless he continued loyally as Viceroy of Milan with Augusta Amelia as his Vicereine. Both were still deeply in love and had a large and growing family. Yet despite the handsome pair's personal popularity the North Italians – indeed all Italians – were growing disaffected. They did not like being treated as inferior citizens of the French Empire, while too many swaggering French soldiers and officials were living at their expense. Napoleon had awakened heady dreams of a re-born Italy, only to dash them. Nor did Italians enjoy being conscripted and forced to serve abroad in the Emperor's foreign wars – thousands, Neapolitans and Tuscans as well as Northerners, were perishing miserably in Spain. None dreamt of the horror awaiting them in Russia.

Eugène's sister, Hortense, parted from her husband King Louis as soon as he abdicated. The latter was infuriated by the news that his brother had taken possession of all his palaces and country houses in Holland. In December 1810 his former kingdom was officially annexed by France, but he was given an annual income of two million francs with several fine estates and allowed to keep the title of king. He rejected both annexation and compensation and, from Graz in Austria where he saw no one save doctors, wrote to his wife ordering her to do the same. Wisely, Hortense took no notice. The Emperor gave her their hôtel in Paris and the château of Saint-Leu besides an income of half a million francs – he also promised to provide for her sons' education and careers. He was still very fond of Hortense, and in a letter informing her of his gift of the château says, 'You need a place in the country – you could not find one more agreeable than Saint-Leu.' He always continued to call her 'my daughter' and to sign himself, 'Your affectionate father, Napoleon.' Yet later he was not entirely uncritical. 'Hortense, so kind, so generous, so devoted, was sometimes in the wrong. I have to admit it in spite of all my affection for her and the very real attachment which I know she has for me. However queer, however unbearable Louis may have been, he loved her, and when this is so, and affairs of state are involved, a woman should be mistress of herself and somehow make herself return love.' But the Emperor was swayed by Corsican tribal feeling. No woman could ever have loved the King of Holland.

Hortense's decision to leave Louis may well have been precipitated by her mother's divorce. If her stepfather could do such a thing, so could she. All the Beauharnais were badly shaken at Joséphine being cast off, including her giddy little niece Stéphanie-Napoléone of Baden. In exile the Emperor said that because of the divorce Stéphanie-Napoléone 'realized the danger of her own position and became much more attached to her husband. Since then the couple have been leading a very happy married life.' Indeed after the fall of the Bonapartes the Grand Duke staunchly resisted his own family's pressure to divorce her.

After leaving Louis, Queen Hortense went to comfort the discarded Joséphine at Aix-les-Bains. She was to remember July 1810, the month after she had finally parted with him, as 'the happiest month of my entire life', much of her happiness being due to the presence of the Comte de Flahaut. Now twenty-five, this reputed bastard of Talleyrand had been a soldier since the age of fifteen and was one of Napoleon's brilliant young staff officers. Hortense had been discreetly in love with him since at least 1806, her affection having wavered when Caroline Murat lusted after him and when he demonstrated his gift for being deeply in love with two or three women at the same time. Now this most innocent of women began to sleep with him and was terrified when she found herself pregnant the following year, dreading lest her condition be discovered by the Police Minister and reported to her stepfather. The child, the future Duc de Morny, was born in September 1811.

Bernadotte had not been cashiered, despite spectacular blunders at Auerstädt and Wagram, purely for the sake of Désirée. The Emperor said that on campaign he did 'nothing but prance'. He now began to infuriate Napoleon by visiting the salons of the openly hostile Mmes Récamier and de Staël. He faced a very real possibility of being sent to his Principality of Pontecorvo and left to rot there. He was saved by his remarkable luck.

In 1810 the heir of the aged Carl XIII of Sweden died unexpectedly. The Swedes dreaded the return of the King's nephew Gustav IV Adolf, whom they had deposed two years before, nor would they accept the latter's son. The Swedish Estates decided that a French prince would make a good monarch in a world ruled by Napoleon and approached Eugène de Beauharnais. Eugène refused to become a Lutheran, considering the Mass of more worth than Stockholm. Then some Swedish officers who had been prisoners of the French remembered the excellent dinners given to them by Marshal Bernadotte. After much persuasion Carl XIII adopted him as his heir. Some historians have been puzzled at the Emperor allowing him to accept. The explanation is that Napoleon was delighted to think that his former mistress would become a queen. Bernadotte made a surprisingly favourable impression on the Swedes and since the old King was failing he took control of the country's government. The Emperor had reason to feel uneasy. On Elba he was to remark that there had been three times when he ought to have had Bernadotte shot, but three times he spared him out of affection for Désirée. The latter (renamed Desideria) returned to France and did not settle in Sweden until 1823.

Uncle Fesch, of all unlikely people, began to cause his nephew trouble. So far his career had not been noted for idealism. There had been the short period as a 'Constitutional' – and excommunicated – cleric during the Revolution, followed by ten years as self-unfrocked priest in which he had been an unscrupulous and indeed almost unsavoury financier, a noted *bon vivant* and gourmet, very fat in consequence. He had then become the principal agent of the Emperor's ecclesiastical policy, imposing an extraordinary new catechism containing the question and answer: 'What must one think of those who fail in their duty to our Emperor? According to the Apostle Paul, they are resisting the established order of God himself and thus render themselves worthy of eternal damnation.' He had helped to introduce the feast of the non-existent St Napoleon (in competition with the Bourbons' ancestor, St Louis), and had always co-operated with the imperial Minister of Cults. Metternich calls him 'a strange compound of bigotry and ambition', explaining that 'although sincerely devout, he was not far off believing Napoleon to be the instrument of Heaven and an all but supernatural being. He thought that his reign was written in the Book of Destiny and regarded his most ambitious plans as the decrees of God Almighty.' Fesch still retained some of the worldly habits of his disreputable past. Even his nephew had had to tell him to stop living in his palatial museum of a house in the Chaussée d'Antin, a species of millionaires' row popular among rich bankers – 'not a neighbourhood suitable for a cardinal' – and order him to return to his cathedral city of Lyons, where he transferred his constantly growing collection of paintings.

In 1809 the Emperor nominated Fesch Archbishop of Paris, but he refused. He succeeded in extracting enormous emoluments from the state, though attempts to return to his beloved Chaussée d'Antin were frustrated. Yet secretly he was alarmed by the Pope's imprisonment. He became even more unhappy in 1810 when thirteen Princes of the Church – the 'Black Cardinals' – were themselves thrown into prison and officially deprived of their scarlet robes, for staying away from Marie Louise's marriage to demonstrate that they did not accept the annulment of Napoleon's marriage to Joséphine. He himself had arranged the annulment and conducted the wedding service. The same year too Rome was annexed to the French Empire. In 1811 he chaired the council of ecclesiastics which the Emperor had summoned to Paris and, with a hitherto unheard of independence, conveyed their refusal to approve the proposal that the investiture of bishops should be transferred from the Pontiff to the metropolitans. 'All the bishops will resist you,' he warned Napoleon. 'You are only going to make martyrs of them.' The last straw came in 1812 when the Emperor gave orders for Pius VII to be moved from Savona to Fontainebleau, so that he could personally bully the unfortunate Pope into signing a concordat which would give him more or less complete control of the Catholic Church. The Cardinal told his nephew roundly that he disapproved. Napoleon promptly banished him to his see and ordered him to stay away from the capital. From there Fesch wrote of his martyrdom to Madame Mère. 'Do not increase your worries by thinking about the reasons why I left Paris. I have laid them at the foot of the Cross. God will be my strength and I put all my trust in him.'

In the Archbishop's palace at Lyons the Primate of the Gauls gave shelter not just to persecuted prelates but to every sort of monk or friar down to the humblest lay brother, in particular to those chased out of Italy. He was surrounded by dedicated young priests who under the Bourbon Restoration would lead the Catholic revival and the Church's counter-attack on everything which had come in since 1789. In addition he contributed generously to the secret fund for the relief of the Black Cardinals. Nevertheless, this strange man continued to worship Mammon as well as God. He continued to buy diamonds, estates in Corsica and, above all, pictures which eventually were to number nearly 30,000 canvases by Italian, French, Dutch and Flemish masters, including works by Bellini, Botticelli and Titian. He also lent money to his nephew King Jérôme at an exorbitant rate which verged on usury.

On 20 March 1811 Stendhal, in bed with his mistress Angéline, was awoken by cannon roaring out a salute to celebrate the birth of a son and heir to the Emperor Napoleon and his Empress Marie Louise. 'We heard the cheers in the streets,' he writes in his journal. 'My wigmaker informs me that in the rue Saint-Honoré people cheered just as they would a famous actor coming on to the stage.' The child was christened Napoléon-François-Charles-Joseph at Notre-Dame on 9 June with Madame Mère for his godmother – his grandfather, the Emperor Francis in Vienna, was the godfather – amid scenes of seemingly frenzied rejoicing. So anxious had the father been for a son that he had attended the birth, a difficult and indeed an agonizing one which distressed him so much that he retired to a closet for long periods. He told the nervous midwives to treat the Empress 'just as you would any housewife from the rue Saint-Denis', and when asked which life should be saved if a decision had to be made, answered promptly, 'The mother's – it is her right.' She could always bear him more children. It now seemed as though the Bonaparte Empire was at last established on a firm dynastic basis. To demonstrate that the boy was heir to Charlemagne and the Carolingian Empire, he was given the title King of Rome, which was pretentious even by Napoleonic standards, causing offence not just to Italians, Austrians and Germans but to every Catholic concerned about the Pope. Despite detesting Marie Louise just as they had Joséphine, the entire clan shared the Emperor's new sense of lasting security. Joséphine, who stayed on the friendliest terms with Napoleon regardless of Marie Louise's irritation, sent such warm congratulations that she was allowed to return from the country to Malmaison – where, as so often before, she quickly ran up astronomically high debts.

Napoleon decided to bring back more pre-1789 etiquette: court dress, footstools for duchesses, so many horses for one's carriage. However, the old nobility and the new ruling class continued to detest each other, yet another failure for his hopes of fusing Revolution and legitimacy. Having married into the *ancien régime* so successfully himself, the Emperor was eager for the imperial nobility to.follow suit. He did not merely encourage them to marry into the greatest families of old France but went so far as ordering the Ministry of Police to instruct all *préfets* to conscript well-born young ladies. Statistics had to be supplied of girls of good family with details of physical appearance, education, religious attitude and such cultural abilities as playing the piano or the harp. Warned that he was about to receive an order to marry his daughter to a general, the Duke de Croy married her the same day to a cousin who was staying in the house. Other fathers were not so resourceful. Mlle Dillon was forced to marry General Sebastiani, the two Mlles d'Arberg Generals Mouton and Klein. All this made the notables still more fearful of a complete return to the days before 1789.

Fatherhood made Napoleon less anxious to go campaigning again, more aware that he was ageing. In July 1811 the novelist Paul de Kock watched him appear on the balcony of the Tuileries. Instead of the hero of his dreams he saw a stout little man, 'yellow, obese, bloated, with his head too far down on his shoulders'. A secret envoy was sent to London to explore the possibility of peace with the British, suggesting concessions: Joseph could come to an agreement with the Spanish patriots, the Braganzas could be restored in Portugal, and all French and British troops should leave the Peninsula. The Marquess Wellesley, Wellington's brother and British Foreign Secretary, replied that His Majesty's Government would only negotiate after France had recognized Ferdinand VII as King of Spain. Napoleon was not entirely averse to Ferdinand's replacing Joseph – he would have given a very great deal to be rid of the Spanish involvement – but he was not going to be ordered about. He broke off communications.

The British had reason to adopt an aggressive tone, since the Peninsular War was going very well indeed for them. Poor Joseph was in worse trouble than ever. The French generals in Spain were virtually independent warlords who oppressed and pillaged the unfortunate Spaniards in their territories and ignored the man in Madrid signing himself meaninglessly 'Yo el Rey' – Soult for example was King of Andalusia in all but name. The only reasonably efficient government was in the four provinces north of the Ebro, which had been annexed and converted into French departments. King 'José' was desperately short of money, having to raise loans on his French estates and what was left of his diamonds. When his brother sent him half a million francs in bullion, a general intercepted the convoy and calmly requisitioned 120,000 francs to pay the troops under his command. As Pieter Geyl points out, Spain was 'a training ground in disobedience for the marshals', which would have disastrous consequences for the entire imperial army. When the Emperor at last gave way to his brother's ceaseless pleading for more power and in March 1812 made him Commander-in-Chief in Spain with control of all political and military affairs it made little difference – he could only remove generals from their commands by complaining to Napoleon and there was no guarantee his complaints would reach him. Soult and his colleagues went on behaving like satraps. Moreover, although on paper French troops vastly out-numbered British, in reality they were dispersed all over the Peninsula and tied down by the relentless attacks of implacable guerrillas.

Throughout 1811 and 1812 Joseph's position deteriorated steadily. The month after he was appointed Commander-in-Chief Badajoz fell to Wellington. Disaster came on 22 July at the great battle of Salamanca where Marmont was routed – the Marshal lost an arm and 7,000 men, the remains of what had been an army of over 50,000 being saved only by nightfall. Wellington then marched on Madrid, which he entered to wild acclaim on 12 August. King Joseph had fled from his capital only two days before, accompanied by terrified supporters in a train of carts and wagons which stretched for miles, eventually finding refuge in Valencia. But

Wellington had too few troops, and although the French had temporarily lost all central, southern and western Spain they soon regrouped, Masséna arriving to restore the situation. At a council of war in October Soult proposed concentrating several armies to attack Wellington from the rear while he was engaged with the French Army of the North before Burgos – a plan which might well have proved fatal for the British. Joseph, convinced of his own military genius, would not hear of it and insisted on reoccupying his capital as soon as possible. He returned there on 2 November 1812, though even he no longer had any illusions about his popularity. He was to spend only five more months in Madrid.

By contrast the sun appeared to shine on the peaceful land of Westphalia, however much in debt its carefree monarch may have been. He continued to amuse himself recklessly; at one particularly wild party he became so drunk that he was arrested in the streets of his own capital by his own police who had not recognized him. He was already a laughing-stock in Cassel. Metternich informs us that 'Jérôme was clever, but his depraved way of life, absurd vanity and mania for imitating his brother in every possible way covered him with ridicule'. Nevertheless, he did not have to face invaders or rebellious patriots like Joseph, or to worry about the Continental System like Louis or Murat since he had no seaports. At the end of August 1811, shortly after the King of Rome's christening, Madame Mère paid a visit to the court of King Hieronymus Napoleo at Napoleonshöhe. She was first received at Cassel with the honours due to a reigning sovereign – troops lining the streets, cannons roaring out a salute and a gala night at the opera. (An oratorio had been composed for the occasion by none other than Pauline's fugitive lover, Blangini.) Her youngest son was enough of an Italian to love and fear his mother more than any other woman. For her part Letizia had grown extremely fond of her ill-used daughter-in-law, Catherine of Württemberg. The latter returned her affection, no doubt perfectly sincere in claiming that Madame Mère inspired respect 'in much the same way as the Russian Empress'. Letizia presented Catherine with a superb pearl-fringed parasol with a gold handle, together with her own likeness set in pearls, a testimony of true devotion from someone so parsimonious. The visit included a grand military review – Jérôme's soldiers wearing the impressive and unusual uniforms he had designed for them – hunting parties, picnics, sightseeing tours, banquets and concerts. The 'actresses' were kept well out of sight. Madame Mère found it all so very pleasant that she stayed for two months. When she left, Catherine wrote in her journal of 'a painful separation from a most delightful companion'. Even Letizia, bleakly pessimistic as she was, can never have dreamt that within only two years the realm of Westphalia would disappear without trace. Yet even during the imperial summer many observers, including Jérôme himself, sensed that Westphalia was already on the verge of disintegration. Crushed by taxes, disgusted by the court's morals, resentful of the adventurers governing them, its inhabitants were beginning to loathe the Latin playboy who posed as their king. At the end of 1811 the Prussian Minister at Cassel reported to Berlin that each night Jérôme had three horses waiting, saddled and bridled, with six others harnessed to Catherine's fastest carriage, in case they should suddenly have to flee from their subjects.

In Baltimore Betsy Patterson despaired of a royal destiny and started proceedings for an American civil divorce, which she obtained in 1813. She would not consider remarriage. She told her father, 'Nothing could persuade me to marry anybody in America after having had an Emperor's brother for a husband.' She devoted herself to her disinherited son, Jerome Patterson Bonaparte.

In an attempt to ingratiate himself King Joachim of Naples paid an uninvited visit to Paris in April 1811 to attend the celebrations for the birth of the King of Rome. He was terrified of the baby's mother, without any justification. Marie Louise was the niece of Queen Maria Carolina whose husband's white Bourbon standard with its kaleidoscope of quarterings still flew over Sicily under the protection of the British navy. Idiotically, Joachim blamed the Empress for the failure of his expedition to conquer the island in the previous year, suspecting that she had stopped Napoleon from lending him enough French troops. Nevertheless, Murat had reason to feel uneasy after the absorption of King Louis's domains into the French Empire. Early in 1811 Catherine of Westphalia had noted in her diary, 'The Kingdom of Naples is to be united to the Kingdom of Italy. On being invited by the Emperor to the Empress's lying-in, the Queen of Naples has written to Madam Mère that, since they want to take her crown away from her, she would rather receive such an insult at Naples than in Paris.' When Murat presented himself he was greeted coldly by his brother-in-law, but then there was a brief reconciliation.

However, immediately after his return to Naples the following month the French Ambassador there, Baron Durand, reported to Napoleon that the King was nursing 'bitterness in his heart'. In June Joachim issued an edict dismissing foreigners from the Customs and Excise and ordering all other Frenchmen who held Neapolitan government posts to take out naturalization papers. The Emperor countered this bold move by decreeing that every citizen of France was already a citizen of Naples since it was part of the French Empire. He would not allow the King to accredit his own ambassadors to Vienna or St Petersburg. He never took seriously Murat's attempts to sink roots. Yet the King was building new roads, creating a cotton industry and founding a new city (on the most modern gridiron pattern) next to the strategically important seaport of Bari. In his capital he sought desperately to endear himself to his subjects, staging military parades whose magnificence was calculated to impress Neapolitans, keeping splendid court and continually making rich offerings at the shrine of San Gennaro. Admittedly he had been forced to impose an alien legal system and set up a commission abolishing feudal privileges. In August 1810 Caroline complained in a letter to her husband that too few ladies had come to her birthday reception at the Palazzo Reale because of 'the poverty afflicting all noble families, who have not enough money to buy proper dresses since that wretched commission ruins more and more people every day'. Not only was he building up his army to an eventual strength of over 80,000 men but he was intriguing with nationalist secret societies throughout the peninsula, in particular with the Carbonari. His ultimate aim was to establish an 'Italic' party which would one day bring all Italy under his rule as a 'Patriot King'. His adviser in this, and the chief advocate of such a party, was his new Minister of Police, the subtle and intriguing Antonio Maghella who was Caroline's sworn enemy. Only the looming war between France and Russia saved Joachim from a serious crisis which might well have resulted in his deposition.

Murat was still bickering with his wife. There were stories in Naples of another liaison on her part, with the obese and coarse-mannered Count Hector Daure, who was Minister for both War and the Marine. Neapolitan rumour had it that the rotund Daure, attempting one night to join Caroline in her bedroom in the Palazzo Reale through a secret passage, which she had had built for the willowy La Vauguyon, found himself stuck and was only released by the Queen's tugging – it was said that the King's edict dismissing foreigners had been drafted with Daure in mind. She also gathered around her uncompromising supporters of the Emperor, who formed a French party in opposition to Maghella's Italic party.

The Continental System had caused increasing resentment among Napoleon's allies. The Tsar was thoroughly disenchanted, and on the last day of 1811 Russia withdrew formally from the System. The following month the Emperor annexed the Duchy of Oldenburg on the northern border of Holland – its heir had married the Tsar's sister. War between France and Russia was now inevitable though Metternich, who as early as January 1811 had seen it coming, informed the Emperor Francis that the Russians had 'not the remotest chance of success'. In the same month as Oldenburg was invaded French troops marched into Swedish Pomerania, completing the alienation of the Swedes.

Fouché warned against a war on two fronts. 'Sire, I don't believe the Spanish campaign is going well enough for it to be safe to fight across the Pyrenees and across the Niemen at the same time.' Napoleon replied

contemptuously, 'I need 800,000 troops and I have them. I can drag all
Europe after me and in these days I regard Europe as a rotten old whore
who has to do my pleasure when I possess such an army . . . There must be
one legal code, one court of appeal and one currency for all Europe. The
European nations must be melted into a single nation and Paris must
become capital of the world.' He added, 'Can I help it if so much power is
sweeping me on to world dictatorship?'

Looking back from the days when the Napoleonic legend had captured
the French imagination, Chateaubriand reminded people what the Empire
had really been like.

> They forget that everybody had good reason to mourn victories, forget that the
> slightest hostile reference to Bonaparte in a theatre which escaped the censors
> was greeted with delight, forget that the populace, the court, the generals, the
> ministers and all those close to Napoleon were weary of his conquests, weary of a
> game always being won and then having to be played again, weary of an existence
> which had to be put at risk again every single morning because it was impossible
> to stop.

However, the Emperor was intoxicated by his marriage and his son. He
did not care if there was scant love between Marie Louise and the
Bonaparte clan. Madame Mère seems to have distrusted the girl although
she paid weekly visits to her mother-in-law at the Hôtel de Brienne. Letizia
referred to her as little as possible, speaking to her only when necessary,
but the Empress was shrewder than Joséphine, clever enough to feign a
dutiful respect. Like Napoleon himself, the clan were overawed by a
Habsburg Archduchess; she told Metternich, 'I'm not frightened of
Napoleon though I'm beginning to think he's frightened of me.' It was
difficult for the Bonapartes to discredit her as they had Joséphine because
not only did her husband, terrified she might be seduced by a younger
man, isolate her in Byzantine seclusion, but she kept to herself with her
principal lady-in-waiting the young Duchess of Montebello (Marshal
Lanne's widow) for her sole friend.

Mme de Montebello, far from keeping the peace, constantly reminded
Marie Louise of her Habsburg blood while retailing scandalous stories
about the Bonapartes. Twenty-nine in 1811, Louise Scolastique Guéhen-
nec belonged to the Breton *petite bourgeoisie* and was icily beautiful, chaste,
avaricious, envious and a diehard Jacobin. Despite her republican views
she was furiously resentful that her late husband had not been created a
prince as well as a duke and extracted titles, appointments, promotions and
pensions from Napoleon for as many of her relations as possible. He had
given her the post out of affection for Lannes and on account of her well-
publicized virtue. Secretly she hated the Emperor, together with his
kindred and most of his courtiers. Her one potential rival was the little

King's governess, the Comtesse de Montesquiou – '*Maman Quiou*' – who in spite of belonging to the old aristocracy was genuinely devoted to Napoleon. However, Mme de Montebello succeeded in monopolizing Marie Louise's friendship, to the exclusion of other women. Her baneful influence antagonized many people, earning the Empress ill-deserved unpopularity.

Laure d'Abrantès tells us that Marie Louise spent most of her time doing needlework or playing the piano. 'She visited her son or else had him brought to her at fixed times of the day, and it was sometimes difficult to persuade the child, who knew his nurse far better than his mother, to lift his small pink face up to the Empress so that she could kiss him.' Laure adds, 'Marie Louise was not a general favourite with those who went to court . . . and she dressed with a marked lack of elegance.' It also seems that she snubbed Mme d'Abrantès.

The Emperor was in love with Marie Louise and she with him. He even broke into Italian in his letter to her – '*Addio, mio dolce amore*' – while she took the place of his valet in massaging him in his bath with eau de cologne. She did exactly what he told her. He was determined that she should not be exposed to the campaigns of slander waged on Joséphine by the clan. In any case there were distinct signs that Napoleon was at last growing disillusioned with his family as a whole and not just with his brothers and Murat. He admitted to Metternich, probably in 1810, 'Were I beginning again, my brothers and sisters would only be given palaces in Paris with a few millions to spend, living idle lives. The arts and charity ought to be their business, not kingdoms. Some of them don't know how to rule while others embarrass me by imitating me to the point of caricature.' Since the Empress had presented him with an heir with Habsburg blood she enjoyed security of a sort undreamt of by Joséphine.

Napoleon suffered irritation at the Tuileries from the members of the clan of whom he was perhaps fondest, Pauline and Hortense. In February 1812, together with Caroline, they gave a ball there accompanied by an entertainment in the palace theatre, a dramatic allegory on the union of Rome with France. Pauline played the part of Rome, Caroline that of France. The former seemed 'like an angel descending from heaven on a sunbeam', Mme d'Abrantès reports. She is less flattering about Caroline. 'If a charming head, rosy-faced and condescendingly pretty, had not peeped out from such a heap of gilt, pearls, excessive jewellery and sheer bad taste it would have made a startling contrast to that incandescently beautiful phantom which was her sister.' 'Their charming faces, diamond-studded shields and jewels of many colours made a dazzling show,' Hortense remembers. 'The other ladies were very pretty as Naiads of the Tiber, Hours and Irises, though the faces of chamberlains and equerries transformed into Stars, Zephyrs and Apollos gave rise to some amusement. The mime was ill suited to the dignity of both the participants and the subject.' The following evening the Emperor asked the Queen of Naples angrily, 'Where did you get that idea for your allegory? It just didn't make sense. Rome obeys France but is far from contented. What on earth made you represent her as happy, satisfied at being subjected? Yes, I know you only wanted to look pretty and dress up in a splendid costume, but surely you could have found some other topic without bringing politics into a ball.' Then he scolded Hortense for letting her little son wear a Polish uniform. Napoleon and his family were behaving as though their Empire would last for a thousand years.

8
The Death of the Empire

' "He wants to sacrifice all our children to his mad ambition'';
that was the cry rising up from every family, in Paris as in the
remotest provinces.'

ADOLPHE THIERS, *Histoire du Consulat et de l'Empire*

'I find it difficult to convey any idea of the painfully uneasy
expressions on the faces of the courtiers and on those of the
gold-braided generals, who had assembled in the Emperor's
apartments. The Prince of Neuchâtel [General Berthier, Chief
of Staff] whispered to me, "Don't forget that Europe needs
peace, France in particular, that's all she wants." '

METTERNICH ON HIS MEETING WITH NAPOLEON IN JUNE 1813.

During the spring and summer of 1812 Napoleon and his Empire appeared
overwhelmingly formidable. He had massed 800,000 troops. Admittedly
150,000 of his best men were tied down in Spain while many of the *Grande
Armée* were not even Frenchmen; it included over 150,000 Germans,
nearly 100,000 Italians and 60,000 Poles. Before finally declaring war on
Russia, the Emperor decided to hold a congress at Dresden and hold court
to his client kings and princes in an attempt to overawe the Tsar. As
Chateaubriand puts it, 'a proletarian monarch, he humiliated kings and
noblemen in his anterooms'. Even his father-in-law the Austrian Emperor
Francis and his consort were forced to yield precedence to the Emperor
and Empress of the French. Francis was mystified by his daughter's
affection for her husband. 'Whatever she may say,' he grumbled, 'I cannot
stomach the creature.' Ségur relates that the more intelligent French
officers were deeply alarmed by the spectacle. 'They could see these rulers
leaving Napoleon's palace with their faces and their hearts full of the most
bitter resentment.'

Napoleon stayed at Dresden until 29 May, expecting Alexander to make
peace. However, at Danzig (Gdansk) on 22 June he issued another of those
stirring proclamations to his troops, declaring war on Russia. 'Let us
march!'

For the first time, a member of the clan was actively betraying him. The
Swedish Crown Prince refused to march, bribed by Russia's offer of
Norway. Had Sweden invaded Finland, which it had lost to the Tsar only
in 1809, and threatened St Petersburg the war would have ended very

differently. Napoleon later claimed that the city had been at the mercy 'of a small Swedish patrol'. But by July Bernadotte was telling the Russian ambassador, 'I know of no way of saving Europe except by defeating the "monster".'

On 24 June the Emperor crossed the river Niemen at Kovno, invading Russian Poland. The Grand Army of Russia consisted of 450,000 troops, supported by another 160,000 in reserve. Eugène de Beauharnais and Jérôme each had one of the two centre army groups while the King of Naples was appointed Grand Master of the Imperial Cavalry at the head of the greatest body of horse seen in Europe since mediaeval times.

The Viceroy at the head of his beloved army of Italy was as always the austere professional soldier with little time for frills. By contrast, Jérôme equipped himself in his own special way, taking a wardrobe with plain clothes and hunting uniforms as well as over 50 military uniforms, 200 shirts, 60 pairs of boots and 318 silk handkerchiefs, cared for by nine valets and filling seven wagons. Other wagons contained tents, bedding, furniture, carpets, dinner services, dressing cases and a silver chamber pot. There were also crates of indispensable champagne. He confidently expected to exchange his crown for that of Poland and he and his cronies had therefore spent the months before the campaign using up what little was left of the Westphalian treasury, Baron Kudelstein (formerly La Flèche, husband of the King's mistress Jennie) decamping with the balance of the budget for 1812. All Jérôme's campaigning equipment was paid for by loans from his old friends the bankers of Cassel and from Uncle Fesch. Countess Potocka saw 'the little King of Westphalia' on his way to the front and comments, 'he played at reigning just as little girls play at being grown-up women.' She adds that there were absurd rumours that he bathed in rum every morning and in milk every evening: 'His servants, they said, put the liquid in bottles and sold it.' In his absence Catherine was Regent of Westphalia, completely ignored by the ministers. One day she asked for a report on the kingdom's financial situation. After reading it she retired to her bed in tears.

King Joachim also went campaigning in regal style with a huge baggage train, which was even equipped with scent and staffed by chamberlains, equerries, secretaries, pages and footmen, and the best Parisian chefs available. He had designed a new uniform for himself. His boots were yellow, his breeches crimson with gold braid, his tunic sky-blue likewise gold-braided and his dolman of crimson velvet not only gold-braided but trimmed with sable. His gold-braided cocked hat, enormous even by the fashion of the day, was crowned by white ostrich feathers held by a great diamond buckle, while his gold-mounted sword and gold sword-belt also glittered with diamonds. His pistols, protruding from jewelled holsters, were damascened in gold and studded with rubies, emeralds and sapphires. When he rode one of the sixty superb chargers he had brought, the animal was caparisoned with a tiger-skin saddle-cloth and a gold bit and gold stirrups. But in these royal days he did not always campaign on horseback, travelling instead in a luxuriously equipped carriage on long marches.

The Tsar's main army under Marshal Barclay de Tolly guarded the road to St Petersburg while a slightly smaller force commanded by Prince Bagration defended the road to Moscow. They adopted scorched earth tactics, falling back in front of the French. On 28 June Napoleon rode into Vilna to find that they had burnt the supplies on which he had been counting. The weather was sweltering hot, men dropping like flies from heatstroke and horses foundering. Cossacks attacked continually. The King of Naples was in his element chasing them off. He led several charges and was once in such danger that he had to draw his jewelled sword. Just in time, an equerry cut down a Russian about to sabre the King. Not only had the *Grande Armée* lost a third of its strength by the end of July, but it was growing alarmingly short of horses.

Jérôme had begun the campaign in very high spirits, enthusiastically leading his army group across the Niemen at Grodno. Here the Russians offered only a token resistance yet he insisted on treating the city's capture as a glorious victory. When the veteran General Vandamme complained that he and his troops were confused by the King's contradictory orders Jérôme relieved him of his command. He then failed to support Poniatowski's attempt to trap Bagration. The Emperor commented, 'By disregarding all the rules of war and my instructions he has managed to give Bagration the time he needs to retreat, which he is now doing with the greatest of ease.' Meanwhile the King was boasting that Napoleon 'can't fail to be pleased by what his right wing has accomplished'. The Emperor tried to conceal his brother's inadequacy by annoucing that Bagration's escape was due to a 'great storm' that had made it impossible for the King of Westphalia to leave Grodno. Then Jérôme tried to order Marshal Davout about whereupon that brutal warrior, who had had trouble with him in the past, produced secret imperial orders placing him under his command.

Burning with rage and humiliation, King Jérôme promptly wrote to Napoleon tendering his resignation and stating that 'quite apart from the insult to his feelings which he had just suffered, he was in any case determined not to serve as anyone's subordinate'. Despite his brother's order to stay with the *Grande Armée* he left two days later. Without instructions his troops were immobilized for several days and did not support Davout when he attacked Bagration at Mogilev, depriving him of a decisive victory. At Warsaw the King received a letter from his wife who implored him not to leave until he had been an outstanding success but he rejoined her at Napoleonshöhe on 11 August, a week before the Emperor came in sight of Smolensk. His subjects were informed that his Westphalian Majesty had returned only because his health had been broken by the privations of the campaign. As usual he took refuge in lavish parties and with mistresses who were paraded before poor Queen Catherine in her own house. On 13 November there was a ball to celebrate the unveiling of a new statue of Napoleon at Cassel, the day before the *Grande Armée* set out on a ghastly retreat from Smolensk. Very few if any of the Westphalian corps returned from Russia, but the parties at Napoleonshöhe were gayer than ever that winter, the Cassel opera better than the Paris opera. However, Jérôme suffered a serious blow when one of his mistresses, Baroness Kudelstein – alias Jennie La Flèche – bolted with Catherine's brother, Prince Paul of Württemberg.

Borodino on 7 September was the Emperor's last victory as a conqueror. Kutuzov, who had replaced Barclay de Tolly, would not repeat Barclay's mistake by fighting a decisive battle. Murat was like a demon, dismounting to lead a crucial bayonet charge on foot, then remounting to direct his cavalry in attack after attack while cheering on the Old Guard; 'Soldiers of Friant, you are heroes!' he told General Friant's square after its bayonets had bloodily repulsed the enemy cuirassiers. But though nearly 50,000 Russians were killed, wounded or taken prisoner, Napoleon had suffered 24,000 casualties while 7,000 of his men were prisoners too. It was a truly Pyrrhic victory, even if Prince Bagration lay dead on the field and it opened the way to Moscow. (Among the dead was Pauline's friend, Canouville – her miniature was found round his neck.)

The King of Naples led the triumphant French entry into Moscow on 14 September, riding in at the head of a squadron of Polish lancers. That night fires broke out, deliberately started by the Russians, which continued for five days. Four-fifths of the city was destroyed but enough shelter remained for the invaders, together with food for some weeks, and the Emperor stayed at Moscow in the belief that the Tsar would sue for peace. Eugène guessed correctly that the Tsar wanted the French to linger in his ruined city for as long as possible – his envoys dragged out the negotiations, making insincere overtures for an armistice. Eventually Napoleon decided to retreat, Joachim being given the task of clearing away the Cossacks who had now begun to reappear. The King wrote to his invalided chief-of-staff General Belliard that he and his men were half-starved, sick of galloping from one barn to another.

The retreat began on 19 October, 80,000 troops marching out from Moscow, accompanied by 50,000 non-combatants who included women and children. On 24 October Eugène and his Italian Royal Guard, supported by French troops, were confronted by Kutuzov at Maloyaroslavets 70 miles from Moscow. The little town had to be taken and retaken seven times before the Russians were finally driven out. Nevertheless Kutuzov forced the invaders to retreat by the route by which they had come, over country already stripped bare, dooming them to disaster. On 1 November the first heavy snow fell. Most men were without even greatcoats, having thrown them away during the oppressive summer heat of the invasion. Two days later Eugène was attacked at Vyazma, but drove the enemy off after seven hours of furious fighting. Describing the action Ségur comments that the Viceroy 'was most certainly not one of those generals who owed their promotion to favouritism, who never anticipated danger, who were always being taken by surprise from lack of experience. He recognized the threat at once and knew exactly what to do.' On 6 November a terrible snowstorm began. The Russian winter had set in.

It was the effect on horses as much as on human beings that was so disastrous. The snow smothered all vegetation and there was nothing for them to eat – the cavalry had dwindled to less than 4,500 mounts by the time it arrived at Smolensk on 9 November. Not only was there no cavalry but there were no teams to pull supply wagons. Starvation was added to cold. Even the most senior officers had to go on foot, not excepting the Emperor, the King of Naples and the Viceroy.

When the *Grande Armée* reached Smolensk it found that the commissariat had broken down. There was no food. The retreat through the snow must continue. Before reaching even Smolensk the Army of Italy had been almost completely destroyed by its pursuers at the crossing of the river Wop. Eugène managed to save a handful. Caulaincourt, an eye-witness, says, 'Everything that courage could achieve, given the example by a brave and dedicated commander, was done but in vain.' On 11 November the Viceroy wrote to his wife in Italy that he had not shaved for ten days and had a beard like a Capuchin friar. He still found the strength to lead his broken fragment of a command to the rescue of Marshal Ney, who had been cut off.

At the end of November Napoleon and 12,000 troops struggled across two pontoon bridges over the river Berezina, a dreadful crossing in which even more perished in the icy water than by Russian gunfire, to join up with the armies of Oudinot and Victor. Together they staggered back towards the Niemen. The temperature dropped to 20 and sometimes 30 degrees of frost. 20,000 men died in three days alone. Eugène – laying aside for a moment the musket he shouldered like a common soldier – wrote to a friend, 'Our companions and comrades collapse on the march and perish from misery, exhaustion and cold. My Italians are dying like flies. Not more than a hundred men of the Royal Guard survive. How happy we would be if only we could see our homes again one day! That's my sole remaining ambition. I no longer seek glory. It costs too much.' The Emperor left 380,000 men behind the Niemen, killed or taken prisoner. When on 30 December Marshal Ney crossed the Niemen, musket in hand and the very last Frenchman to do so, just 4,000 troops – officers, NCOs and men of the Old Guard and the Young Guard – were still in battle order.

Napoleon abandoned his army at Molodechno on 5 December, handing it over to Murat and returning to France by fast sledge. News had come to him from Paris of an attempt to seize power by General Malet, a fanatical republican who announced that the Emperor had been killed in Russia. Although it failed, Malet's attempt gave Napoleon a terrible shock. He was particularly shaken that no one had thought of proclaiming the King of Rome as Napoleon II. After fleeing through Germany in a hired carriage with the blinds down – no one knew what had happened to him – the Emperor drove into the Tuileries, totally unexpected, on 18 December 1812. Forty-eight hours before, a bulletin composed by him had been published in the *Moniteur* revealing as gracefully as possible the catastrophe which had taken place in Russia. It ended reassuringly, 'His Majesty's health has never been better.'

The King of Naples, already demoralized by having to go on foot, was dismayed by his new responsibilities. Napoleon's orders were specific: to rally the army at Vilna and attack the Russians, to hold the west bank of the Niemen and take up winter quarters along the river. Later he was to say of Joachim, 'It is beyond my comprehension how such a brave man could so often be so cowardly.' On reaching Vilna on 8 December and finding its hitherto friendly inhabitants hostile, the King declared, 'I'm not going to let myself be caught in this hole', and promptly abandoned it, although the city was full of food and munitions. Ten days later Joachim summoned senior commanders to a council of war at Gumbinnen in East Prussia, to which he had now withdrawn his troops, telling them that whatever the Emperor might think, the line of the Niemen could not be held and that he meant to retreat still further. In response to loud disagreement he shouted, 'what can we do to save a madman? There isn't a sovereign in Europe who will trust his promises or his treaties. As for me, I'm sorry I spurned the approaches made to me by the English. If I hadn't, I would be just as safe on my throne as the Emperor of Austria or the King of Prussia.' Marshal Davout interrupted icily, 'Those are sovereigns by the grace of God, from long tenure and by reason of the traditional loyalty of their peoples, while you are only a king by the grace of Napoleon and at the price of French blood. You are blinded by the blackest ingratitude.' Murat hastily changed the discussion to plans for moving his headquarters to Königsberg.

Secretly he dispatched two Neapolitans on his staff who had relations in Vienna, the Duke Carafa de Noia and Prince Cariati, to go to Metternich and see if a confidential arrangement might be reached with the Austrians to guarantee his crown in the event of the French Empire collapsing. On 26 December, learning that Prussian troops were going over to the Russians *en masse*, Joachim decided that Königsberg too must be abandoned, withdrawing his headquarters still further westward. Moreover, he was distracted by colourful rumours that during his absence Caroline was ruling Naples as Regent with an alarming degree of independence and taking a whole host of new lovers.

On 15 January King Joachim wrote to Napoleon that he was reluctantly relinquishing command of the *Grande Armée* 'only because the state of health to which I have been reduced during the last five or six days makes it quite impossible for me to attend adequately to administrative matters', adding in a postscript, 'I have fever and symptoms of a serious attack of jaundice.' Two days later he vanished from Poznan (Posen), where he had set up his final headquarters, having waited just long enough for Eugène to come and take over. He was back in Naples after a fortnight's hard riding. 'Not bad for a sick man!' commented an amused Eugène when he heard the news. Two days before her reunion with Joachim Caroline had received a curt letter from her brother. 'Your husband the King of Naples deserted the army on the 16th. He is a brave man on the battlefield but weaker than a woman or a monk when the enemy is out of sight. He has no moral courage whatever. I leave it to you to make him aware of just how displeased I am by his behaviour.'

It is odd that Napoleon had not given the command to the Viceroy in the first place. General Caulaincourt suspected that he 'did not want his stepson to gain credit for yet another success'. Italian officers complained that Ney alone had been praised for his courage during the retreat when Eugène had shown equal heroism. Perhaps the Emperor was anxious not to enhance the reputation of a man who might one day be a rival to the King of Rome. The Viceroy bore no ill feelings and reorganized the army, finding hospital beds, raising morale by smart parades, forming a new observation corps, recruiting, regrouping, despite heart-rending appeals from Augusta Amelia to come home. When the Prussian King declared war on France in March 1813, he ignored his stepfather's order to burn Berlin and withdrew behind the Elbe. By the spring he had 60,000 healthy troops, with guns and horses.

Napoleon waited grimly for Europe to rise against him. Soon Bernadotte would land at Stralsund with 35,000 Swedish troops and link up with the Russians and Prussians. Austria was secretly arming, if remaining neutral for the moment. However, the Emperor was far from finished, still confident of his 'star'. There was one sovereign from the old Europe of whom he hoped to make an ally, Pius VII. Five days of cloistered discussion at Fontainebleau ensued between the two men. On 25 January the Pope signed a draft concordat. Marie Louise, expecting to be crowned empress in Notre-Dame by the pontiff himself, wrote excitedly to her father, 'The Emperor has settled the affairs of Christendom.' But, true to the shrewd instinct of Curia diplomacy down the centuries, Pius's advisers had recognized the implications of the retreat from Moscow. (At Rome St Anna Maria Taigi was prophesying Napoleon's imminent downfall.) On 24 March Pius wrote to withdraw his agreement.

The Senate endorsed the Emperor's request for 350,000 conscripts although 150,000 would have to be adolescents. The poor children were nicknamed the 'Marie-Louises' – scarcely a sign of affection for the dynasty. If it did not lose one itself, almost every family in France knew of another that had had to sacrifice some unhappy boy to save the regime. The middle-aged bourgeois of the National Guard were made liable to service abroad. In consequence, Napoleon had a new army of 200,000 by the spring of 1813, though its officers had never before clapped eyes on the men they led into Germany, while most NCOs only received their stripes on the eve of departure. The most striking weakness was the dearth of good horses. The cavalry chargers and gun teams which had perished in Russia were replaced by a motley collection of screws, nags and veteran animals out at grass.

Moreover, the Emperor knew that, whether he liked or not, he had to abandon Joseph to his fate. He foresaw accurately that Wellington, who had been made commander-in-chief of the Spanish as well as of the British and Portuguese armies, would strike at northern Spain, which was in revolt against the French occupation. On 18 January he told his Minister of War, 'Repeat my orders to the King of Spain to move his headquarters to Valladolid and occupy Madrid only with his most forward troops, and to transfer as many men as possible to the north and Aragon to reduce northern Spain to submission.' Again and again he sent orders for Joseph to withdraw to Valladolid. But his brother, as always, preferred the show of power to the substance and argued that to leave his capital was tantamount to abdication. When he finally abandoned Madrid at the end of March, although he had assumed personal command of all operations in the field he spent his time setting up a court in exile at Valladolid and had little time to spare for military matters. As a result, he awaited Wellington's spring offensive with no more than 30,000 troops while behind him northern Spain was still overrun by insurgents.

In contrast Jérôme for once showed himself realistic. His brother had explained to him that a decisive war would be waged on his frontiers, and he could see that his people regarded him as a foreign puppet – he was having considerable difficulty in recruiting a new Westphalian army. Although he stayed at his capital of Cassel, with unusual consideration he sent Queen Catherine and her household to the safety of Paris on 10 March despite Napoleon's insistence that she should on no account leave Westphalia. Her departure demoralized still further her husband's few remaining loyal subjects.

Louis, living quietly at Graz, had foretold that the Russian war would end in his brother's ruin – a prophecy inspired by innate gloom rather than prescience. Now he offered his services to the Emperor, but only in return for the restoration of his Dutch throne. He was told firmly that such a condition was impossible, though he was very welcome to return to France. The former King of Holland stayed glumly at Graz, insisting that he was Dutch and not French. Not even Madame Mère could persuade him that to go home would be 'a noble action'.

Lucien was as anxious as ever to play the statesman and to go against the Emperor's policies whatever they might be. When he heard of the Russian disaster and the Malet conspiracy, he suggested from Worcestershire – through his friend Colonel Leighton – to the British Foreign Minister Lord Castlereagh that should Napoleon be eliminated he might be succeeded not by the King of Rome but by the peace-loving Joseph. This would enable Ferdinand VII to return to Spain immediately. Castlereagh gave a polite answer, though he had no intention of adopting the proposal. In January 1813 Lucien was again in correspondence with the Foreign Minister, reverting this time to a plan which would enable both the Emperor and Joseph to keep their present thrones. He even offered to mediate with Napoleon, an offer which was courteously declined by Castlereagh.

The one member of the clan who had no comment to make on the retreat from Moscow and its consequences was Pauline. Indeed her mother rebuked her for not writing to the Emperor to express her sympathy. She had spent most of 1812 quietly nursing her health and her hypochondria at Aix-les-Bains, enjoying boating parties on Lake Bourget and acquiring two more admirers. At forty-nine François-Joseph Talma, the star of the Comédie-Française who had begun his career as a dentist, was the most famous French tragedian of his day, excelling in all Corneille and Racine's classical roles and even trying his hand at Shakespeare. Deeply admired by Napoleon, who paid his debts twice, he reciprocated by hero-worshipping his patron – royalists said that he gave the great man tuition in deportment and elocution. Although heavily middle-aged and more than portly, he fell violently in love with the sylph-like Princess when he went to take the waters at Aix in the summer of that year, sending her elaborately passionate, over-written letters which were discreetly addressed to

'Madame Sophie': 'Pauline, you cannot realize the depth of my love for you or the wounds which you have inflicted on my heart. . . . Was there ever a fate like mine? My God, how unhappy I am!' More practically he also sought her help in obtaining a licence to export goods to England for a merchant house in which he had shares. Pauline neither answered his letters nor procured him his licence and it is most unlikely that she ever admitted him into her bed. On the other hand she undoubtedly slept with Colonel Antoine Duchand. This young gunner officer in the dark-blue uniform, who came from a family of Grenoble bankers, was her own age and as handsome and virile as poor Canouville had been. He came to Aix about the same time as Talma, to convalesce after being severely wounded during the siege of Valencia, and was soon genuinely devoted to the strange, valetudinarian Princess. He consoled her when the news of Canouville's death arrived – she was so distraught that she could not eat for days. By the end of 1812, however, Duchand was fit enough to return to his guns, fighting with such bravery at Leipzig the following year that he was created a baron of the Empire.

The Emperor and his new army linked up with Eugène's troops on 1 May 1813 near the banks of the river Saale in Saxony. Next day at Lützen, with 110,000 men he fought and defeated 75,000 Russian and Prussians under General Wittgenstein. He was delighted by the performance of his 'Marie-Louises', or at least pretended to be. 'During the twenty years in which I have commanded the armies of France I have never seen greater bravery, greater loyalty', he told them. 'My young soldiers, honour and courage flow from every pore in your skins!' But Marshal Bessières had been killed, no enemy guns or prisoners had been taken, and lack of cavalry made it impossible for the French to launch a proper pursuit and exploit the victory. He compained petulantly to the Viceroy, 'My son, yesterday would have been such a beautiful day if you had brought me 3,000 prisoners. Why weren't you able to send me any, in terrain where the enemy could not use his horse properly?' After Eugène had occupied Dresden, he was allowed to return to Milan at last. He was never to see his 'father' again though he managed to send him 45,000 fresh infantry and 2,000 cavalry from Italy before the end of summer, a feat which was regarded as miraculous. Meanwhile Napoleon went on to win yet another victory, at Bautzen on 21–2 May, though the French lost 15,000 men compared with 10,000 enemy casualties – among the dead was Marshal Duroc, a loss which genuinely upset his master. As at Lützen shortage of cavalry made it impossible to exploit the victory. 'What, no results, no guns, no prisoners?' grumbled the Emperor. 'These people won't even leave me so much as a horseshoe nail!'

On 4 June an armistice was signed at Poischwitz. It was a grave error on the part of Napoleon, who believed that he would be able to double his forces and, above all, obtain more cavalry. He failed to appreciate the difficulties of the Russians and Prussians in mobilizing their own troops and that, with reason, they expected to be joined by Austria.

In practice this meant an unofficial armistice with Sweden as well. Bernadotte panicked, complaining that after offering to make him Emperor, the Allies were betraying him – shouting that in any case he would rather retreat to Lapland than reign over 'so degraded a people' as the French. If the armistice turned into a peace, it would also spell the end of his scheme for seizing Norway. To add to his worries, in Stockholm Carl XIII was senile and apparently on the point of death while not every member of the notoriously unruly Swedish officer corps cared for 'that damned Frenchman'. But Napoleon had no desire for a general peace.

On 26 June Metternich had his historic interview with the Emperor in the Marcolini palace in Dresden, knowing that his army in Spain had been routed. He told Napoleon that the Emperor of Austria was prepared to mediate and could secure peace if the French would restore Prussia's frontiers to what they had been in 1806, return Illyria to Austria, dissolve the Grand Duchy of Warsaw and give up the Protectorate of the Confederation of the Rhine. In return France might keep the natural frontiers of the Rhine and the Alps, together with Holland, Westphalia and Italy. Murat would be left in possession of Naples. Nothing was said about Swedish interests. Metternich could afford to be blunt. He told Napoleon, 'I've seen your soldiers. They're children. Your Majesty is convinced that you are indispensable to your country. But don't you need your country as well? When this army of adolescents you have conscripted has gone, what are you going to do then?' The Emperor was so infuriated that he threw his hat into a corner of the room, shouting, 'I grew up on battlefields and someone like me doesn't mind if he loses a million men!' He explained most revealingly, 'Your sovereigns born on a throne can let themselves be defeated twenty times and always return to their thrones. I can't do that – I'm self-made.' He complained that he had made 'an unforgivable blunder' in marrying the Empress Francis's daughter. 'In marrying an Archduchess I hoped to combine past and present, Gothic prejudices with the ideas of my own country. I made a mistake and today I know just how wrong I was. Perhaps it will cost me my throne, but I'm going to bury the world with my ruin.' As he left, Metternich burst out, 'You're lost, Sire!' None the less the armistice was extended and peace talks began at Prague, though on St Helena Napoleon admitted, 'The truth is I never had any intention of making peace at Prague.'

During these crucial days the Emperor seems to have ignored what was happening on his second front in Spain, where more than 100,000 of his best troops were tied down. On 13 May Wellington began his advance from the Portuguese frontier. King Joseph, who was in personal command of his army – advised by Marshal Jourdan, currently incapacitated by fever – evacuated Valladolid and moved his headquarters to Burgos, then to Vitoria. Here on 21 June, five days before Metternich's interview with his imperial brother at Dresden, Joseph's confused troops were irretrievably defeated. It was not their fault for there was no proper battle plan, the King having spent the previous day dallying with the Marquesa de Monte Hermoso. The French lost thousands of prisoners, 150 guns, 1,500 supply wagons, a military chest containing currency to the value of a million pounds sterling, and Joseph's carriage together with his crown and regalia. The King fled, crossing the Pyrenees on 28 June to take refuge in France. Apart from a few frontier towns nothing remained of his realm. Napoleon commented later, on hearing that there had been a decisive defeat, 'All the blunders in Spain stem from my ill-advised kindness to the King who, besides not knowing how to command an army, is in addition incapable of judging his own abilities accurately and of leaving the command to a soldier.'

The news of Vitoria made up the minds of the Austrian Emperor and Metternich to bring Austria into the war on the side of the Allies. They had feared that large reserves of veteran troops from Spain might reinforce Napoleon but they now saw that there was no longer any possibility of this. 'José Primero' had ruined his brother.

Joseph went back to Mortefontaine and his wife. If Hortense – who visited them there in the latter half of 1813 – is to be believed, Julie cannot have seen his return as an unmixed blessing.

> The Queen shared his retirement. She was admirable in her gentleness, kindness of heart and unselfishness. She shared my own indifference to rank and position and no more than I did she find they bring happiness. Her husband, whose character was totally unlike that of Louis, made her unhappy but for quite different reasons. With no consideration for her, and only interested in other women, he neglected her and was frequently rude to her. Her domestic sorrows put me in mind of the life I myself had led for so long.

In the same passage Hortense refers to Julie as 'a slave and so unhappy'.

The bankrupt, jerry-built conglomeration of territories which formed the Kingdom of Westphalia began to disintegrate as early as the spring of 1813. There was panic in Cassel, and French officials began to slip away in April. Every morning brought news that more men had deserted from the Westphalian army. Even King Hieronymus Napoleo admitted that his troops – conscripts brought in to replace all those who had died in Russia – were an unknown quantity. At the end of April the arrival of French and

Polish detachments made him feel a little more secure. He was hurt that his brother would not even grant him an audience, let alone give him the important command which he felt was his due, not realizing just how disillusioned the Emperor had been by his performance in the Russian campaign. When he was at last received by Napoleon, during the latter's stay at Dresden, he did not however discuss military matters. Having learnt that Betsy Patterson had at last agreed to a divorce and that this had been approved by Congress, he now proposed divorcing his excellent but as yet childless wife Catherine – regardless of the insult to Württemberg – and taking as his third wife the Princess zu Löwenstein, who was pregnant by him. He hoped that this could be done as soon as possible, so that she might present him with a legitimate heir. He was told sharply to abandon the idea. In the meantime his Westphalian troops continued to desert steadily. Only the armistice postponed the final demise of Jérôme's realm.

In Naples Joachim and Caroline were being nothing if not realistic. King Joachim had now entered upon a lengthy and secret correspondence with Metternich through his confidential envoy Prince Cariati, who was appointed Neapolitan Ambassador in Vienna at the end of April. At the same time through his Police Minister, the Duke of Campochiaro, he had also made contact with the British representative in Sicily, Lord William Bentinck. He was in an agony of indecision during the armistice in Germany, since his brother-in-law's victories at Lützen and Bautzen made him wonder if the French Empire might not survive after all. Napoleon guessed only too clearly what Murat was up to, though he could not quite bring himself to suspect his sister. On 18 June Joachim promised the Austrians that if they joined the Russians and Prussians he would attack in Italy with 30,000 men. But would they? On 3 July Caroline wrote to ask her brother to show himself more kindly disposed towards her husband. The following day the King himself wrote to Dresden, offering his services. 'Resume, Sire, the confidence that was founded upon twenty years of tried fidelity,' he pleaded. 'Remember, Sire, that I consider my honour involved in commanding myself the Neapolitan troops fighting for you, and that I am capable of ending the noble career, through which I have lived under your auspices, by losing my throne and my life but not by sacrificing my honour.' The Emperor replied to Caroline, not to Joachim, grumbling that her husband was not sending reinforcements to Eugène and was negotiating with the enemy. If he was wrong, then the King should come to Dresden. Caroline replied that Joachim was too clever to be trapped by her brother's enemies and that he would come and disprove all these slanders, since he could not go on living without loving and serving Napoleon. Murat left Naples for Dresden on 2 August. The next day he was met by a courier with secret dispatches from Cariati in Vienna. Since he could not read the cipher, he told the courier to take them to Naples. He himself galloped on towards Germany. The dispatches were to have informed him that Austria would declare war on France.

The other male of the clan to rule in Italy, Eugène, was as unfailingly loyal as he was realistic. He can have had few illusions about the future and was saddened by the recent deaths of his two closest friends among the marshals, Bessières and Duroc. None the less, he amassed men and horses with quiet efficiency, taking good care that recruits were properly trained before sending them to Germany. The Emperor bombarded him with instructions, sending as many as three letters a day. In addition to raising and training a new Army of Italy he was also responsible for the troops in Illyria, besides organizing an observation corps to patrol the river Adige – there were justified fears of an Austrian invasion. Although the Viceroy was working desperately hard at Milan, he was reunited to his Augusta Amelia and supremely happy. He was able to reassure the Emperor that the Kingdom of Italy had seldom been more tranquil. On 11 August he received a dispatch from his stepfather informing him that Austria was about to declare war.

Hostilities reopened on 16 August along an enormously long line stretching from Bohemia to Hamburg. Napoleon had made Dresden his base, filling it with supplies and munitions. He had 300,000 men which he could deploy between the Oder and the Elbe. His intention was to provoke the encircling enemy forces into making isolated attacks so that from his central position he could reinforce any one of his armies which was threatened and cut off and destroy the attackers in turn.

Unfortunately his opponents were aware of this favourite strategy. At a meeting in the Silesian castle of Trachenberg the previous month they had evolved a new strategy to counter it. The Allied armies were to converge on Napoleon in a huge semicircle, always withdrawing when faced by the Emperor in person, concentrating instead on attacking his flanks and communications and any detached corps. It was a strategy of harassment and attrition made possible by superior numbers which would eventually envelop and strangle the imperial army. Ironically, the 'Trachenberg Plan' was the invention of that former Marshal of France, the Crown Prince of Sweden – exploiting insights gleaned from earlier days in the French service – written down by the Swedish General Count Löwenhjelm, and Bernadotte's one great contribution to the art of war. He himself led 120,000 Swedes, Prussians and Russians around Berlin while Marshal Blücher was to attck from Breslau with 95,000 Prussians and Prince Schwarzenberg to advance from the south with 240,000 Austrians.

After a fortnight of exhausting manoeuvres caused by the Allies' revolutionary tactics, Napoleon caught Schwarzenberg just outside

Dresden and destroyed his entire left wing on 26–7 August, inflicting 38,000 casualties. Schwarzenberg retreated as fast as he could into the Bohemian mountains. The victory was largely due to a brilliant performance by Murat who led 45,000 men to turn the Austrian left and took 12,000 prisoners and 30 guns besides killing or wounding 4,000 of the enemy – during the pursuit on the day after the battle he captured another 6,000 prisoners. However, success at Dresden was offset by a whole string of peripheral defeats. General Vandamme, pursuing too rashly, was defeated and taken prisoner, Marshals Oudinot and Macdonald were both routed, while Marshal Ney had to retreat in confusion after losing 20,000 men. Then the Emperor fell ill with food poisoning and was only able to resume full command at the beginning of September. The reverses suffered by his subordinates made it impossible for him to advance on Berlin as he had planned. The enemy persistently refused to face him and he was unable to catch them despite superhuman efforts, sleeping on a bed in his carriage with a bandana tied round his head and using the vehicle as a travelling headquarters. Meanwhile Bernadotte, whose troops had repulsed Ney at Dennewitz, succeeded in linking up with Blücher. The outlook grew gloomier every day.

No one was more disheartened than the mercurial King Joachim. On 19 September he wrote to the Duke of Campochiaro, 'Everything is going wrong. The army longs for peace. Only the Emperor is opposed to this universal longing.' By now his brother-in-law had heard of Prince Cariati's intrigues in Vienna – though luckily for Joachim he did not have precise details – and insisted that the Prince should be recalled to Naples. Instead Cariati joined the Austrian army, from where he contrived to send a secret message to the King that Metternich and the Emperor Francis would see he kept his throne if he abandoned Napoleon. The latter was further incensed by news that the Neapolitans were refusing to reinforce the Viceroy's Army of Italy.

When the Austrians under General Hiller attacked Italy, Eugène reacted with his accustomed vigour. He drove the enemy out of Villach, which they had occupied, but his troops were still inexperienced and no match for Austrian veterans. He therefore withdrew to the Isonzo at the end of September. Here, although there were no full-scale battles, he fought a number of small yet ferocious actions in which he led his young soldiers with well attested dash and daring. He remained unshaken by the grim tidings coming out of Germany.

By the beginning of October Napoleon had been encircled, mainly because of his stubborn insistence on holding Dresden, and all but ringed by a wall of 350,000 enemy troops who hoped to cut off his retreat to France. He was still as aggressive as ever, as indeed was Murat who once again fought like a lion in a savage engagement at Liebertwolkwitz where he captured a thousand prisoners. Despairing of defending the Elbe, the Emperor at last retreated to Leipzig, where he held one of the last of his stirring military reviews on 15 October.

The 'Battle of the Nations', as the Germans called the greatest battle of the nineteenth century, began outside Leipzig on the following day. The enemy were eventually able to bring 300,000 men into action against Napoleon's 200,000 and this superority of three to two was reflected in their preponderance of artillery. The conflict continued for three days. The French resisted attack after attack though their Saxon and Württemberger allies began to desert. Again Murat's performance was heroic. Seeing his glittering figure leading a charge against the Russians the Tsar joked to his agent Cariati, 'Our ally rather overplays his part in disguising his game.' A prisoner, General von Merveldt, was so astonished at seeing the King at French headquarters that he blurted out some words hinting that Joachim had been in touch with the Austrians. The Emperor sent Merveldt to ask the Austrian Emperor to mediate and secure an armistice – he was prepared to accept the terms offered by Metternich at Dresden and in addition give up Holland, Westphalia and Italy. It was too late. The Allies were determined not to halt until they had driven every French soldier back across the Rhine. News arrived that the Bavarian King had gone over to them. They waited for Bernadotte to arrive on the third day. He rode up to the front in a uniform which would have been the envy of King Joachim, 'a tunic of violet velvet braided with gold, on his head a hat with white feathers surmounted by an immense plume in the Swedish colours . . . in his hand a violet velvet baton'. Then they made their supreme effort, consisting in six concentric attacks. The French held them, just, but the battle had been lost. At midnight on 18 October Napoleon gave the order for a general retreat. The principal bridge over the river Elster had been blown up prematurely and whole companies were drowned trying to swim across. However the Allies' hopes of cutting off the Emperor's retreat came to nothing and he fought his way back to the Rhine.

Joachim Murat had said goodbye to his brother-in-law at Erfurt on 25 October, embracing him again and again, explaining smoothly that he would be of more use in Italy where he could bring his Neapolitan troops to the aid of the Viceroy. The Emperor did not want him to go, observing that he always left when things were getting difficult. Before he even reached Naples the King informed Prince Cariati in a secret dispatch that he would join the Allies as soon as he got home, and told him to try to obtain more territory on the Italian mainland in compensation for Sicily which was obviously going to be retained by the Bourbons. In his absence Queen

Caroline had authorized the acceptance of the Austrian proposals on her own responsibility, besides ordering the seizure of all French vessels in Neapolitan ports, the confiscation of all French property and the occupation of the French enclaves of Pontecorvo and Benevento. On 21 November, at her insistence, King Joachim led a Neapolitan army north, though he had not yet quite made up his mind to attack Eugène, his basic objectives being to keep his throne and acquire more territory.

In the north the Austrians were advancing through the Tyrol and the Viceroy had to withdraw to the line of the river Adige. His wife, expecting their fifth child, was deeply upset by the defection of her father, King Maximilian of Bavaria. She wrote, 'God gave me an angel for a husband. That is my sole happiness.' Indeed her entire family was devoted to Eugène. On 22 November one of King Maximilian's ADCs, Prince Augustus of Thurn and Taxis, came through the lines under a white flag to see the Viceroy at his headquarters on the road between Verona and Vicenza. He brought a message from the Allies offering him the iron crown of Lombardy if he would desert Napoleon. Eugène rejected out of hand this offer of a kingdom. He sent a grateful but firm refusal to his father-in-law. 'I would rather sacrifice my future happiness, and my family's, than break the vows I have sworn.' Shortly afterwards he received a grumbling letter from his stepfather, asking why he had retreated to the Adige when he was about to be reinforced by Neapolitan troops. The Viceroy held on calmly, continuing to fight small, indecisive actions since the Austrians were not yet attacking in strength.

After Leipzig the Kingdom of Westphalia vanished as though it had never been. For some time King Jérôme had been selling off crown lands and lodging the money in a secret bank account in France with a view to purchasing a country estate not too far from Paris. He took refuge at Coblenz – accompanied by his mistress, Princess Löwenstein – at the end of September and beginning of October when Cassel was briefly occupied by Cossacks, but returned to his capital on 17 October. Nine days later, after the news of Leipzig, even before the arrival of the enemy, Jérôme left Cassel for the last time and set up a species of court at Cologne. He soon moved to Aix-la-Chapelle and then to the great royal château of Compiègne, with a huge and gaudy household in attendance. He bullied his wife into going to plead with her thoroughly unsympathetic father, the King of Württemberg, to intercede with the Allies and save Westphalia for them.

Joseph, Louis and Jérôme Bonaparte had now all lost their thrones. Yet with scarcely credible fatuity each one confidently expected to be restored, insisting that they were still sovereigns. Predictably, King Louis's behaviour was the oddest of the lot – he wrote to Madame Mère announcing that he had left the domains of the Austrian Emperor in order to facilitate his return to Holland. Joseph and Jérôme had at least enough sense to realize that it was just possible they might have to live out their days in 'exile' in France. What they did not appreciate was that their brother the Emperor had lost contact with reality. And, as always, they were incapable of accepting that their position in the world depended entirely on Napoleon.

9

The Bonapartes Lose their Crowns

'My dear fellow, if the Cossacks reach the gates of Paris it's
the end of Empire and Emperor.'

NAPOLEON IN 1814

'That pig of a Joseph.'

NAPOLEON IN 1814

Napoleon's domination of Europe ended at Leipzig. It was impossible for
him to find troops to replace the armies lost in Russia and Germany during
the last twelve months. Undeterred, he held a victory parade at the
Tuileries five days after his return, when captured Austrian colours were
somewhat tactlessly presented to his Austrian Empress – who received
them with sufficient grace. The *Marseillaise*, banned for many years on
account of revolutionary associations, was now played everywhere to
arouse patriotic fervour. To reassure the Parisians he spent the next two
months at the Tuileries with Marie Louise and the King of Rome. Crowds
still cheered him in the streets, but it impressed only simple people – and
the clan.

The Emperor knew that he was facing the greatest crisis of his entire
career. The Allies again offered astonishingly generous terms which would
leave France with the frontiers of the Rhine, the Alps and the Pyrenees,
but he would not accept. Yet, as he himself admitted publicly, 'Wellington
has invaded the south of France, the Russians threaten the northern
frontier, and Prussians, Austrians and Bavarians are on the eastern.' More
or less abandoning the south to take care of itself and to cope with the
British invasion, he scraped together nearly 120,000 'men' to defend his
northern and eastern frontiers. For the most part they were pensioners and
'Marie-Louises' even younger than before, most of them conscripted
forcibly. In an unguarded moment, addressing the Senate in a rage, he had
said, 'Those boys are only fit for filling up the hospitals and the roadside.'
He also recruited maimed and crippled veterans from the Invalides,
including men of over sixty. He planned to turn his capital into a fortress,
ordering 'No preparations whatever are to be made for abandoning Paris,
[whose defenders] must if necessary be buried in its ruins.'

Even so the Emperor was more realistic about his brothers' qualities
than in past days. Angered by reports of an enormous and impossibly

expensive household at Compiègne, he refused to receive King Jérôme and forbade him to install it in a sumptuous château at Stains near Paris. Jérôme was reduced to moving into Cardinal Fesch's house in the Chaussée d'Antin, which he did without bothering to ask his uncle's permission. Napoleon offered him command of the forces around Lyons but only if he dismissed his 'Westphalian' courtiers and 'on condition he promises me that he will stay with the vanguard and the outposts, has no train of attendants and makes no display of luxury, takes no more than fifteen horses, bivouacs among his soldiers, and that not a gun is to be fired unless he himself is the first under fire'. The King declined to accept such undignified terms, arguing that unless he retained the state of an exiled sovereign, he would have little chance of regaining his realm at the forthcoming peace; in any case a monarch could not take orders from marshals but only from the Emperor in person. In consequence he stayed on at Uncle Fesch's house while the Bonapartes' world disintegrated around him.

Joseph too would not accept that he was no longer a sovereign, no longer King of Spain. Napoleon was particularly scathing about him when Count Roederer informed him of this in November 1813.

What a chimera! [commented the Emperor] They [the Spanish] don't want him back. They think he's incapable. They don't want a king who spends all his time with women playing hide-and-seek and blind-man's buff. The King [Joseph] is entirely dependent on his women, his houses and his furniture. He said to me at the Prado, in all seriousness, that my grenadiers simply mustn't make a mess in his palace. . . . And I sacrificed thousands, hundreds of thousand, of men so that he could reign in Spain.

As for Vitoria, 'How he lost that battle! He doesn't even know the ABC of the soldier's job and yet he wants to fight battles!' When Roederer suggested that Joseph might be given the crown of Italy instead, Napoleon's reply revealed what he thought of Eugène in comparison. 'If I separate the French and Italian crowns – I've never quite decided whether to join or divide them – am I to throw over the Viceroy, a young man who is loved and respected, who has always served me with honour and fidelity? He has honour while the King has none at all.' For a time Joseph was left to languish like Jérôme, though in the soothing luxury of his beloved Mortefontaine, where he had passed the time since leaving Spain in picnicking, shooting, boating, making music and of course philandering. Madame Mère and his wife Julie journeyed incessantly between Mortefontaine and the Tuileries trying to make peace between the two brothers. In the end Joseph swallowed his pride and on 5 January 1814 sent the Emperor a formal letter – for publication – offering his services as 'first of the French princes and first of your subjects'. In reward he was allowed to keep the title King Joseph instead of that of King of Spain. Furthermore, on 24 January before Napoleon left for the front he appointed him Lieutenant-General of France, the traditional French Protector of the Realm, with the responsibility of defending Paris and command of all troops in and around the capital. One may question the appointment of such an unmilitary, lazy, ineffectual and – as will be seen – defeatist creature to so vital a post. The answer is that he was the only man available who, Napoleon hoped, could be depended on to work for the dynasty's survival. It was far too great a responsibility for the young girl who, three days before, had again been created Empress Regent.

The earliest to abandon the sinking ship which the French Empire had become were, all too predictably, the Murats – though even now the Emperor himself did not suspect the extent of their double-dealing. Yet on his way back from Erfurt Joachim, running into King Louis by chance at Basle, had advised him to join the Allies if he hoped to regain his throne, adding that this was what he himself was going to do as soon as he reached home. *En route* at Milan Murat met Vauguyon, his former ADC and rival for his wife's affections, who spoke inspiringly of a unified Italian Kingdom stretching from the Alps down to the toe of Italy and whom he commissioned to recruit support. Significantly, in the light of future developments, Joachim also stopped at Florence where he spoke with the Grand Duchess Elisa. Meanwhile, at his own capital not only had Queen Caroline committed him to an Austrian alliance in his absence, for she too had come to despair of her brother's survival, but another refugee was on his way there too, to arrive in November some days after the King's return. Fouché, Duke of Otranto and former imperial Police Minister, had been sent to Illyria as Governor by Napoleon to keep him out of the way and stop his intriguing. Driven from Illyria by the Austrians as the Empire crumbled, he had been commissioned to report on the situation in Italy before going back to France to report to his master, who still trusted him. A man of immense complexity and tortuous motives, after the Neapolitan army had marched off to occupy the former Papal States – a move in which Napoleon saw nothing suspicious until the last moment – Fouché encouraged Murat's policy of allying himself with the Austrians and extending his realm up to the south bank of the river Po. At the end of December a charming and persuasive Austrian plenipotentiary with one eye, General Count Neipperg (a name of which more will be heard), came to finalize negotiations. The Treaty of Naples was signed on 11 January 1814. It guaranteed King Joachim and his heirs perpetual possession of his kingdom, in return for which he was to lend the Austrians 30,000 troops and attack his brother-in-law's forces in Italy with another 60,000 – a secret clause stipulated that Austria would try to persuade the Bourbons to abandon their claims if Murat renounced his pretensions to Sicily.

That famous beauty and extremely influential hostess Mme Récamier, the mistress of Chateaubriand and the friend of Mme de Staël, was staying in the palace at Naples when the treaty was signed. The royal couple staged a scene which they no doubt hoped would be widely reported in France. Mme Récamier was with Caroline in her apartments when Joachim burst in, immediately after signing, and dramatically asked his wife for her opinion. 'You are a Frenchman, Sire,' she replied. 'You should be faithful to France.' Murat violently pushed open the window of a great balcony looking on to the sea and cried, 'Then I am a traitor', pointing to the British fleet entering the port of Naples under full sail. Throwing himself on to a sofa he buried his face in his hands and burst into tears. The Queen brought him a glass of orange-flower water laced with ether, begging him to be calm. By mid-February Joachim, in alliance with the Austrians, had taken over all central Italy and was occupying both Rome and Bologna. This was done with the complete if carefully concealed approval of Caroline Murat.

Fouché had by then gone on to Florence. Elisa had written to Paris in January that, having heard of the 'criminal' Austro-Neapolitan treaty, 'I am only too aware of my duty towards Your Majesty, I will spare no pains in performing it and whatever may happen I shall do everything I can to save Tuscany for France.' This was before she heard that the Allies had crossed the French frontier. The prematurely aged Grand Duchess – she was going bald – was only too eager to make use of so brilliant a politician as Fouché. She made it quite clear that she was a realist about her imperial brother's prospects and wanted unvarnished advice. After explaining, 'Madame, the sole means of saving ourselves is to kill the Emperor on the battlefield', Fouché counselled her to throw in her lot with King Joachim, who, for the moment, seemed more likely to survive than Napoleon. Elisa did so, apparently reaching a secret agreement with Murat to cede Tuscany to him if she might keep Lucca, and ordering her troops to offer no resistance to the Neapolitans when they marched in. She drove out of Florence amid the jeers of her former subjects who threw stones and horse dung at her coach, abandoned by her equally realistic lover Cerami, and leaving her husband behind with a small garrison. Prince Félix surrendered the very next day, 2 February, departing amid Florentine catcalls. At Lucca she announced that she had severed all links with the French Empire.

Learning that after three months of promising to come to his rescue the Neapolitans had joined the enemy, Eugène withdrew to the river Mincio. He had to leave the pregnant Amelia Augusta at Milan which was threatened by the Austrians, though the enemy commander chivalrously guaranteed her safety together with that of her suite. On 8 February he went into action across the Mincio, inflicting 5,000 casualties on the enemy and taking 3,000 prisoners. Even so his men were beginning to desert. Not only was his retreat southwards cut off by vastly superior Austrian and Neapolitan forces but he decided that it was impossible to cross the Alps. He refused to bring his largely Italian army to France as his stepfather most unreasonably demanded, even asking Joséphine to persuade her son to obey. To petulant complaints from a frantic Napoleon he answered simply, at the end of February, 'My one object in life is to justify the confidence you place in me and I shall be only too happy if I can prove my devotion and my pride in serving you.' Eugène's position was further confused by Murat's bewildering behaviour.

King Joachim, always vacillating and never able to escape wholly from the Emperor's spell, suddenly began to wonder if he was on the wrong side after all when he heard of Napoleon's string of victories over the Allies in France and of the Viceroy's small triumph on the Mincio. Despite writing to the Austrian Emperor of his devotion to the Allies at the end of February, in the same week he wrote to Eugène with a proposal for a joint attack on the Austrians followed by a division of Italy between the two of them. On 1 March Murat wrote an extraordinary letter to his old master, protesting in maudlin terms that although 'I appear to be your enemy' in reality 'never was I more worthy of your affection. Your friend till death'. In the next few days he withdrew his troops without warning during an action near Parma, throwing the Austrians into confusion. Napoleon instructed his stepson to coax 'this extraordinary traitor' into abandoning the Allies and attacking them. But then Joachim heard from the Emperor Francis that not only would he definitely accept the Treaty of Naples and guarantee his throne but Russia and Prussia would do so too. He immediately informed Metternich he was 'an irreconcilable enemy of Napoleon's system of universal domination which has cost France so much blood and treasure and brought so many calamities on Europe' and hurled his men against the Army of Italy.

In the meantime the Emperor was fighting for his existence. The Allies had begun to cross the Rhine even before Christmas 1813, refugees fleeing before them in carts or on foot. By the middle of January Prince Schwarzenberg was holding a line between the Marne and the Seine with 200,000 Austrians and Prussians, while General von Bülow was occupying Holland and Bernadotte threatening Belgium. In all they mustered over 350,000 troops, backed up by reserves at home of at least 400,000. Napoleon was therefore outnumbered by nearly three to one, what troops he had being of very questionable quality. All too many were raw recruits who had merely been given an overcoat, a shako for headgear and a musket or a fowling piece they did not know how to use. In Paris conscripts who had tried to desert were being shot in batches every day.

The atmosphere in the capital was defeatist to a degree. The royalists were encouraged by the knowledge that throughout the provinces Bourbon supporters were preparing to rise while the Chouans were up again in the Vendée. Talleyrand was in contact with the exiled Louis XVIII. Republicans took no less pleasure in the difficulties of a dictator who had betrayed the Revolution and imposed a new monarchy and nobility on France. The talk in the salons was all of defeat, that things could not go on as they were for long, that peace was not far off. Most informed Parisians agreed with Talleyrand: 'It's the beginning of the end.' Outside the army and a very few untypical regions Napoleon had long been extremely unpopular with most Frenchmen. Now even the army was succumbing to pessimism.

The Empress was frightened though her husband did his best to reassure her, with a certain lack of tact. As Hortense was leaving Sunday Mass at the Tuileries during this nerve-racking time she met Marie Louise's trusted lady-in-waiting, the Duchess of Montebello, who cried, 'Haven't you heard? The Allies have crossed the Rhine! Paris is terrified. What *is* the Emperor doing?' Marie Louise had said to Mme de Montebello, 'Wherever I go I bring misfortune!' That same evening Hortense dined alone with Napoleon and the Empress. The former asked Hortense if the Parisians really were afraid. 'Are they expecting to see Cossacks in the streets? Well, they aren't here yet and I haven't quite forgotten my business as a soldier.' He joked to Marie Louise, 'Don't you worry! We're going to Vienna to beat Papa Francis!' After dinner the King of Rome was brought in, already a typical blond Habsburg with a long face. The child was taught to say, 'Let's go and beat Papa Francis' by his father, who roared with laughter when he repeated it.

Napoleon had had many women, possessed what he at least considered to be a shrewd and thoroughly unsentimental knowledge of the sex, and never allowed himself to be influenced by them. Yet he remained extremely fond and extremely proud of Marie Louise. He genuinely respected her, in a way he could not respect Joséphine, 'never a lie, never a debt,' he was to say on St Helena. During the years since their marriage she had been invaluable to him, even if only as a symbol. In after years when Duchess of Parma she was literally adored by her normally far from uncritical subjects, and the Emperor recognized and exploited her popular appeal – which was not altogether dissimilar from that of the Princess of Wales in Britain in the 1980s. She presided with dignity and grace not only over court functions but over military parades as well, and was capable of delivering an excellent speech, if in a strong German accent. After one of her addresses to the Senate, that arch-cynic Talleyrand admitted that 'Neither too bold nor too timid, she showed genuine dignity combined with tact and self-confidence.' Napoleon boasted to Count Roederer, 'It was a mistake on my part ever to have thought that my brothers were essential for my dynasty's survival. My dynasty is perfectly secure without them. It will be forged amid the storms by sheer force of circumstance. The existence of the Empress makes it certain. She has more wisdom and political sense than all of them put together.' At that time Marie Louise was undoubtedly still in love with her husband even if he was so much older and though they had so little in common, and whatever might happen in the not too distant future hers was a far from fickle nature. It was this which would make her seemingly heartless defection such a devastating blow.

One person in Paris who showed no fear of the approaching allies was Letizia. In December 1813 she wrote to her brother Fesch,

> I have spoken with the Emperor, as you wished. He asked me to persuade you to stay at Lyons so long as there is no danger, while if the enemy comes there and if it seems likely that the city may be captured you should leave though stay within your diocese doing good. I am pleased to hear that Louis is with you. The Emperor asked me why he had not come to Paris at once. Tell him that I am expecting him and that his brothers are arriving this evening. This is no time to stand on formality, dear brother. The Bourbons lost everything because they did not know how to die fighting.

For all her courage Madame Mère obviously expected the worst. Metternich recounts with amusement how she had hidden a large sum in cash behind a portrait of the late lamented Carlo Buonaparte in case she had to leave in a hurry, but that her idolized imperial son heard of it, called on her and – when she was out of the room – discreetly took the money for his own use. No doubt she was pleased to see Louis again, who reached the capital on New Year's Day 1814, though his presence there was of even less relevance than that of Jérôme.

On 23 January, accompanied by Marie Louise and the King of Rome, Napoleon reviewed 900 officers of the National Guard at the Tuileries. 'Messieurs, France has been invaded,' he told them. 'I am leaving to place myself at the head of my troops and by God's help and their valour I hope that I shall speedily drive our enemies back across the frontier. Should they approach the capital, however, I entrust the Empress and the King of Rome to the National Guard – my wife and my son!' One observer of this scene, the royalist Pichon, was unimpressed, comparing the Emperor's harangue to that of a Mameluke Pasha: 'A countenance animated more by fury than by genuinely noble feelings, a speech inspired by frenzy, distorted by rage . . . appealing over and over again to the nation's vanity

. . . the tone of some desperado whipping up his gang into making a defiant end.' On the following day Napoleon inspected troops in the snow-covered courtyard of the palace, which he left at 3 o'clock the next morning in the darkness. The winter roads were in a dreadful state but by midnight he was at the front.

Since the Allies were invading, it was much more difficult for them to avoid direct confrontations with Napoleon as they had done so successfully during the Leipzig campaign. Moreover, they could not as yet agree on a wholly concerted operational plan because they were still arguing about what peace terms they should offer. On 27 January the Emperor gave Blücher a nasty shock at Saint-Dizier, forcing him to retreat, though failing to prevent his joining forces with Schwarzenberg. Then on 1 February Napoleon was repulsed at La Rothière. A week later there came the grim ultimatum from the Allies that France must return to her frontiers of 1792, an announcement which enraged Napoleon whose 'roars were like those of a trapped lion'. It also inspired him to all but superhuman activity. In the five days from 10 to 14 February he savaged and routed the Russians and the Prussians in four astonishing victories – Champaubert, Mont-mirail, Château-Thierry and Vauchamps – inflicting 20,000 casualties on an enemy force of 50,000 with only 30,000 men of his own. He turned on Schwarzenberg, who was threatening Paris, and repulsed him bloodily at Montereau, sending him reeling back in headlong retreat. The Allies had made the fundamental mistake of dividing their armies, an error which the Emperor knew exactly how to exploit, as in the days of his greatest triumphs. As he said, he had 'put on the old boots I used to wear in Italy'. By the middle of March he and his little army had fought fourteen battles and won twelve victories against three enormously superior enemy armies. No soldier in the world could match him as a commander, nor could any troops face the French with confidence when they were led by such a man in such a mood. Marshal Marmont tells us that 'conscripts who had only arrived the day before went up to the front and showed just the same courage as veteran troops. There is heroism in the blood of France.'

Indeed Napoleon was so elated that he began to think he might win. After the first of these victories, at Champaubert near Epernay on 10 February, he was literally drunk with joy. Marmont says that he bragged to his officers, 'If we can beat Sacken tomorrow as we did Olosufiev today, the enemy are going back across the Rhine quicker than they came and I shall return to the Vistula.' Noticing looks of horror all round, he added hastily, 'And then I will make peace on the natural frontiers of the Rhine.' Marmont comments, 'As if he would!' The Marshal tells us that his master was incapable of envisaging defeat.

Even Joseph was more realistic though as usual he exaggerated the importance of the Bonapartes.

> Louis and Jérôme have asked me to remind Your Majesty that they are ready to carry out whatever task you may think fit to give them [he wrote on 6 February]. If the worst comes to the worst and the enemy enter the capital, it would be advisable that not all Your Majesty's brothers should abandon it. Between the Empress's departure and the enemy's entry, it seems to me that there would be an interval during which a Provisional Government commission could be established with a prince to head it.

He wrote letter after letter, all uncharacteristically moderate and tactful, begging the Emperor to make peace. To that of 9 March Napoleon replied, 'I am the master here, just as I was at Austerlitz.' Two days later Joseph sent him a final, despairing appeal, 'We are on the brink of total destruction. Our only hope is peace.' By then it was too late.

Sexual jealousy had made the Emperor even less likely to heed his brother's advice. Marie Louise, writing to her husband at the front almost every day, mentioned in several letters that she saw a lot of Joseph. In a letter home Napoleon warned her not to trust him, saying that the one thing he could not survive was the knowledge that she was sleeping with Joseph. 'Beware of the King. He has a bad reputation and unpleasant habits which he picked up in Spain.'

However brilliant for the moment, the Emperor's strategy was misconceived. He did not have the right troops – few men could respond to the demands he made on them, marching and countermarching vast distances at a breathless pace down roads covered with mud and slush, fighting again and again, then sleeping famished in the open beneath freezing winter skies. His green recruits collapsed, from exhaustion, from hunger, from exposure. He himself admitted that even his best troops were 'melting away like snow'. On 9 March the Allies agreed to accept nothing less than unconditional surrender. Their armies began to close in on Paris, whereupon he decided on an extremely risky manoeuvre, to cut their communications and frighten them into withdrawing from his capital. He sent an uncoded note to Marie Louise, 'I have decided to make for the Marne in order to drive the enemy back from Paris.' It was intercepted by Cossacks and reached Schwarzenberg, confirming the Allies' suspicions. They called his bluff and marched on. They had grasped Pozzo di Borgo's advice to the Tsar. 'His military power is still very great, however much it may have been shaken, but his political power has been destroyed,' said the Corsican waging his implacable vendetta. 'Lay a finger on Paris and Napoleon the colossus will fall at once.' The Emperor realized his danger belatedly but at Fontainebleau on 31 March he was given the news that on Joseph's instructions Marshal Marmont had signed an armistice and that his capital was in the hands of the enemy.

If Paris had been given the merest vestiges of fortification – no more than a few entrenchments and barricades – it could have been held. Joseph, who as Lieutenant-General was in charge of fortifying the capital, must take the blame. Even without entrenchments the city might well have been defended until Napoleon's arrival, since he was only a day's march away when it fell. Joseph decided to capitulate and did not bother to ask Marmont for his opinion. The Emperor was in no doubt as to who was responsible. 'That pig of a Joseph who imagines he can command an army as well as I can!' But Joseph had no desire to command an army on this particular occasion.

The imperial family – Marie Louise, the King of Rome, Madame Mère and Catherine of Westphalia (pregnant at last) – had left the Tuileries with their suites in ten green carriages at 9 o'clock in the morning of 28 March. Escorted by 1,200 horse grenadiers, *chasseurs à cheval* and lancers, they set out for Rambouillet, where they were joined by Louis 'in such a state of panic that he wanted to leave for some fortress' said the Empress afterwards, 'so demented that he was embarrassing.' (Hortense made her way to Rambouillet, then, practically alone, to Joséphine's château of Navarre in Normandy where her mother was overjoyed to see her.) The refugees at Rambouillet were driven from there by the threat of Cossack patrols, Catherine in a state of exhaustion. They travelled on to Chartres in their carriages – ironically these had been made for Napoleon's coronation – where Joseph joined them announcing the fall of Paris. He and Jérôme had departed in haste on 31 October as soon as enemy cavalry began to threaten the suburbs, despite the former's earlier opinion that an imperial prince should stay behind and despite his heroic proclamation to the Parisians: 'The Regency Council has provided for the safety of the Empress and the King of Rome. I remain.' On the Emperor's instructions he had written to Bernadotte, though without much hope, in a last attempt to detach him from the Allies. He had left Julie and his daughters with Crown Princess Desideria (Désirée) in Paris at the Bernadotte hôtel at 26 rue d'Anjou. He and the dejected clan went on to Blois, where they set up a court in the *préfecture* guarded by their troops. The two imperial brothers appear to have considered setting up some sort of provisional government south of the Loire, but although Jérôme threatened to use force if necessary to make Marie Louise go with them she wisely refused. Then the Empress was visited by an ADC to the Tsar, Count Shuvalov, who informed her that she must accompany him to Orleans from where she would be escorted by Prince Esterházy to her father who had installed himself at Rambouillet. Chivalrously, the Emperor Francis also sent an invitation to Madame Mère to accompany her, which Letizia at once declined. As she left, Marie Louise said to her, 'I hope that you will always think kindly of me.' Her mother-in-law replied coldly, 'That depends on you and on how you behave.'

Meanwhile the head of the clan wanted to fight on, but his marshals had more sense. He accused Joseph of having lost his head – 'Joseph is a *coglione*' – and tried to persuade his commanders to advance towards Paris. On 2 April Ney, 'bravest of the brave', told him publicly, 'The army will not march.' They rejected the Emperor's proposal to re-group behind the Loire and then counter-attack although some suspected that he might try to have them shot. Once again he was the victim of his own delusions of grandeur.

> If only Napoleon had strode out of the conference chamber into the hall outside filled with junior officers, he would have found a whole host of young men keen to follow him [says Baron Agathon Fain]. After a few more steps he would have been greeted at the foot of the staircase by cheering soldiers. Their enthusiasm would have given new life to all his hopes. But Napoleon was the dupe of his own regime. He thought it beneath his dignity to march off without the senior officers who owed their entire careers to him.

The Emperor told Caulaincourt, 'I am humiliated by the knowledge that the men whom I have raised so high could fall so low.' He stayed on at Fontainebleau. A first abdication in favour of the King of Rome was followed by a second, unconditional abdication. He had to remain where he was until the Allies decided his fate. On 12 April he took poison but vomited it up and decided against suicide.

The terms of the peace included provision for most members of the imperial family. Marie Louise was to have the Duchy of Parma. Joséphine would receive a million francs a year, Joseph and Jérôme 500,000 each, Eugène 400,000, Madame Mère, Pauline and Elisa 300,000 each and Louis 200,000. As they feared, a near bankrupt France would never be able to afford these huge sums. In the midst of his ruin Napoleon still found time to think of the clan. 'The King of Westphalia must go to Brittany or Bourges,' he advised Joseph in a letter. 'I think Madame Mère ought to join her daughter [Pauline] at Nice. Queen Julie and her children should go to the region around Marseilles. And obviously King Louis, who has always been fond of the Midi, should go to Montpellier.' He added, 'Counsel everybody to practise economy', and sent a message to the Empress to share out two million francs among them.

On 20 April the Emperor bade a theatrical goodbye to the Imperial Guard at a final review in the courtyard at Fontainebleau today known as the 'Cour des Adieux'. The Allies had granted him the island of Elba in full sovereignty together with an allowance and the meaningless title of 'Emperor'. He was also allowed a small army of 600 veterans. *En route* for the coast he met Marshal Augereau, Duke of Castiglione, who in his usual foul-mouthed way abused him for sacrificing France to his mad ambition. This toughest of men grew steadily more demoralized by threatening crowds along the roads, so that in the end he disguised himself in a Prussian forage cap, a Russian military cloak and an Austrian uniform borrowed from the officers who escorted him, even putting on the Austrian order of Maria Theresa. By chance his journey took him through Bouillidou in Provence where Pauline was living in a luxurious country retreat and he was able to spend the night there – though she tearfully refused to kiss him until he had changed back into French uniform. She promised to join him on Elba, but could not go with him at once because of her habitual ill health. On 28 April he set sail from Saint-Raphael on board the frigate HMS *Undaunted*, to reach his little island five days later. On 30 April the restored King Louis XVIII gave his assent to the Treaty of Paris, which pushed France back to the frontiers of 1792.

The rest of the Napoleonic Empire had collapsed with the defeat of its creator. In Italy the undaunted Viceroy continued to hold the line of the Mincio, although increasingly worried at receiving no instructions from his stepfather after 12 March. (The last had included speculations as to the probable insanity of King Joachim.) Firm news was brought by General von Neipperg on 17 April, accompanied by an ADC to the King of Bavaria who delivered a letter from the latter telling Eugène that the Emperor had abdicated and that 'to hold out longer would be unforgivable'. The Viceroy was in the ducal palace at Mantua where his wife had given birth to their fifth child, a daughter, four days earlier and therefore in no mood for unrealistic heroics. He signed a detailed surrender the same day. Napoleon had abdicated any rights which he had to the crown of Italy at Fontainebleau and there were riots in Milan when Eugène's supporters proposed that he be proclaimed king. The man who did so, his Finance Minister Giuseppe Prina, was beaten to death in the street with umbrellas. After a grateful farewell to his troops the former Viceroy left Italy as quickly as possible, sending Augusta Amelia and their children to Munich while himself going to Paris since he had news that his mother Joséphine was dangerously ill.

Meanwhile, in Elisa's domains the last French troops had been evacuated by way of Livorno after a few skirmishes with the Neapolitans. The Grand Duchess's territories were overrun by enemy troops, including a British force as well as Austrians. She fled from Lucca when she heard that Austrian troops were approaching, although she was nine months gone with child – during her flight she gave birth to a boy at a poor roadside inn. She only got as far as Bologna before being arrested by the Austrians who sent her via Trieste to confinement at Brünn [Brno] in Bohemia – she had to do her own packing in front of Austrian officers. On 15 April she had written to a friend, 'The dreadful catastrophe has come to pass. All is lost. I have decided to leave for Naples. I will never live on Elba. I want to settle at Rome, if the French government doesn't object and if the Pope will allow it.' Even so, she did not despair of compensation. However, the Austrians would not permit her to leave Brünn until the autumn of the following year.

The one part of the Empire which did survive was the Kingdom of Naples though, as Fouché had shrewdly warned Elisa, the accord between the Austrians and the Neapolitans was not going to last. Murat had joined the Austrians under their Irish General Nugent at Bologna in February, but had irritated his new allies by failing to go into action until he heard that his throne had been guaranteed by the Emperor of Austria. In March Lord William Bentinck had landed in Tuscany with a British force which, to Joachim's fury, included Sicilian troops under the Bourbon flag and insisted on the Neapolitans evacuating the Grand Duchy. Murat was so angry that he was only restrained with difficulty from attacking them, and reopened his negotiations with Eugène. He knew very well that Bentinck was his implacable foe, determined to restore the exiled Bourbons to Naples. Then, when Pius VII returned to the Papal States in April, he had to evacuate Rome. Nothing had come of his dream of setting himself up as King of all Italy while he had thoroughly upset the Austrians. At the Congress of Vienna there was proposal after proposal that Bonaparte's henchmen should make way for his realm's rightful king and be compensated with some petty principality, such as the Ionian Islands. He had kept his throne for the time being but he and Caroline lived in a state of constant anxiety.

As for Bernadotte, perhaps not unreasonably the Allies looked on him as a species of northern Murat and disliked and distrusted him. Most contemporaries agreed with Lord Byron's description, 'that rebellious bastard of Scandinavian adoption, Bernadotte.' Tsar Alexander was disgusted by his sly refusal to use Swedish troops, while currying favour with French prisoners by paroling 1,500, and dropped him. Somewhat surprisingly in view of her sweet nature, Désirée had shared in her husband's vain ambition of supplanting the Emperor, the former lover to whom they owed their prosperity, and had even gone so far as to send Bernadotte detailed reports from Paris of French troop movements during Napoleon's last desperate days.

10

Family Ruin

'We are lost. Napoleon ought to be killed to save France and
his family.'

LUCIEN BONAPARTE IN 1815

'For my part, I saw him as a madman tied hand and foot and
delivered up to Europe's mercy.'

FOUCHÉ ON NAPOLEON IN 1815

The exiled imperial family were soon scattered far and wide. As always,
their behaviour varied considerably. Madame Mère displayed her
customary stoic dignity, while Pauline revealed unsuspected qualities of
loyalty and self-sacrifice. The brothers would all hasten to Paris to take part
in the doomed adventure of the Hundred Days; even though the restored
Empire was not going to last, it was still worthwhile to be an imperial
prince again if only for a few months. The Murats precipitated their own
ruin, out of crass ineptitude. However, the first and most dramatic
consequence within the clan of Napoleon's fall in 1814 was the carefully
planned destruction of his marriage.

On 2 May Marie Louise and the former King of Rome crossed the Rhine
on their way to Schönbrunn. The Emperor would never see them again,
but still believed firmly that they were going to join him on Elba and was
adding an extra floor to the 'Imperial Palace' to accommodate them. Marie
Louise had been given the Duchy of Parma by the Allies as compensation,
though it would be a long time before she was allowed to go to Italy to
reign. She was still in love with Napoleon – should she and her son be
reunited with him the political consequences might well be explosive. The
Austrian Chancellor, Metternich, had a profound knowledge of full-
blooded young women based on deep experience, in particular of young
wives who were separated from their husbands, and knew exactly what to
do in this case.

Before 'proud Austria's mournful flower' (Byron's description) had left
Orleans she had made it quite clear that she wanted to rejoin her husband,
writing to him, 'I long to be near you and look after you.' More practically
she sent him 30 bullion boxes containing over two and a half million francs
in gold. She had been persuaded only with difficulty from going to him at
Fontainebleau. Her secretary, Baron de Méneval, reported to Napoleon's

secretary the day after setting out from Orleans, 'She is in fact a prisoner – suffering and deeply troubled.' Her father, the Emperor Francis, persuaded her to go from Rambouillet to Vienna 'just for a few months'. She wrote to Napoleon that her father had been 'really very good and kind to me, though it hasn't cured the awful shock he gave me in preventing me from joining you, from seeing you, from travelling with you', adding, 'It is impossible for me to be happy without you.' This very highly-sexed girl was speaking no more than the truth. She and her son remained in the Austrian capital until the end of June when, leaving the boy with his governess Mme de Montesquiou, she went to take the water at Aix-les-Bains for her health.

At the villa which had been leased for her there she found that she had been given an equerry and major-domo, General von Neipperg. He had received precise instructions from Metternich.

> Count von Neipperg must dissuade the Duchess of Colorno [Marie Louise's incognito] with all possible tact from any idea of journeying to Elba, a journey which would deeply pain the paternal heart of His Majesty, who cherishes the tenderest wishes for his beloved daughter's happiness. He must not fail, therefore, to try by any means whatsoever to dissuade her from such a project.

Prince Metternich meant just what he said when he used the words 'by any means whatsoever'.

Lieutenant-General Adam Count von Neipperg, a colourful mixture of dashing light cavalryman and polished diplomat, was a man whose destiny had become intertwined with that of the Bonaparte clan. Born in 1775 the 'German Bayard' – Mme de Staël's name for him – belonged to an ancient Swabian family and, a hussar since the age of fifteen, had had a most distinguished career. The same year that he joined the imperial Austrian army he lost an eye from a French sabre cut at the battle of Neerwinden but this had not dissuaded him in the least from taking part in countless other campaigns against the Revolution and Bonaparte, including Marengo. He hated the modern French more than anything in the world. In 1810 he went as Austrian Ambassador to Stockholm where he was most successful in encouraging Bernadotte to ally himself with the Russians against Napoleon. His skilful handling of his cavalry and personal heroism at Leipzig in 1813 resulted in his promotion to *Feldmarschall-Leutnant* and his being given the privilege of taking the news of the victory to Vienna. The following year he had been brilliantly successful as Austrian Ambassador to Naples, forcing the weathercock Murat into finally signing the treaty of alliance against France, and in 1815 he would in person smash King Joachim's ambitions for ever on the battlefield. In 1814 too he had led the first Austrian troops into Eugène's capital of Milan. He had met the former Empress before, when he had been one of twelve chamberlains-in-waiting to her during a visit to Prague in 1812, though then she had taken little notice of him. She must none the less have been aware of Neipperg since this *ancien régime beau sabreur* cut a striking and virile figure in his glittering hussar uniform and black eyepatch. He was strongly built with curly fair hair, a short fair moustache and a florid, rather battered face, being only six years younger than Napoleon. He was also a cultivated man, something of a poet, who enjoyed good music and played the piano. Above all, he was strikingly attractive to women, a famous lady-killer of whom Mme de Staël – that connoisseur of men – remarked, 'With his one unbandaged eye he could devastate the fair sex in half the time another man could do it with two.' He had been involved in countless love affairs and his private life was a byword for scandal. In 1813, after her previous marriage had been annulled, he had married the Contessa Teresa Ramondini, with whom he had eloped some years before – they already had five children, born out of wedlock.

Precisely what Metternich had hoped, in selecting Neipperg for this delicate assignment, took place. As late as 18 August 1814 Marie Louise could write to Napoleon with genuine affection, 'How happy I should be if I could join you the very moment that I have my son with me! I had given orders for him to be sent here, when I received a letter from my father asking me to Vienna for the Congress where my son's interests are to be discussed . . . I am simply miserable at not being with you on your happy island by now. It really would be heaven for me.' The letter was the last which his wife would write to the Emperor while still in love with him. It was in response to a message brought by three agents whom he had sent to Aix in secret, imploring her to come to Elba by herself – an Elban brig was waiting for her at Genoa. However, one of the agents, Murault de Sorbée (a captain in the Elban Imperial Guard), was denounced and arrested. She had to promise her father that she would never go to Elba without his permission. She also agreed to return to Vienna, travelling by way of Switzerland. If she was not allowed to live on Elba she still hoped to reign at Parma, which she was terrified of losing. She enjoyed her time in Switzerland very much indeed. On 24 September she visited William Tell's chapel and, caught by a severe thunderstorm, was forced to spend the night at the local inn, the *Soleil d'Or*, where she became the General's mistress. Within days of their return to the Austrian capital, Viennese wits had christened her 'Madame Neipperg'. To make her position less embarrassing, and to ensure that the affair continued, he was appointed her chamberlain.

Predictably Joseph had made extremely practical financial arrangements for exile. When he fled from Paris he took seven van-loads of silver and valuable furniture with him. By pure chance an American of French origin, James le Ray, offered his services to him as soon as he arrived at Blois at the beginning of April. Always a better businessman than statesman, Joseph at once exchanged his possessions for property in the United States. Through le Ray he also engaged a young American secretary, James Carret. However, it would be some time before he needed either the property or the secretary. He reached Switzerland at the end of the month and quickly purchased the fine old château of Prangins on the shores of Lake Geneva, selling Mortefontaine as rapidly as possible and transferring his magnificent art collection to this new refuge. The 'Comte de Survilliers' – his incognito – received a whole host of visitors here, while leaving Julie in somewhat less comfortable retirement at Auteuil on the outskirts of Paris. Among them was his sister-in-law Marie Louise, not yet isolated, for whose stay he donned his Spanish marshal's uniform. He was not entirely secure. The Swiss had no love for Bonapartes, while the French government wanted him to leave even Switzerland. Another sister-in-law, the Princess of Sweden – Désirée – tried to intercede for him with Louis XVIII but the King would merely promise not to disturb Julie.

Jérôme sent Catherine – whom only a year before he had been trying to divorce – to get what she could out of her family. He confidently expected to go and live in Württemberg at their expense. They were not sympathetic. As Napoleon himself said, when referring to Jérôme later, 'The attitude of his wife whose father – the horrible, despotic, callous, King of Württemberg – wanted her to divorce her husband after my fall, was really quite admirable.' At Paris her brother the Crown Prince would not even see her. Again and again her father ordered her to get rid of her good-for-nothing spouse, but she refused steadfastly. She succeeded in winning the sympathy of her cousin Tsar Alexander, who gave her a pension, obtained passports for herself and Jérôme, and promised to do what he could to procure them some sort of compensation for the loss of Westphalia. Although heavily pregnant she then set out to join her husband at Berne, whither he had summoned her. *En route* she had a terrifying adventure, being held up by the sinister Marquis de Maubreuil – a former equerry to her husband – who robbed her of jewellery worth 150,000 francs and 84,000 francs in gold. She had to plead with him, in the barn where he had imprisoned her, to give her back a thousand francs so that she could at least continue her journey. By August Jérôme and Catherine had found some sort of refuge at Trieste, though they were desperately short of money. Here she gave birth to a son who was christened Jérôme Napoléon – regardless of the feelings of Betsy Patterson.

Louis, a gloomy and half-crazed semi-cripple, who could only walk with the aid of a stick and spoke in a feeble voice, continued to travel aimlessly through Europe, much as he had done before the Emperor's abdication.

After accompanying the Empress and his mother on their flight from Paris he had left them at Blois and gone to Italy to stay with Lucien. The latter had returned in triumph from England and basked in the Pope's favour. Pius VII, reinstalled in Rome at the Quirinale, created him Prince of Canino. Lucien's days of straitened circumstances were over and his relations with his family were reversed – he was now able to patronize them. Besides Louis he gave shelter to his mother at both his Roman palace and at Canino, where he resumed his archaeology and his amateur theatricals, supported by his loving Alexandrine. The Pope was so well disposed towards him that he even accepted the dedication of his epic (and unreadable) poem *Charlemagne*.

Madame Mère and Uncle Fesch had travelled to Italy together, the Cardinal having joined her at Orleans after fleeing from Lyons. *En route* they ran into Pius VII at Cesena by chance and when Fesch solicited an audience and asked for permission to seek refuge in Rome with his sister he was greeted with open arms and had his request granted. They arrived in the Eternal City on 12 May, moving into the Cardinal's Palazzo Falconieri in Via Giulia. Letizia had an affecting reunion with her 'Luciano', whom she had not seen for many years and who was now the one secure member of the clan – apart from the Murats, whose future was the subject of uncomfortable rumours. However Madame Mère's sole thought was to join Napoleon on Elba. Fearful of confiscation she immediately set about selling her enormous house in Paris, the Hôtel de Brienne, for which she obtained 800,000 francs (200,000 more than the buyer had originally offered). She soon managed to extract permission to go to the Emperor.

When Eugène de Beauharnais had arrived in Paris in early May in response to Joséphine's urgent summons, instead of seeing his mother on her deathbed he found her in the pink of condition and enjoying the Allied occupation since its leaders were flocking to see her at Malmaison. They included her son's brother-in-law the Crown Prince of Bavaria, the King of Prussia with his two boys (one of whom was to ride into Paris at the head of a German army in 1870) and the Tsar with his brothers. Alexander was especially amiable, very friendly towards Eugène and Hortense. During the day when he came, 14 May, the Duchess of Navarre suddenly felt unwell and seemed to have caught a chill. Soon she and her two children had to retire to bed with high fevers and by 20 May she was seriously ill with a strangely sore throat. The doctors said that it was nothing more than a cold. However, on 28 May she felt so dreadful that it was decided to tell the Tsar she would be unable to receive him at dinner. He called none the less, visiting Eugène's bedside and dining alone with Hortense. After receiving the Last Sacraments from the tutor of Hortense's children, the Abbé Bertrand, who had been summoned hastily, Joséphine died at noon the following day. Her illness was probably diphtheria. The police, under new management but nevertheless gracefully magnanimous when reporting the death of 'Mme de Beauharnais' to Louis xviii, commented,

> This woman was unfailingly gentle and possessed much charm and attractiveness in manner and in mind. Extremely unhappy during her husband's reign, she sought refuge from his roughness and neglect in the study of botany. The public was aware of how she strove to rescue Bonaparte's victims, and grateful to her for having thrown herself at his feet to beg for the life of the Duc d'Enghien.

Joséphine would have been gratified by the respect shown to her children. Eugène was received with the utmost cordiality by King Louis xviii, by his brother, the Comte d'Artois (the future Charles x), who claimed to remember his father well, by Artois's two sons and by the Duke of Orleans. The Allied sovereigns were equally friendly. His Bavarian father-in-law and brother-in-law remained as affectionate as ever, constantly urging delegates to the Congress of Vienna to compensate him with a principality; Italy was out of the question, but Tréves (Trier), the Duchy of Zweibrücken or Corfu with the Ionian Islands were spoken of as distinct possibilities. Hortense was lionized, even the Duke of Wellington calling on her in person and being 'most deferential'. She received more than mere compliments. At the end of May King Louis created her Duchess of Saint-Leu by letters patent, confirming her possession of her château besides placing her on the Civil List and increasing her annual income to 400,000 francs. She owed all this to the Tsar's friendship. The news drove her exiled husband Louis – who already styled himself Count of Saint-Leu – into paroxysms of fury and deeply wounded her stepfather.

The most unlikely consequence of the Empire's demise was the transformation of Pauline into a woman of action. She showed a shrewd business head, commissioning her old friend and lover Colonel Duchand to sell her Paris hôtel with it's contents and her other properties, the former being bought by the Duke of Wellington, now British Ambassador, who paid 800,000 francs, twice what she had given for it. There was trouble over the sale of her château at Neuilly, since Camillo Borghese demanded the return of his property there, notably 175 valuable paintings, but after a long legal battle she obtained a good settlement. Her jewels, purchased so frivolously, also proved an extremely useful investment. In the mean time the Princess announced her intention of visiting Naples and set sail on board the Neapolitan frigate *Letizia*, sent to collect her by her brother-in-law King Joachim, from Saint-Raphael on 30 May. Three days later the vessel put into Portoferraio, the capital of Elba. Pauline was distressed to find the Emperor living in such poverty and discreetly gave General Bertrand, Elban 'Minister of the Interior', a priceless diamond clasp to pay for the building of a cool summer villa in the island's woods.

After staying only a night she sailed on to Naples. Almost certainly, as Louis xviii's police believed, she had gone to Naples to discuss the possibility of a future alliance with the ever vacillating Murat and carried to her brother-in-law a secret message to be ready for the news of the Emperor's return to France. At bottom this wilting nymphomaniac, normally so self-indulgent, lacked nothing of her sister's toughness and cunning.

Elba was a very small island indeed, only sixteen miles long and seven miles wide, rocky, with poor soil covered with scrub. The 12,000 Elbans were not unlike the Corsicans of Napoleon's boyhood. A quarter of the population lived in the capital, the fishing port of Portoferraio, which boasted no more than a single flea-ridden inn. There was a tiny group of better-off families with very modest pretensions to nobility, mainly of Tuscan, Genoese or Corsican origin, and these held most of the municipal offices. The Emperor's 'palace' was the Villa dei Mulini at Portoferraio whose accommodation was extremely limited. He nevertheless insisted on preparing two apartments of four rooms each for his wife and son, ordering the drawing-room ceiling to be decorated – with some irony – in a pattern in *trompe l'oeil* representing Marital Fidelity. The Villa was a charming place for a holiday but scarcely suitable for the man who had conquered Europe. He found as much to do as he could, organizing his miniature court, his little army and his even smaller navy.

He built a country retreat with Pauline's diamond clasp, a villa at San Martino, yet he seldom went there when it was finished. He had another refuge, the disused hermitage of Madonna del Monte in the hills at the western end of the island, which could only be reached by a steep mountain path, and where he spent a good deal of time. Part of its charm was its seclusion. Late on the evening of 1 September a brig landed a party of four persons, not at Portoferraio, but at the fishing village of San Giovanni. They were Maria Walewska, her son Alexander, her sister Maria and her brother Colonel Teodor Laczynski. They dined privately with Napoleon and spent the night at the hermitage, sailing away the next morning. Presumably Laczynski reported the failure of his mission to Marie Louise – to persuade her to come to Elba – but it is harder to guess at the reason for Maria's visit, which was clearly inspired by more than affection or loyalty. Undoubtedly she discussed the financial provision which he had made for their child. It is also probable, though there is no evidence, that she brought secret messages in connection with his return to France. He certainly told her that he considered his exile to be temporary 'and the information he is seeking is that which will enable him to choose the most propitious moment to bring it to an end'. There must have been other discreet visitors to the hermitage.

Already there was another imperial resident on Elba, Madame Mère, who put into Portoferraio on board HMS *Grasshopper* on 2 August under the assumed name of Mme Dupont. Her little suite of five included her maid Saveria. The British Commissioner on Elba, Colonel Sir Neil Campbell, writes in his diary, 'The old lady is very handsome, of middle size and with a good figure and fresh colour.' Her son sailed round from the hermitage to meet her on his little cutter. Learning that he was short of funds – he insisted on keeping his army for fear of being kidnapped – she offered the entire contents of her jewel box. When he declined, she demanded most uncharacteristically to pay her own household bills. She was living at a house which the Emperor had rented for her, the Casa Vantini, a short distance from the Villa dei Mulini and conveniently near a church where she could hear Mass. At the end of October a third member of the family arrived, Pauline, who moved into the rooms which Napoleon had got ready for Marie Louise at her little palace. The three lived a domestic, and surprisingly harmonious, family life.

Pauline took over the little court's social routine, organizing balls, receptions and theatrical entertainments; there was even talk of an opera season. Her efforts transformed the island – before her coming the garrison had been 'bored to death' – while the Elbans were enchanted by such novelties. Everyone was diverted by her eccentricities, such as paying calls in a sedan chair because she was so tired, and then dancing until the small hours of the morning, and by her scandalously immodest dresses. The Neapolitan musicians which she had brought with her caused a sensation. She made her brother not only take part in parlour games but convert a disused chapel into a new theatre. However, sometimes the three Bonapartes simply spent a quiet evening playing cards with one of the officers, Letizia's favourite amusement. Early in 1815 when informed by Colonel Campbell that he intended to visit Florence for a few days to see a doctor, the Emperor said that he hoped the Colonel would be back by 28 February and come to a ball which was being given by Pauline.

In the event, when the Colonel returned he was informed that Napoleon had set sail on 26 February on board the Elban brig *L'Inconstant*, bound for an unknown destination. The Emperor had only told his mother the previous evening. In her *Souvenirs* Madame Mère recalls, with perhaps a little too much poetry, that on hearing the news she replied, 'Heaven will not permit you to die by poison, or in inactivity unworthy of you, but sword in hand. Go my son, fulfil your destiny – you were made to perish sword in hand.' More practically, Pauline gave him her best diamond necklace, valued at half a million francs. She wept as they said goodbye; she would have preferred him to stay on Elba. In fact Napoleon's little state was proving too expensive for his limited resources while he genuinely believed that if he remained on the island he would be dragged off to imprisonment by the Bourbons or the Austrians, or even murdered. As Louis xviii's Minister, Count Blacas d'Aulps, observed a short time before, when discussing the problem of King Joachim, 'If nothing is done, then one day we shall see that man from the Isle of Elba land in Italy to menace the security and disrupt the tranquility of France and Europe.' Both the Emperor and Murat were undoubtedly in danger. When he boarded his brig those on board began to sing the *Marseillaise*, and it was taken up by the Elbans on the quayside. He could have made no more menacing departure.

The unfortunate Sir Neil Campbell questioned the two imperial ladies. He upset Pauline so much she exclaimed, 'That's no way to talk to a princess', and at 2 o'clock in the morning of 3 March, escorted by a chivalrous French officer, fled from Elba on a felucca. After a night at sea she landed in Tuscany at Viareggio, installing herself in a nearby villa which had belonged to Elisa. The unsympathetic Austrian army immediately placed her under house arrest and although her confinement was later relaxed she was forced to remain in Tuscany until the autumn. Madame Mère simply stayed on at Portaferraio till a Neapolitan warship, the *Gioacchino*, dispatched by Caroline, came at the beginning of April to take her to Naples.

Napoleon and his little flotilla landed at Golfe-Juan near Cannes on 1 March 1815. He had a thousand troops with four small cannon. Instead of taking the main road to Paris he went through the lonely hills of Provence up into the mountains and then down to Grenoble where he received a tumultuous welcome. Lyons too at once opened its gates to him. He was joined at Auxerre by Marshal Ney, who had promised King Louis to bring him back 'in an iron cage'. On 19 March Louis xviii hastily left Paris for Belgium and on the following day the Emperor was back in the Tuileries without a shot having been fired. Hortense and Julie were waiting for him at the palace.

However, Napoleon had been restored by a dissatisfied army, not by the French people, who were tired of war and tired of despotism. While determined to keep power in his own hands he was not averse to political window-dressing and *en route* to Paris had promised peace abroad and a popular constitutional monarchy at home, together with reduced taxes. 'I am not just the soldiers' Emperor,' he told Joseph's friend Benjamin Constant, 'I am also the peasants' Emperor and the French plebeians' Emperor.' He banished recently returned émigrés and abolished pre-1789 titles. 'Public discussion, free elections, responsible ministers, liberty of the press, I want all these things,' he assured Constant glibly. During the next few weeks he introduced a new constitution by the 'Additional Act', which established an hereditary upper chamber and an elected lower chamber, besides abolishing press censorship. These measures were purely cosmetic and everybody realized that he remained as autocratic as ever. Fouché remonstrated with him, to no avail. Not only peace but his survival was impossible. Even before the end of March the Congress of Vienna published a proclamation: 'Napoleon Bonaparte has placed himself outside the pale of political and social relations and as an enemy and disturber of the world's tranquillity has rendered himself liable to public vengeance.' England and Prussia pledged themselves to put 150,000 men in the field, Austria and Russia promising another 400,000.

Nevertheless, the clan rushed back to Paris. Joseph was first to arrive, on 23 March, only three days after the Emperor. Learning that the Swiss were going to arrest him, he had left Prangins hurriedly after burying five million francs' worth of uncut diamonds in a 'fox hole' in its grounds. He was given the task of summoning the family, though most of them were already on their way. He wrote to Marie Louise but received no answer. Napoleon himself had written to her from Auxerre, 'I shall be in Paris by the time you receive this letter. Come and join me with my son.' By now she was far too much in love with Neipperg, and desperately worried lest her husband's new adventure might lose her Parma. The Emperor was consoled to some small extent by the unlooked for appearance of Lucien in Paris on 10 April on a mission from the Pope who asked him to protect the Papal States against King Joachim. Within a month there was a complete reconciliation and he had been given the Palais-Royal as his town house together with the title of prince of the Empire. Yet soon Lucien was in despair at his brother's policies. Like Joseph, Jérôme had been in danger of arrest and had fled from Trieste, sailing at midnight disguised as a seaman on board a small Neapolitan vessel – leaving Catherine and their baby behind – and was making his way to France from Naples. One member of the clan who did not rally to the Emperor was Eugène, who had sacrificed enough and was anxious to save his vast private fortune for his wife and family. Hortense had remained in Paris throughout her stepfather's exile on Elba and to begin with he was very cold towards her. 'I never would have thought that you would forsake my cause,' he rebuked her. 'If one shares in a family's success, one ought to share its misfortunes.' After she began to cry he relented. 'You haven't a single good excuse, but you know that I am a very fond father. There, there. I forgive you. We'll say no more about it.' Nevertheless, she was horrified by the possibility of his trying to reconquer Belgium.

Meanwhile Letizia had landed at Naples to stay at the palace of Portici, the Neapolitan Fontainebleau just outside the capital and overlooking the bay. Caroline received a good telling-off for betraying Napoleon. When she argued that she could not control Murat, Madame Mère replied, 'Only over your dead body should your husband have been able to strike at your brother, your benefactor and your master!' Uncle Fesch was also at Portici, still pink-faced and surprisingly young looking, though not in the best of moods. On hearing of the escape from Elba he had exclaimed, 'My nephew must be mad!' Jérôme and Julie were there too. The former had tried to reach France by land but turned back after nearly being caught by Austrian troops at Florence. He and his mother went to a performance in the San Carlo in the royal box with their hostess. However, shortly afterwards, 'depressed in body and mind' according to Jérôme's memoirs, Caroline informed them they must leave her kingdom as soon as possible. Letizia, Fesch, Jérôme and Julie drove through bandit-infested country to the coastal fortress of Gaeta, where they deposited Murat's children, and then embarked on the French warship *Dryade* which the Emperor had sent to fetch them. *En route* they were forced to put in at Corsica to escape an English patrol, spending two hours at Bastia receiving local notables before they sailed on. It was the last time Letizia would see her native island. They disembarked at Golfe-Juan, where Napoleon had landed in March, on 22 May. The party finally reached Paris on 2 June.

The reason for Caroline's depression and their precipitate departure from Naples was Austrian invasion. The Murats had rightly feared for their future, knowing that the hand of every delegate at the Congress of Vienna was against them. Only Metternich appeared well disposed, yet secretly he too had decided they must go. Joachim was overjoyed by the news of his brother-in-law's escape, which he received during a court ball. On 15 March he declared war on Austria, summoning all Italians to rise and help him create a unified kingdom. In doing so he destroyed any hope of the Emperor's convincing the Allies that his return to France was purely a matter for the French, in no way a threat to European peace. Napoleon had already written to Rome to reassure the Pope that he had no designs on Italy. Murat's declaration of war convinced the Congress of Vienna there could be no peace with Bonaparte, that he must be outlawed. Confident he was being of the utmost assistance to the Emperor, King Joachim marched north with 40,000 troops to occupy Rome and Bologna. Most of his men were untrained recruits commanded by young officers, inexperienced and in any case too intelligent to enjoy risking their lives in hare-brained adventures. In April he learnt that two Austrian armies were advancing on Bologna. One was led by Adam von Neipperg who, for the time being, had been excused valuable service elsewhere. (He wrote wistfully if stiffly to Marie Louise at Vienna, 'I tremble when I think of anything disagreeable happening to Your Majesty whose extreme kindness and angelic nature merit nothing but happiness, and I pray to God daily, even in the heat of battle, for Your Majesty's well-being. Your Majesty does not tell me whether you ride much and, if so, with whom.') Jérôme recalls in his memoirs that Caroline 'predicted in detail what would happen and how her husband would behave'. She did her best to keep up morale in Naples, putting on uniform and reviewing troops, issuing fictitious communiqués.

The King began to retreat after some unpromising skirmishes, but made a stand at Tolentino. Here Neipperg personally led 2,000 cavalry in a devastating charge against the Neapolitans, who promptly bolted. Late in the afternoon of 18 May Murat rode back into Naples alone save for an escort of four Polish lancers, to spend a last night at his palace. 'Madame', he told Caroline, 'don't be surprised at seeing me alive – I did everything I could to be killed.' Next day, after dark, he fled to Ischia with money and diamonds sewn into his coat. His subjects sang a tunefully derisive song about his departure while preparing to welcome home the Bourbons whom they had always much preferred. A furious Caroline waited in the Palazzo Reale until a British ship was ready to take her into exile. Neipperg, formerly so charming, rode into Naples and told her curtly that she was to be interned at Trieste. She left on board HMS *Tremendous* on 25 May, first picking up her children and their English governesses at Gaeta. Neipperg reported exultantly to Vienna that the Austrian government now had in its power as hostage ' a queen who is much more the king of this country than her fool of a husband'.

On 1 June the 'Additonal Act' was inaugurated on the Champ-de-Mars at the ceremony known as the *Champ de mai* attended by 50,000 troops and 200,000 civilians. High Mass was celebrated by the Archbishop of Tours and cannon roared salutes; then Napoleon – in robes which were all but sacerdotal – swore meaningless fidelity to the new constitution. He was accompanied by Joseph, Lucien and Jérôme, each one in court dress. After he had taken the oath he distributed colours to his regiments. The occasion was not entirely a success. Many must have agreed with the Duc de Broglie.

> I saw the imperial squad pass by in elaborate ceremonial costume – nodding plumes, floppy hats, short Spanish cloaks, white satin breeches, shoes with rosettes and all the rest of it. This pantomime at a moment of such ill-omened crisis, with France on the verge of invasion and dismemberment as a result of, and for love of, these fine fellows, this pantomime I repeat, filled me with indignation and contempt.

On 11 June, a Sunday, there was a quiet family dinner at the Elysée. The Emperor and his three brothers, their mother, Julie and Hortense were present, joined later by Julie's daughters and Hortense's sons. It was clearly a cheerful occasion which Napoleon appeared to enjoy, though to Hortense his gaiety seemed forced. This was the last meeting of the clan with its chief.

The Emperor was not the man he had been. The same day he remarked to General Bertrand's wife, 'Well, Mme Bertrand, let's hope we don't regret the Isle of Elba!' That morning General Thiébault had watched him at Mass in the Elysée chapel.

> His glance, whose piercing quality was once so terrifying, had lost not just its force but even its steadiness. His face, which I had so often seen lit by dynamism or as if cast in bronze, had lost all expression and any vestige of strength. His head itself was no longer carried in the way which formerly marked him as master of the world, while his gait was as awkward as his bearing and his gestures were hesitant. Everything about him seemed twisted, shrivelled. His skin's normal pallor had been replaced by a noticeably greenish tinge.

The 'Catholic and Royal Army' of the Chouans rose again for the King in the Vendée and although defeated held down over 10,000 imperial troops – enough to make the difference between victory and defeat in the forthcoming campaign against the Allies. Already Wellington and Blücher were on the move in Belgium with over 200,000 men. If the Emperor could not match such numbers, what troops he did have were excellent, veterans who had returned from Germany and Spain or enthusiastic volunteers, of very different calibre from the 'Marie-Louises' of 1813–14. Despite Joseph's dismal performance the previous year he was left in Paris as President of the Council of Ministers, though with only a casting vote and no longer in overall charge. Lucien sat on the Council while Jérôme went to the front as a divisional commander. On Monday 12 June Napoleon marched out from Paris with his Army of the North, to anticipate the Allies' offensive. Within three days he was over the river Sambre and in Belgium.

On 16 June the French right under Napoleon's personal command routed Blücher at Ligny after a ferocious engagement. Their left under Ney were held at Quatre-Bras by the British, who eventually fell back at the end of a long and bloody action. Jérôme fought with surprising efficiency and dash, leading his brigade against the farm at Quatre-Bras, then forming it into squares to repulse the Duke of Brunswick's hussars, the Duke being mortally wounded. Jérôme himself received a bullet in the arm but did not dismount, dressing his wound in the saddle. However, Ney's check at Quatre-Bras saved the Prussians from destruction. Napoleon thought that they were falling back with the intention of withdrawing over the Rhine, as indeed their chief-of-staff General von Gneisenau advised. Instead they were retreating northward since fierce old Marshal Blücher, despite having been knocked off his horse and concussed, was determined to bring his 80,000 men to the aid of Wellington in the decisive battle which was obviously going to be fought in the next few days. The French wasted 17 June instead of smashing the British while the Prussians were safely out of the way.

The Duke of Wellington withdrew to a position near the Belgian village of Waterloo and on 18 June prepared to face an opponent generally acknowledged as the greatest military genius of the day. He had 68,000 troops – 26,000 Germans, 18,000 Dutch and Belgians, and 24,000 British (of whom a large proportion were Irish like their commander). Most were stationed behind a ridge three miles long, while the rest occupied three strong points slightly in front: the château and wood of Hougoumont, the farm of La Haye-Sainte and the farm of Papelotte. His strategy was simply to hold on until the Prussians could come from the east and reinforce his left. The Emperor's strategy was that employed so successfully in many of his victories: to soften up the enemy by a heavy artillery bombardment, followed if necessary by cavalry charges, then to send his massive infantry columns crashing into and through them. He was not entirely certain that Blücher had withdrawn altogether and, to make sure, sent the reliable Marshal Grouchy after him with 30,000 men, though he dismissed a rumour picked up by Jérôme that the Prussians would definitely come to support the British. He himself retained only 72,000 troops but he considered them more than adequate since they were to be concentrated on a narrow front. 'Because you have been beaten by Wellington you think he is a great general,' he told Soult. 'Well, I tell you he is a bad general and the English are poor soldiers. We shall eat them for breakfast.' He did not take British musketry into account, or Wellington's use of reverse slopes to protect his men from artillery fire.

Even so it must be said that the Duke ought to have been defeated. He was saved by the time factor. Torrential rain falling throughout the night until just before daybreak had turned the ground into a quagmire which had to dry out. It was therefore well after 1.00 p.m. before the French 'grand battery' of eighty heavy guns could be dragged into position and start firing, and the French infantry did not launch their frontal attack until about 1.45. Had the ground been dry and the attack begun earlier, the British might well have been destroyed and Napoleon in Brussels by nightfall.

Before the attack started, Jérôme was dispatched at about 11.00 a.m. to occupy the approaches to Hougoumont, though not to capture it. Instead, after storming the wood at bayonet-point in a charge which he led himself, he assaulted the château again and again. Its walls were massive and the British guardsmen inside cut his division to ribbons as he committed more and more men in what became a battle within a battle. He only ceased in the evening when bad news came from the principal sector. For all his gallantry he wasted valuable troops on a mere diversion.

176

The morale of the French infantry was excellent and they went into the first main onslaught singing. They overran the farm of Papelotte but did not take La Haye-Sainte. However, they were held by British infantry and then driven back by a determined cavalry charge. Meanwhile, at about the time that his infantry had attacked, the Emperor had been informed that the Prussians seemed to have bypassed Grouchy and were definitely approaching. He detached 10,000 men to hold them while he dealt with Wellington. He also moved his command post to the rear so that he could control both operations, delegating Marshal Ney to handle the frontal attacks against the British.

Ney's intelligence never matched his bravery. He led the French cavalry in charge after charge against Wellington's unweakened centre, selecting the section which had not even been exposed to the first French infantry attack. His men suffered terrible casualties from British cavalry. This bloody mêlée lasted for nearly two hours, from 4.00 p.m. until about 6.00 p.m. Eventually, after being given the last French cavalry reserve and accompanying it with infantry, Ney finally overran La Haye-Sainte at 6.30 when its Hanoverian garrison retreated having exhausted its ammunition.

The loss of La Haye-Sainte dangerously exposed a section of Wellington's centre and soon French horse gunners were pouring grapeshot at point-blank range into his squares. Napoleon grinned, repeating several times, 'They're ours! I've got them!' This was the moment to send in more infantry, but the Emperor's available troops had been decimated by what even Ney called 'the most frightful carnage' he had ever seen, while all the reserves were engaged in holding off the Prussians before whom they were gradually beginning to give ground. However, the French managed to drive the Prussians back at Papelotte, making safe Napoleon's right flank.

The Emperor thereupon brought twelve battalions of the Guard to the foot of Wellington's ridge. Both he and his men still believed that they could win. He formed 4,000 grenadiers and chasseurs of the Middle Guard into five columns, each sixty abreast, and sent them uphill in what was intended to be the first wave of the final breakthrough. Hitherto an attack by the Guard had been the invariable prelude to a glorious victory. Each column was headed by a general on horseback while Ney rode in front. In fact they marched not at the centre but towards the left, within range of British artillery at Hougoumont. The Guard were met both by lethal musketry on their way uphill and by cannon fire, from the flank as well as from the front. They reached the top, then stopped. Within a few minutes they were running back, to horrified French shouts of 'The Guard is retreating!' It had never done so before. At the same time 30,000 Prussians were rolling up Napoleon's right flank. Fearful of being cut off, the French cavalry and infantry began to retreat, British cavalry adding to their discomfiture. Suddenly the retreat became a rout and the imperial army disintegrated, cut to pieces by the pursuing enemy. The battle which should have been won was lost. The Emperor could scarcely believe his eyes.

For the first time in his life Napoleon knew irretrievable defeat. He drew his sword as though intending to die fighting. Jérôme, his face black with powder, his arm in a sling and his uniform in rags, rode up and shouted, 'It wouldn't be a bad idea if those of us called Bonaparte died here.' Much moved, the Emperor answered, 'Brother, I've learnt to know you too late.' (Some days later the novelist Fanny Burney wrote excitedly from Brussels that it was rumoured 'Little Jerry' had been killed.) Two regiments of the Old Guard, without ammunition, were still holding firm under General Cambronne and Jérôme stayed with them to receive Lord Uxbridge's charge before leaving the stricken field. In the mean time, Napoleon's staff pushed him into a barouche and, weeping, he fled for his life. When pursuing Prussian lancers came too close he mounted a horse to go faster. Cambronne's remnant stayed to cover his retreat until they were shot down. The Emperor let himself be persuaded to return to his capital, a return which he realized might be a mistake. 'Very well,' he said, 'I'll go to Paris but I'm convinced you're making me do a foolish thing.'

When Joseph received news of the disaster on 20 June he summoned the Council of Ministers 'to save France and the Empire'. This enabled Fouché to organize the opposition even before an exhausted, mud-caked Napoleon reached the Elysée early the following morning. To begin with, encouraged by Lucien, Lazare Carnot and some of the marshals, he hoped to fight on – during the pursuit the Allies had become disorganized, receiving an unexpected repulse outside Paris from Davout. He told the Council that there was no reason to despair. Lucien addressed the upper chamber with all his old eloquence, insisting that nothing was lost, appealing to his audience's honour. La Fayette thereupon jumped to his feet and delivered the one sensible speech of his long career.

> You accuse us of failing in our duty to our honour and to Napoleon. Haven't you forgotten what we've done for him? Haven't you forgotten that everywhere our children's and our brothers' bones are bearing witness to our fidelity – in the African desert, on the banks of the Guadalquivir, the Tagus and the Vistula, on those freezing fields in front of Moscow? During the last ten years and even longer, three million Frenchmen have died for a man who now wants to go on fighting the whole of Europe. We've done enough for him – today our duty is to save our country.

This speech completed the Emperor's ruin. Lucien, backed by Davout, wanted another *coup d'état*, another 18 Brumaire. 'Be bold', he urged his brother. Napoleon replied simply, 'I've been too bold.' He was exhausted, completely used up, and often did nothing save laugh hysterically or mutter, 'Ah! Mon Dieu!' He feared that attempting a *coup* might merely lead to anarchy: 'Memories from my youth terrified me,' he explained afterwards. On 22 June he abdicated in favour of his son, knowing that the Austrians would never let the boy leave Vienna. Then, accompanied by Hortense, he took refuge at Malmaison while Lucien tried desperately and unsuccessfully to proclaim Napoleon ii. We learn from Hortense that the fallen Emperor was reluctant to leave Malmaison, the scene of the most cheerful days of his career. 'How beautiful it is here,' he said, 'how happy we should be if we could stay here for ever.'

Napoleon was soon joined by Joseph, Lucien and Jérôme. On 25 June the four brothers all decided to seek asylum in the United States, although American public opinion was extremely hostile. In 1816 former President Thomas Jefferson would say of Napoleon, 'I considered him as the very worst of all human beings, and as having inflicted more misery on mankind than any other who had ever lived.' The problem was to cross the Atlantic, since Fouché refused to let them have the two frigates they requested. Lucien then set out for London to ask the British for a ship, although just before her stepfather had left the Elysée Hortense had warned him, 'If you choose to go to America, hurry to the port before the English hear what is happening . . . they would imprison you in the Tower of London.' Joseph too thought it insane to trust the British. Meanwhile Wellington and Blücher were advancing on Paris. Over 60,000 French troops with 60,000 National Guardsmen were available and Napoleon offered to organize the defence of the capital, merely as a French general, whereupon Fouché insisted that he leave Malmaison at once. Before his departure on 29 July many came to say goodbye, among them Madame Mère, Uncle Fesch and Maria Walewska. According to Talma, Letizia shed precisely two tears, her farewell being restricted to, 'Goodbye, my son!' Hortense had sewn a diamond necklace into the lining of his coat. He and Joseph then left separately for the port of Rochefort.

After reaching Rochefort Napoleon established himself in a little fortress on the offshore island of Aix. Meanwhile Joseph chartered a Yankee brig, the *Commerce* of 200 tons, bound for Charleston, South Carolina, with a cargo of cognac, in the name of M. Bouchard. He then made the one indisputably noble gesture of his life. A few days earlier he had been arrested and then released, after being mistaken for the Emperor. Although taller and not so fat he realized that he could pass for his brother and he offered to remain behind on Aix impersonating him while Napoleon sailed for America on the *Commerce* in the guise of M. Bouchard. The proposition was rejected as too undignified for a former Emperor of the French. On 15 July Napoleon boarded HMS *Bellerophon* under the delusion that the Prince Regent would offer him asylum in England.

Joseph was more practical. His American secretary James Carret had

179

procured visas for 'M. Bouchard' and four companions from the US Vice-Consul at Rochefort and on the night of 24 July he set sail for America where he landed at New York on 27 August. During the voyage his ship was intercepted by two British frigates, who examined the passports of all those on board – while the inspection took place 'M. Bouchard' stayed below, pleading seasickness. When the *Commerce*'s skipper learnt who his passenger was, he announced that he would have blown the vessel sky-high rather than surrender him. 'Just what I wanted to avoid!' exclaimed Joseph. Needless to say, he had left his wife Julie behind though admittedly she was safe with her sister Désirée.

Lucien had reached Boulogne before prudently changing his mind about seeking British aid and had gone to Italy instead – to be arrested at once and thrown into prison in the citadel at Turin. After leaving Malmaison Jérôme had wandered through the country around Paris before returning to the capital to hide in the house of a Corsican shoemaker. Louis XVIII wanted to have him shot but Fouché arranged for him to escape to Switzerland. He then made his way to Württemberg to rejoin his spouse, whose enraged father speedily incarcerated him in the peculiarly bleak castle of Göppingen where Catherine had been languishing since the beginning of the Hundred Days. Later they were moved to the no less grim stronghold of Ellwangen, still under house arrest.

Madame Mère remained for some time at the Hôtel de Brienne, which she had reoccupied in the almost impertinent belief that the restored Louis XVIII would allow her to go on living there. She argued that if the old Duchess of Orleans, the regicide Philippe Egalité's widow, could stay, then so might she. Letizia also expected that Fesch would be able to remain as well. They were speedily disillusioned and ordered to leave France immediately. Predictably the Cardinal refused to go without astronomical financial compensation. In response the government simply issued Madame Mère and Fesch with passports for Rome and had them escorted to the frontier. Kind as ever, Pius VII – to the irritation of many cardinals – received them with open arms at the Eternal City.

The Bourbons considered Hortense thoroughly ungrateful and, to her surprise, insisted that she too leave France. She had forfeited the friendship of the Tsar, who would no longer protect her. She took refuge at Karlsruhe and then at Augsburg.

The Allies had had a very bad fright indeed and were determined there should be no repetition of the Hundred Days. The British proposed that Bonaparte should be exiled for life to the lonely island colony of St Helena in the South Atlantic, 'the ugliest and most dismal rock conceivable', some hundreds of miles from the African coast, to be kept under strict surveillance. Here he landed on 17 October 1815. He was about to fight his last and in some ways most brilliant campaign.

11

The Exiles

'When one has shared in the elevation of a family one must share in its misfortunes.'

NAPOLEON

'Who knows whether all these kings won't some day come to me begging for bread?'

LETIZIA BONAPARTE

On the whole the women of the clan accepted their loss of status more philosophically than the men.

I have noticed that men usually show less moral courage than women during political troubles [wrote the former Queen Hortense]. They are more easily disconcerted and depressed. The reason is simple enough. A man is motivated principally by ambition, and it is perfectly natural for him to be discouraged if he realizes that he is a failure, which upsets him more than anything else. A woman on the other hand is motivated mainly by her affections and breaks down only when her heart is broken.

Napoleon's years on St Helena may fairly be called a martyrdom. His residences, The Briars and Longwood, have been described as comfortable country houses of the sort known by Jane Austen; a ridiculous exaggeration: they were primitive colonial dwellings, if on a comparatively large scale for a remote colony. The Emperor was deprived not merely of luxuries but of simple domestic articles and at the beginning had to endure real discomfort. The worst hardship was the Governor Sir Hudson Lowe, who was the narrowest type of Lowland Scot, harsh and rigid, fearful lest his prisoner escape as he had from Elba. Attended by a small but faithful household, Napoleon appeared to pass the time only in cards, billiards and chess and in conversation with those rare visitors to St Helena who were allowed to see him. Yet – unlike the Pope whom he had once denied writing materials – he was provided with pens, paper and secretaries. This indulgence would change the course of European history, for, under pretext of dictating his memoirs, he was creating the Napoleonic legend.

Whatever he might say about his 'dynasty' to the loyal Count Dieudonné de Las Cases for inclusion in the propagandist *Memorial of St Helena*, he told General Bertrand what he really thought of them. (Never intended for publication, the latter's memoirs were not deciphered until 1949.) 'I believe that had I been ready to sacrifice Joseph I would have succeeded,' claimed the Emperor. 'It's quite true that Joseph never worked at anything. What's more, he thought he was a great soldier. He admitted I might be better, but that was about all. He thought himself very much superior to Suchet, Masséna or Lannes.' He was no less scathing about his youngest brother. 'When Jérôme reached Pultusk he wanted to take over command of the cavalry from Murat. "You're crazy!" I said. "What! Do you think you're capable of even leading a squadron of cavalry into action?" What amazing conceit!' He added, 'I was very wrong to make Jérôme King of Westphalia. I should have appointed some little German prince instead.' As for Murat, 'It was his wife who made him defect. Caroline! My sister!' He was particularly illuminating about the Bernadottes. 'It was Bernadotte who set the Swedes against me . . . It was Désirée's charm which got him his job, besides the fact that he was Joseph's brother-in-law.' He explained that it was because he had 'taken her maidenhead' that he had created Bernadotte marshal, prince and king. 'What made Bernadotte adopt such a strange attitude was fear that Russia and England might run him out of Sweden while he knew that . . . whatever I did I would never push him off his throne.'

On St Helena Napoleon was no less anxious than his father Carlo had been to ensure the Bonapartes' standing as nobles. 'The family must take over Rome by marrying into Roman princely families,' he told Bertrand repeatedly. 'Soon it will have popes, cardinals and papal legates among its members.' On the other hand, 'Those who can't Settle in Rome . . . ought to live in Switzerland and have their names recorded in the Golden Book of Berne.' He thought that there were opportunities for them in the New World too. Joseph 'might perhaps prefer to go on living in America and see his daughters settle there, marrying into the Washingtons and Jeffersons so that he may number future Presidents of the United States among his kinsmen'.

This time the Emperor did not expect his wife to join him. Marie Louise joyfully began her reign as Duchess of Parma in April 1816. Her Grand Chamberlain, Commander-in-Chief, Foreign Minister and Minister for Home Affairs was none other than Adam von Neipperg. He proved to be a remarkably successful politician, firm but benevolent, whose administration brought the Parmesans prosperity and the Duchess popularity. In May 1817, having retired to the discreet shelter of her villa at Colorno, she bore him a daughter, to be followed by a son and another daughter. The children were made Prince and Princesses of Montenovo (a subtle Italian rendering of Neipperg, which could be spelt Neuberg, i.e. Montenovo). Her son by Napoleon was disinherited at Metternich's insistence, the succession to Parma passing to the former ruling family of Bourbon-

Parma, though he was compensated with the title of Duke of Reichstadt and the style of Serene Highness. He lost even the name Napoleon, being designated Francis-Charles – popularly shortened to Franz. He was deliberately brought up to think of himself as a Habsburg and an Austrian, his tutor Count Dietrichstein trying to turn him into a complete Teuton, but not altogether successfully since he read everything he could lay his hands on about his father. The former King of Rome was not allowed to visit Parma though his mother came to see him at Schönbrunn.

When Joseph landed at New York he booked into Mrs Powell's quiet family boarding-house in Park Place but the press soon learnt of his arrival and he was immediately lionized. None the less when the 'Comte de Survilliers' – his name from now on – followed the advice of Mayor Jacob Radcliffe and tried to call on President James Madison to seek official protection, the President refused to receive him. Even so Joseph was perfectly safe in the United States and rented a house at Philadelphia – 260 South Nine Street, which still exists – and began visiting the spa at Saratoga Springs. He had a good income from property investments made for him by his Franco-American acquaintance James le Ray, while he avoided the confiscation of Mortefontaine and Prangins by transferring their nominal ownership to trusted friends. When, as a result of his extravagance and own inept speculation in real estate, he found himself short of cash he sent his secretary to Switzerland to retrieve his diamonds from the fox hole at Prangins – so skilfully hidden that the secretary had difficulty finding it and, in order to dig holes, had to pretend to be an English mining engineer prospecting for coal before he recovered the cache. In the summer of 1816 he bought an estate of several hundred acres (eventually amounting to 1,800), with a large house in the Federal style at Bordentown in New Jersey named Point Breeze, which he turned into one of America's most luxurious mansions, becoming so attached to it that he rebuilt it without hesitation when it was burnt down in 1820. He also purchased a hunting lodge in Jefferson County in New York State, acquiring nearly 27,000 acres which he called his 'wilderness'. He made many American friends, including the future President John Quincy Adams, and as early as July 1816 was writing to his sister-in-law the Duchess of Gotland (Désirée Bernadotte), 'I am growing more and more attached to this country every day. It is the land of liberty, peace and happiness.' He wrote several times to invite Julie and his two daughters to join him, but perhaps understandably his wife preferred to keep away. She stayed in Europe, moving from Frankfurt to Brussels and eventually to Florence. No doubt it was as well, since Joseph continued to womanize as much as ever. His principal mistress was Mme Sari, the wife of a Corsican officer, though he also had an American girl, the Quaker Annette Savage, whom he installed at his lodge in the 'wilderness' in Jefferson County. Yet he was not entirely selfish. In 1817 and again in 1819 he wrote to Napoleon offering to share his exile on St Helena, an offer which was declined – presumably much to his relief. He also made firm friends with Betsy Patterson, who paid several visits to Point Breeze.

Pius VII forgave Lucien for his part during the Hundred Days, intervening to secure his release from imprisonment at Turin. He returned to his pleasant life at Rome, Canino and Tivoli, publishing a second unreadable epic, the *Cyrénéide*, telling at appalling length of the rescue of Corsica from Moorish invaders in the eleventh century. Surrounded by his sons, entertaining lavishly at his Roman palazzo, patronizing artists and writers, and dabbling in Etruscan archaeology, the Prince of Canino was undoubtedly the happiest of the Bonaparte brothers, even more to be envied than Joseph in America. Yet he too offered to join Napoleon on St Helena.

Louis had stayed in Italy during the Hundred Days. The 'Comte de Saint-Leu' was broken in health and twisted in mind, his sole diversions being a somewhat second-rate taste in literature and grumbling about his wife. In 1816 he made himself the laughing-stock of Rome by falling in love (Platonic) with the young and beautiful Princess Vittoria Colonna, whom he confidently expected to marry him, until her parents disillusioned him. For once Madame Mère and the whole clan joined publicly in supporting his ex-wife Hortense when he demanded their furniture and paintings so that he could furnish a house for Vittoria. In 1826 he moved from Rome to Florence where he spent the rest of his life in comfortable if scarcely opulent circumstances. Occasionally Hortense visited him to discuss their children's future, visits which reduced her to a state of nervous collapse. After much wandering she and her sons had settled at the small and dilapidated villa of Arenberg on the shores of Lake Constance, which she bought in 1817, and where they lived in the utmost seclusion. She wrote in her memoirs, 'I withdrew from the world and all I wanted was tranquility and kindness.' Her affair with Flahaut had faded after she rejected his proposal of marriage in 1814 – to divorce Louis meant losing her sons. It revived briefly during the Hundred Days but finally came to an end when he married Lord Keith's daughter. She sometimes saw her brother Eugène who remained unshakeably faithful. Once a year he went to stay with Pauline at Rome.

The former Viceroy of Italy did not after all receive a principality. Instead he was compensated in cash, which gave him an enormous private fortune. In 1817 his devoted father-in-law King Maximilian created Eugène Duke of Leuchtenberg and premier peer of Bavaria, ranking only after the princes of the blood, with the style of 'His Royal Highness' – he also made him colonel of a Bavarian regiment of light infantry. He lived happily in the beautiful *Residenz* at Eichstätt with his adoring Amelia Augusta and their seven children, spending much of his time hunting boar in the mountain forests. In 1823 Joséphine, the eldest daughter of the clan's most faithful paladin, married Crown Prince Oscar of Sweden, son and heir of the clan's greatest traitor Bernadotte. It was to be a supremely happy marriage. Eugène was already ill with cancer and died in 1824.

Jérôme spent two years as a prisoner in Württemberg, with Catherine and their infant son, the future 'Plon-Plon'. Time and again the King of Württemberg told his daughter that if she would divorce her husband she could have anything she wanted and Jérôme would be given a pension. She refused steadfastly. In the end even her father grew embarrassed by what was widely regarded as his cruel and unnatural behaviour and set the couple free with a miserly allowance, provided they lived in Austrian territory. The Tsar continued to pay Catherine a pension, though this too was not large. They installed themselves at Trieste under the name of the Comte and Comtesse de Montfort. His first wife Betsy Patterson, visiting Europe with their son Bo in 1819, went to Italy where she was received with the utmost amiability by Madame Mère, Lucien, Louis and Pauline, who treated her and the boy as members of the family. However, Betsy did not see her husband apart from a chance and embarrassing encounter with him in the gallery of the Pitti Palace at Florence some years later when not a word was spoken, Jérôme and Catherine fleeing from the room. In November 1821 she reported to her father at Baltimore that her former spouse 'is entirely ruined, his fortune, capital, income entirely spent, and his debts so large that his family can do nothing for him if they were inclined, which they are not'. Her information was quite correct. Letizia had given him several thousand francs but after these quickly vanished she would only help with advice: 'Imitate me. Retrench.' Bo did eventually see his father and, although treated amiably enough, decided to make his life in America since, apart from his grandmother, the entire clan were living above their means and would do nothing for him. Jérôme did not offer to join Napoleon on St Helena. Characteristically his wife Catherine did, petitioning the British government to be allowed to go and nurse her brother-in-law when she heard that he was ill. 'I should consider myself very happy indeed if through my care I could help to alleviate the rigour of his captivity.' The offer was refused. It was all the more generous since Catherine had just given birth to a daughter (the future Princess Mathilde, who was to be immortalized by Proust).

Of the clan's traitors Joachim Murat died as flamboyantly as he had lived. After escaping from Naples disguised as a sailor in May 1815 he reached France safely, but Napoleon refused to see him or make use of his services. Following the Hundred Days he was in mortal danger from the royalists of the White Terror and hunted for his life through the countryside around Toulon, having to sleep rough in the fields. Eventually he made his way to Corsica, from where he embarked in October with 250 adventurers under the delusion that his former subjects were longing for his return. Landing at the little port of Pizzo in Calabria with only 26 men, overdressed as usual and unmistakable, he was at once set upon by a mob of peasants armed with sticks and knives who dragged him to the local lock-up. He was speedily court-marshalled and sentenced to death by the Bourbons' local garrison commander. He died with his accustomed bravery, refusing to let the Neapolitan soldiers bandage his eyes. His widow, who renamed herself the Countess of Lipona – an anagram of Napoli (Naples) – settled with her children in comparative penury near Trieste. Caroline was incapable of living without a man to dominate, and secretly married a soldier of Scots origin formerly in the Neapolitan service, General Francesco Macdonald. Napoleon was disgusted by the news of such a *mésalliance* when it reached him on St Helena, yet undoubtedly it made his sister much happier than she would otherwise have been during the remainder of her life.

In 1818 that other great traitor and most lastingly successful of all the clan, 'the High and Mighty Prince and Lord Carl xiv Johan' – still wearing his Jacobin tattoo – was crowned King of Sweden, of the Goths and of the Vandals at Stockholm with the dignified coronation rites of the Swedish Lutheran Church, followed by a second coronation at Christiania in his other realm as King of Norway. A small but vocal band of Swedish legitimists deeply resented what they regarded as usurpation by 'that damned Frenchman' and remained loyal to the young Vasa who was the rightful heir. Sir Walter Scott was much moved when he met the youth, seeing him as a Swedish Prince Charlie. Liberals too soon had good cause to dislike Bernadotte. Nevertheless, even if he never learnt his subjects' language and though fiercely criticized, Carl Johan kept the crown of Sweden until he succumbed to a stroke in 1844. Queen Desideria, who had rejoined him twenty years before, survived into a venerable old age at Stockholm. Their son Oscar – named so long ago after a hero in the epic *Ossian* at Napoleon's request – succeeded his father on the throne without opposition, and Oscar's grandson was to marry the last heiress of the Vasas. (Through his father the Prince of Wales is descended from both Bernadotte and Eugène de Beauharnais.)

Elisa, that lesser traitor, now styled Countess of Campignano, made herself an exceptionally tiresome 'prisoner of war' at Brünn. Hearing that the Austrian governor of Tuscany had sold her horses she complained savagely, writing to Metternich that she hoped the Emperor Francis knew about it. By relentless nagging in 1819 she extracted an annual pension of 300,000 francs from the Austrians. Her request after the Hundred Days to be allowed to join Napoleon on St Helena was almost certainly insincere and nothing more was heard of it. However, she was not permitted to return to Bologna or settle at Ravenna as she demanded. She went to Trieste – which the Emperor considered 'a one-eyed hole' – where she purchased a fine town house on the Campo Marzio together with the Villa Vicentina by the sea, and where she was reunited to Bacciochi and her two children. Here she patronized artists and the theatre, indulging in amateur theatricals, besides starting the excavation of the Roman city of Aquileia. Her relations with Madame Mère, whom she had not seen since 1810, were distinctly cool but she was delighted when Jérôme, who had now taken Lucien's place as her favourite brother, also came to live at Trieste in 1819. She was still more pleased when Caroline too settled nearby. The oddest addition to her little circle was Fouché, who arrived at Trieste in the same year as Jérôme and became her inseparable companion. She grew immensely stout and lost most of her hair, acquiring an extraordinary resemblance to Napoleon in his own last days. Her husband Bacciochi consoled himself by sleeping with the governess but she took no notice. In July 1820 while visiting the excavations at Aquileia amid its marshes she caught 'a putrid fever' and died the following month. In after years Felice Bacciochi erected a monument to her in the church of San Petrone at Bologna; on it were depicted a married couple with a figure representing the genius of conjugual love, not the most apt memorial. 'The Prince Bacciochi', as he called himself, survived her by over twenty years, dying at Bologna in 1841.

Their only surviving child, Napoléone (1806–69), was among the most high-spirited of the clan's later members. Even more masculine than her mother Elisa, she went so far as to wear men's clothes, fenced and enjoyed driving carriages. She married a sensitive Italian, Count Camarata, whom she reduced to a nervous wreck before deserting him in 1830 and reverting to her maiden name of Bacciochi. At the end of 1830 she went to Vienna with a hare-brained plan of rescuing her cousin Napoleon II, which was quickly discovered by the Austrian police, who made her leave the city. Very much her mother's daughter, she later acquired a keen interest in drainage.

The happiest of the exiles, apart from Joseph and Lucien, were Madame Mère, Uncle Fesch and Pauline who all established themselves at Rome in considerable comfort. Letizia had taken Napoleon's place as head of the clan, partly because of her natural authority and partly on account of that enormous fortune – so profitably invested by her brother the Cardinal who continued to advise her on financial matters. In 1818 she bought the Palazzo Rinuccini in Piazza Venezia although Fesch, who stayed at the

Palazzo Falconieri, remained as close as ever. She lived in impressive state, with a large staff which included a chamberlain, and always drove out in a carriage whose doors bore the coat of arms bestowed on her by her son. Yet at the same time she was as careful as ever with money, dressing only in black after Elisa's death. 'One must live according to one's position in life,' she observed. 'If one is no longer a king it is ridiculous to pretend that one still is, and enough to be a plain, honest man. Rings look well on fingers yet when they drop off the fingers are still there.' She worried desperately about the Emperor's health, physical and spiritual, sending a doctor and two chaplains out to St Helena when she heard he was ill. She addressed a carefully drafted appeal to the sovereigns begging for his release, an appeal which understandably went unanswered. Two other sons also gave her cause for concern: Louis at the Palazzo Salviati who quarrelled incessantly with the rest of the family, and Jérôme at the Palazzo Torlonia who constantly asked her for money. The latter had come to Rome from Trieste in 1822 after she had dissuaded him, perhaps unwisely, from joining Joseph in the United States and had somehow managed to buy the palace from Lucien. He could not afford to run it and on one occasion tried to sell it to his mother.

The Bourbons attempted to deprive Fesch of his see of Lyons but, with Pius VII's support, he refused to resign it even if he could not visit it. He led a life of exemplary piety, fasting and doing penance, going barefoot in procession in which he wore a humble friar's habit, giving alms to the poor, though still delighting in his paintings and statues which filled the entire first floor of his palace and the houses next door. He spent much time with his sister, listening to ceaseless laments about her children.

Pauline had gone to live with her mother and uncle at the Palazzo Falconieri in 1815, but its sombre atmosphere scarcely suited her temperament. With staggering impudence she tried to install herself in the Palazzo Borghese, so infuriating her husband Camillo that he sued for a legal separation, which was granted in 1816. She complained to Lucien, 'It is a terrible thing always to be the victim of men', a very personal way of seeing the dispute. Camillo lived contentedly at Florence in a villa in Via Ghibellina with the Duchess Lante della Rovere, an apparently platonic relationship. Pauline then bought a charming little house in Rome near the Porta Pia, which she rechristened 'Villa Paolina', together with a summer residence at Bagni di Lucca also named Villa Paolina. In Rome she gave frequent receptions, her visitors including Betsy Patterson and her son Bo, and musical evenings. She staged a performance of an opera by Giovanni Pacini – the last of her lovers, her 'Nino', a Sicilian fifteen years younger who deserted her in 1823 as soon as he could make a living from his music. Her complexion was yellowing and she wore a dozen ropes of pearls to conceal the fact that her neck and bosom were withering. She too was extremely anxious about her brother on St Helena, deeply distressed when Madame Mère and Fesch became the victims of a German adventuress who convinced them that the Virgin Mary had told her in a dream that Napoleon was no longer on his island. 'Mama and the Cardinal say they know for certain that the Emperor has been carried off by angels and taken to a country where his health is improving,' she wrote. 'I won't dwell on all the scenes and quarrels and unpleasantnesses between us.'

Napoleon died on 5 May 1821. Despite countless ingenious alternative explanations, such as arsenic administered by the British, the cause of death was almost certainly cancer of the stomach, the disease that had killed his father nearly thirty years before. His last words were, 'At the head of the army.' Significantly, a little earlier he had spoken his son's name twice. In his will he told the clan, 'I thank my good and very excellent mother, the Cardinal, my brothers Joseph, Lucien and Jérôme, and Pauline, Caroline, Julie, Hortense, Catherine and Eugène for having shown such an interest in me.' The document is as much that of a Corsican chieftain as of an exiled emperor.

Marie Louise learnt that she was a widow when listening to a performance of Rossini's *Il Barbiere di Siviglia* in the ducal box at the opera house in Parma. She showed no emotion, but later ordered a discreet period of mourning to be observed by her court. (One cannot altogether blame her for declining Napoleon's legacy to her, his heart preserved in spirits.) Then she married Adam von Neipperg, his wife having died most conveniently, a marriage which was to give her the utmost happiness. She was overwhelmed by sorrow when in 1829 he was killed by a heart attack at only fifty-three, as indeed were the Parmesans whom he had ruled so justly and so amiably — he had had such little interest in personal gain that, apart from his clothes, his sole possessions were his decorations which he kept in a cardboard box. She could not live without a man, and in 1834 married for a third time, the bridegroom being the grand master of her court, a Frenchman of the dull and pompous sort, Count Charles de Bombelles – she kept the marriage secret until her death. She was so popular with her subjects that she survived the political storm of the early 1830s without difficulty and when she died of pleurisy at Parma in 1847 after a reign of over thirty years, she was genuinely mourned by the Parmesans, who remember her with affection even now. (There are demands for her reburial at Parma while her tomb in Vienna is annually decorated with Parma violets by descendants of her former subjects.) During the July Revolution of 1830 in France there had been a feeble attempt to proclaim her son Napoleon II, an attempt which was bound to fail since the young man was under strict supervision in Vienna. He had shown extraordinary promise and unmistakable ambition, dreaming of reviving the French Empire or of a brilliant military career at least, but his health was broken by tuberculosis when he was still a boy and he died at Schönbrunn in July 1832, only twenty-one years old. His mother was at his bedside and collapsed from grief. Ironically, he was buried in the white uniform of that Austrian army so often defeated by his father.

Joseph spent seventeen years in America. He imported the first company of ballet dancers seen in the United States though the ballerinas' drawers scandalized American ladies. After giving his Quaker girl two bastards he married her off to an accommodating husband improbably named Delafolie – when the man died she tried to blackmail him. He also fathered a child on a Creole lady, Mme Lacoste, whom he was rumoured to have bought from her spouse. The July Revolution in France made him take seriously the possibility of a Bonapartist restoration – in September 1830 he addressed an open letter to French deputies reminding them that the chamber had proclaimed Napoleon II in 1815. After visiting President Andrew Jackson at Washington to thank him for the American people's hospitality, he set sail for Europe in 1832 with a large entourage which included his Corsican mistress Mme Sari. Forbidden to return to France, he settled in England for three years, near Godstone in Surrey, during which time he made close friends with his young nephew Louis Napoleon – the only surviving son of King Louis and Hortense whom he regarded as the hope of the Bonaparte dynasty. He returned to his beloved New Jersey for two lengthy visits. After suffering a stroke in 1840 he was allowed to go to Italy the following year, at last rejoining his wife Julie at Florence as an enfeebled old man. He passed his last three years with her, dying in 1844. She survived him by only ten months.

Lucien had already died, at Viterbo in 1840, his old age having probably been happier than that of any other member of the clan. He left a large brood of children, some of them markedly unpleasant. Louis, a frail and querulous old cripple confined to a wheel chair, died at Florence six years later, distressed by the French government's refusal to give his son Louis Napoleon parole from prison so that they might say goodbye. He had become a devout Catholic and was to some extent consoled by religion. Hortense – even more pious – had died much earlier, at Arenberg in 1837, from cancer after a long, lonely and cruel illness. Her one surviving son, Louis Napoleon, arrived at her deathbed just in time.

Madame Mère, having been blind for many years, left this world with her accustomed dignity in 1836. Lucien and Jérôme were at her side. The Roman carabinieri hissed at her coffin as it passed through the streets, but they were hissing at the Bonapartes and not the matriarch. She bequeathed her heart to Corsica. Fesch, who had closed her eyes, followed her in 1839.

The bodies of Letizia and the Cardinal were to return to their native island in 1851 – in circumstances totally unforeseeable in the 1830s – to a final resting place in Ajaccio cathedral where they had so often worshipped together. Unable to leave his wonderful collection of paintings to the city of Lyons as he wished, Fesch had sold it in a series of spectacular sales which lasted five years and in consequence his pictures are in galleries all over Europe and America. What remained he left to Ajaccio to endow a seminary, with the exception of a thousand canvases to adorn the town. Characteristically Joseph went to law and succeeded in obtaining most of them, but enough are still in the Musée Fesch at Ajaccio to comprise what has been described as the best group of Renaissance paintings in France outside Paris.

Pauline had gone as early as 1825, dying from cancer of the stomach like her brother. Through the intervention of Pope Leo xii she had been reconciled with her husband Camillo for the last few months of her life and he was with her at her death in Florence. Although dying a good Catholic, she insisted on wearing her favourite dress for the final dissolution and on taking a last look in a hand mirror to reassure herself that at forty-four she was still beautiful. Camillo and Jérôme were at the deathbed. In her will even the unconventional 'little sister' displayed the clan's lust for status, directing that she be buried in the Borghese family chapel in the church of Santa Maria Maggiore in Rome – between two popes. She also made a point of leaving something, however small, to every young member of the clan, including Bo in America. Pauline may have been an eccentric, self-indulgent whore, but no one can deny that she possessed both style and generosity. Camillo went a mere seven years after her, so fat that he looked as if he had been sewn into an eiderdown.

Caroline Murat, humiliatingly short of money in her last years – she had a vicious quarrel with Jérôme in 1830 over a pitifully small loan – achieved financial security for only a few months at the very end of her life, when the French government granted her a pension. General Macdonald died in 1838, so the fat, middle-aged, solitary woman succumbed briefly to an unsavoury French gigolo called Clavel. Like so many of the clan she was killed by cancer of the stomach, dying painfully at Florence in the spring of 1839. One of her daughters was with her and also Jérôme, with whom she had had a reconciliation.

In the United States the Murat sons retained all their parents' pretensions. The elder, Achille, carried out Napoleon's wishes by marrying into the American aristocracy, his wife being Catherine Willis Gray, a great-niece of George Washington, and became a planter in Florida. A decided eccentric with a taste for alligator-tail soup, he died at Tallahassee in 1847. Like his uncle Jérôme before him, the younger son,

Lucien Murat, married a Southern belle. She was Carolina Georgina Frazer, the daughter of a rich South Carolina planter. After Lucien had squandered her fortune she was reduced to keeping a boarding school in order to support him. Sometimes Lucien could be difficult. 'You were born a miserable Corsican peasant,' the innkeeper's grandson told his uncle Joseph Bonaparte, 'I on the other hand was born on the steps of a throne.'

Alone of his generation of Bonapartes Jérôme was destined to survive the 1840s and indeed the 1850s. He was always regarded with suspicion by the governments of France and Naples, who eventually persuaded the Pope to banish him from Rome in 1831. He went to Florence, where his wife Catherine died of dropsy in 1834. 'What I loved best in the world was you, Jérôme,' she told her faithless, spendthrift husband on her deathbed. 'I only wish that I could have said goodbye to you in France.' He had reason to mourn her, since the pensions from Württemberg and Russia ceased at once. Ruined yet again, he had to sell his palazzo in Florence and move out to a tiny villa in the suburbs. A small legacy from Madame Mère was quickly dissipated and he was reduced to truly desperate straits. As so often, a woman came to his rescue, a rich widow twenty-five years younger than himself, the Marchesa Giustina Bartolini-Badelli, a beautiful, affectionate and generous but simple-souled Florentine who paid his debts and reinstalled him in a palace. He rewarded her by being just as unfaithful as he had been to Catherine and by squandering her money. Countess Potocka, the same great Polish lady who had thought Jérôme so ridiculous at Warsaw in 1812, saw him again at about this time and says that he had the appearance of 'a superannuated lady-killer'.

In middle age Betsy Patterson had turned into a miserly and aggressive business woman who was making an enormous fortune by shrewd investment in real estate. Her beauty remained unaltered until her late forties and she kept her good looks until well into her sixties. Although she travelled widely, especially in Europe, and went out nearly every night to a party or to a ball, she never took a lover. Her ambition was that her son Bo should marry one of his uncle Joseph Bonaparte's daughters. She was bitterly disappointed when in 1829 he married a Baltimore girl named Susan Mary Williams. Bo did little with his life, apart from some desultory farming, though he begot two sons. He continued to correspond with the Bonapartes, even if he did not expect too much from them.

The Revolution of 1848 suddenly burst on the world. That most level-headed of rulers, King Louis Philippe of the French, was taken completely by surprise and lost his throne in a matter of days. A republic was proclaimed, but Bonapartism could not re-emerge as a serious political force. The clan was once again a dynasty.

12
The Legend and the Disillusionment

'Nowadays it is the fashion to glorify Bonaparte's victories.
Those who suffered because of them have departed; one no
longer hears the victims' curses, their cries of pain and
distress. One does not still see France exhausted, with women
ploughing the soil, does not see parents arrested as hostages
for their sons or entire villages punished for a single
conscript's desertion. One does not see the conscription lists
posted at street corners, or passers-by crowding beneath huge
long lists of those sentenced to death, looking frantically for
the names of their children, their brothers, their friends and
their neighbours.'

CHATEAUBRIAND, *Mémoires d'Outre-Tombe*

'One can only come to the conclusion that he was a scoundrel
as well as crazy.'

ADOLPHE THIERS ON NAPOLEON III

Napoleon had not wasted those lonely years on St Helena. He himself said,
'What a romance my life has been', which was how he presented it in
Memorial of St Helena, that subtlest, most cunning of apologias, which
depicted his entire career as one long endeavour in the cause of human
freedom, inspired by liberal ideals, and explaining away every mistake or
defeat. His wars had all been attempts to benefit mankind, since their
object had been the creation of a happier, juster Europe – any war could be
won swiftly and completely if properly organized. This interpretation of
his life was designed to rally support to his son and to the Bonaparte clan. It
was not just a legend about himself but a dynamic legend as well, intended
to prepare the way for a Bonapartist restoration. He deliberately mis-
represented his family, whom in the days of prosperity he had treated
contemptuously as favoured puppets; on St Helena he portrayed them as a
brilliantly gifted kindred worthy of his genius. He knew that the drama of
his tragic end could not fail to appeal to the new age of the Romantics.
France soon grew restive under the Bourbons, and was even more bored by
Louis Philippe's bourgeois regime with its emphasis on money-making.
Despite Chateaubriand's warnings, the nation forgot that it had been bled
white by the Emperor, whose legend was fostered by the poems of Victor

Hugo and the ballads of Béranger. So potent was the spell that in 1840, in a misguided attempt to enlist its magic in support of his own lacklustre regime, Louis Philippe had Napoleon's body brought back from St Helena and ceremonially reinterred in Paris at the Invalides.

Few if any gauged what really lay behind the legend. The Emperor had been the architect of the first modern totalitarian state geared to war, proponent of a peculiarly aggressive form of nationalism: that the bigger the state the better, that maps could be altered by military force to join those speaking the same tongue regardless of law or tradition, that expansionist wars could be won by a single, rapid campaign. (Hitler's foreign policy would be much indebted to him.) A future Bonaparte monarch would have to match Napoleon's inimitable genius, quite apart from incarnating an unrealizable legend. It was truly a *damnosa hereditas*.

However, for many years it seemed that for all its potency the Napoleonic legend would remain no more than a heady myth. Support for Napoleon II in 1830 was almost derisory and could not be taken seriously, while in any case the boy died two years later. After Joseph the clan's new head was Louis Napoleon Bonaparte, third and only surviving son of King Louis and Hortense, who had been brought up by his mother in Switzerland. The young man had no doubts that one day he would be Emperor of the French, though his early intrigues verged on farce. An attempt to enlist the garrison at Strasbourg and proclaim the Empire in 1836 was over in three hours and ended in his forcible deportation to the United States. A second attempt in 1840 – a few months before the return of his uncle's body – to raise the imperial standard at Boulogne was equally disastrous, resulting in his imprisonment for six years in the castle of Ham from which he did not escape until 1846. During the short period which he then spent in London he was regarded as no more than an ineffectual and dissolute adventurer.

The Revolution of 1848 changed everything. The clan rushed back to the promised land. Louis Napoleon Bonaparte, Napoleon ('Plon-Plon') Bonaparte (Jérôme's son), Pierre Bonaparte – one of Lucien's sons – and Lucien Murat became deputies. In December 'Citizen Louis Bonaparte' was elected President of the Second French Republic. The riots and street fighting earlier in the year had frightened the French so much that they wanted the monarchy back, but the royalists were split between Legit-imists and Orleanists. The Bonapartists took advantage of their disunity and the regime became steadily more and more imperial, Louis Napoleon styling himself 'Prince President' and reintroducing his uncle's liveries at the Elysée. In December 1851, on the anniversary of Austerlitz, he launched his own 18 Brumaire and, like his uncle before him, received the presidency for ten years and moved into the Tuileries. At the end of 1852 the Second Empire was proclaimed, the new Emperor taking the name of Napoleon III.

Needless to say, the entire clan profited. The Emperor's half-brother, Hortense's son by Flahaut, was created Duc de Morny and became President of the Legislative Body, while his other, less well-known half-brother, King Louis' bastard, was created Count of Castelvecchio and given a lucrative government post. At one point no less than twenty-one of Lucien's family and their progeny were receiving Civil List pensions, including the ne'er-do-well Prince Pierre Bonaparte, who had spent time in prison for murdering a Papal gendarme but was appointed to a command in the Foreign Legion. Jérôme, now a worn-out old rake, did especially well. In October 1848 he was reinstated as a general of division on full pay. Two months later he was appointed Governor of the Invalides with a splendid house and 45,000 francs a year. His nephew then made him President of the Senate with the Luxembourg as official residence, before promoting him to Marshal of the Empire and giving him the Palais-Royal. Jérôme's son Plon-Plon – a tougher, even more vicious version of his father – was sent to Madrid as French Ambassador and later made a general, installing himself with princely state in one wing of the Palais-Royal. At one moment the Emperor promised to make him King of Tuscany. For a time Napoleon III even contemplated creating Bo – Jérôme's son by Betsy Patterson – Duc de Sarthène, while one of Jérôme's favourite illegitimate sons was created Baron Jérôme David, given a Civil List pension and made Minister of Public Works. Elisa's daughter, Napoléone Bacciochi, ex-tracted no less than six million francs and her Bacciochi cousins received titles and appointments, one obtaining the onerous post of Superintendent of Court Spectacles (with special responsibility for procuring women for his master). As for Caroline's children, at least ten Murats were paid Civil List pensions and Lucien and Georgina – now Prince and Princess Murat – were encouraged to hope for Naples, though in the end they had to remain content with Lucien being a senator and with rich marriages arranged for their children by imperial favour; their daughter Anna secured the Duc de Mouchy, a dwarf but nonetheless a great noble. Achille Murat's American widow in Tallahassee was also accepted as a member of the clan and given a substantial allowance from the Civil List. No one with any claim to belong to the clan was refused and indeed Alexandre Walewski, Maria Walewska's son by Napoleon, was not only created a count of the Empire but became its Foreign Minister. The Beauharnais cousins were not left out, Baron Tascher de la Pagerie being appointed both a senator and Grand Master of the Imperial Household, while his son was the Emperor's First Chamberlain. Many other relatives, too numerous to mention, benefited from belonging to the clan.

The Second Empire was a tawdry parody of the First. The mountebank with the sphinx-like smile who was the clan's chief had nothing in common with his uncle, apart from his name, clan feeling and insatiable sexual appetite. However, he possessed a social conscience ahead of his time and at least tried to alleviate the misery of the poor, doing something towards healing the class war which had erupted in 1848. This, and the coincidence that his reign was a period of prosperity and industrial development, earned him a certain popularity. He continued to beautify Paris as his uncle had done, though the real purpose of Baron Haussmann's wide boulevards was to make it easier to shoot down mobs who tried to erect barricades. The essential hollowness of the regime was shown up in its flashy, spendthrift court filled with unprincipled politicians, speculators, newly rich social climbers with bogus titles and mercenary women who were not just whores but often prostitutes as well. It was a world dominated by the most vulgar materialism, more like the Directory than the First Empire. Even the Empress Eugénie was a Spanish adventuress obssessed with clothes, jewels and luxury, who had far more in common with Joséphine than with Marie Louise. Its atmosphere was both infectiously cheerful and repellent. Its background music, which epitomized it, was that of Jacques Offenbach's operettas, filled with daemonic yet cloying gaiety, exhilarating but with oddly sinister undertones.

The clan led the most scandalous lives of all. Napoleon III was a byword for goatish promiscuity, and if increasing age prevented Jérôme from rivalling his nephew he none the less managed to have one last deplorable affair. In 1853 he finally married his Florentine marchesa – though insisting on a morganatic marriage so as not to compromise his status as first prince of the blood – only to cast her off shortly after. He fell in love with the red-haired Baroness Collin de Plancy, tall, scraggy and hard-favoured but very strong-willed and dominating, and installed her in his palaces. The pair then accused the marchesa of incest, pretending most implausibly that she was having an affair with one of Jérôme's innumerable bastards; this they made a pretext for turning her into the street without a penny. The Emperor was shamed into giving her an allowance and she went back to Florence. When Bo came to France he was at first welcomed by his reprobate father, who had him legitimized. This so infuriated his half-brother Plon-Plon that he was literally driven out of the country by a campaign of intrigue and calumny against the 'Baltimore bastard'. (Interestingly, like true Bonapartes both Bo and his son were to die of cancer.) Plon-Plon's own private life surpassed his father's in extravagance and promiscuity, yet even he was outdone by Lucien's son Pierre Bonaparte – popularly known as the 'Corsican Wild Boar'. After being cashiered from the Foreign Legion despite his name and connections, he married a street-walker. He crowned his career by shooting and killing a left-wing journalist at the end of the reign, the subsequent publicity and official manoeuvres to secure his acquittal contributing to the ruin of the Empire. Elisa's grandson, Count Bacciochi, committed suicide in 1853 after losing millions speculating on the Bourse, his mistress killing herself spectacularly with the aid of charcoal fumes a week later. Caroline's son, Prince Murat, was one Paris's public jokes: since being stricken with gout he had himself carried to the Folies-Bergère every night. Even the Emperor's statesmanlike half-brother the Duc de Morny caused outrage by accepting bribes, while his death in 1865 was rumoured to be the result of too many aphrodisiac pills.

Unfortunately, not only was Napoleon III a very different personality from his mighty uncle but he had been bequeathed an impossible legacy. He could never hope to match up to the Napoleonic legend – nor indeed could even its creator have matched up to it – and with supreme irony it would ultimately destroy both him and the clan. No man and no dynasty were capable of fulfilling the promises made on St Helena.

Before bringing back the Empire, Louis Napoleon had defined it as 'peace'. Yet to embody the legend he had to be a warlord or nothing, which meant not just glittering uniforms and splendid parades at the Tuileries but military glory abroad. And he had inherited none of his uncle's military genius. The most successful of the ensuing campaigns proved to be also the most self-defeating. The war against Austria in Italy in 1859, inspired by his uncle's latter-day espousal of nationalism, saw two undeserved French victories at Magenta and Solferino, but instead of merely humiliating Austria and creating three Italian states it united the entire peninsula into a new great power. Among other military adventures an attempt to impose a Habsburg monarchy on Mexico, which lasted from 1862 until 1867, ended in humiliating failure: France's chosen candidate, the Emperor Maximilian, being shot by his 'subjects' and the French paying a horrific price in blood and gold.

The Second Empire grew steadily weaker, more and more unpopular at home and less and less successful with its foreign policy. Jérôme died in 1860, being given a state funeral, yet even in death he succeeded in causing scandal. His pathetic wife came to follow his coffin despite his vile treatment, which aroused unfavourable comment; then Bo Patterson Bonaparte and Betsy took legal action in the French courts to claim part of his estate, on the grounds that Jérôme's marriage with Betsy had been valid. Under pressure from the government the tribunal found against them and they had to pay the costs of the case. Almost every member of the clan became widely disliked, in particular the foreign Empress. There was one last, triumphant success – the Paris Exhibition of 1867. However, worn out by sexual excess and tortured by an inoperable gallstone, Napoleon III's health and will to govern were failing. In 1870, increasingly aware that he could not even pretend to embody the Napoleonic legend, the Emperor introduced a new liberal constitution. It was too late.

Bismarck and the Prussians had learnt all too much from Napoleon I's example. The Emperor was manoeuvred into declaring a war which he could not hope to win, then crushed by a campaign in which his uncle would have been forced to admire the Germans' brilliance. As soon as the news of his defeat at Sedan on 1 September reached Paris the Empire fell and the Empress fled with the Prince Imperial. In the words of Jacques Bainville, 'The Second Empire was a repetition of the First, without the genius, and like the First it collapsed through an invasion.' Not without irony, the captured Napoleon III was interned at Wilhelmshöhe – once the Napoleonshöhe of his uncle King Jérôme.

There was one last act in the Corsican vendetta. In 1871 the would-be revolutionaries of the Commune burnt down the palace of the Tuileries, the background for the Bonapartes in the days of their greatest glory. Large amounts of the rubble were bought by the Duke Pozzo di Borgo and shipped to Ajaccio, near where he built a château overlooking the gulf. He and his family had still not forgiven Carlo Buonaparte's insult to their forebear.

Napoleon III died in 1873 and the hopes of the Bonapartes perished under the Zulu assegais with his son the Prince Imperial six years later. The new heir, Jérôme's son Plon-Plon, was an impossible candidate for any throne despite his extraordinary physical resemblance to the dynasty's founder – so much so that the Prince Imperial had bequeathed his claims to Plon-Plon's son Prince Victor Napoleon. But the French had finally rejected both the legend and the clan.

The disastrous legacy of the Second Empire is evident even today. But for Napoleon III France would probably have remained a monarchy into the present century and her government might perhaps have regained something of that legitimacy lost in 1789, the absence of which has ever since been the bane of all French regimes.

The Bonaparte clan failed to marry into the Roman nobility or become Swiss patricians, as the first Napoleon had recommended on St Helena. To some extent they again rose in the world under the Second Empire. At thirty-seven Plon-Plon obtained for his bride a sixteen-year-old daughter of King Victor Emmanuel II of Italy, while Lucien's grandson, another Lucien, was created a cardinal. In addition the Bonapartes were reconciled with the Bernadottes when in 1858 Napoleon III became godfather to the future Gustav V of Sweden – Queen Desideria, once Désirée Clary, was still alive. (King Gustav lived until 1950.) Yet, apart from Jérôme's line, male

Bonapartes showed an odd reluctance to marry or else left no sons.

Apart from Queen Catherine, Jérôme's wives shared his longevity. Betsy Patterson reached the age of ninety-four, dying in 1879, a fearsome and immensely rich old dragon who lived on brandy. Her grandson, the Hon. Charles J. Bonaparte Patterson, was President Teddy Roosevelt's Attorney-General – known at one period as 'Charlie the Crook Chaser' – and the American Bonapartes survived until 1945 when Jerome Napoleon Charles Bonaparte Patterson broke his neck by tripping over his wife's dog lead in Central Park, New York. King Jérôme's third wife, the Florentine marchesa, died only in the present century, in 1904. The present head of the Bonapartes, Prince Napoleon, is directly descended from King Jérôme and Catherine of Württemberg. Ironically, his elder son Prince Charles has married a member of the royal family of the Two Sicilies, a descendant not only of both Marie Antoinette's sister Maria Carolina and the Archduke Karl but also, in the direct line, of Louis xiv and so linking the clan with France's *ancien régime* rulers. It is a match which would certainly have won the approval of the Emperor Napoleon i.

Principal Members of the Clan

BACCIOCHI, ELISA
(1777–1820)

Napoleon's eldest sister Elisa (originally Maria Anna) Bonaparte. Although Napoleon disliked her, she was created Princess of Lucca and Piombino in 1806 and Grand Duchess of Tuscany in 1809. An intellectual and very ambitious, she was to betray her brother.

BACCIOCHI, FELICE
(1762–1841)

Napoleon's brother-in-law Felice Bacciochi married Elisa Bonaparte in 1797. An unsuccessful career soldier, terrified of his wife, he irritated everyone by his pretentiousness and violin playing. He was made Duke of Lucca.

BEAUHARNAIS, EUGÈNE DE
(1781–1824)

Napoleon's stepson and son of the Empress Joséphine, Eugène de Beauharnais was Viceroy of Italy 1805–14 and one of the clan's ablest and most loyal members. He married Princess Augusta Amelia, daughter of King Maximilian I of Bavaria.

BEAUHARNAIS, HORTENSE DE
(1783–1837)

Napoleon's stepdaughter and sister-in-law, Hortense was Joséphine's daughter and married Louis Bonaparte, becoming Queen of Holland. Her life was made miserable by her husband's crazy jealousy. Their son was Emperor Napoleon III.

BEAUHARNAIS, STÉPHANIE-
NAPOLÉONE DE
(1789–1859)

Napoleon's adopted daughter and a cousin of Joséphine's first husband, Stéphanie-Napoléone married the future Grand Duke Charles Louis of Baden. Despite a flirtation with Jérôme Bonaparte, her marriage was extremely happy.

BERNADOTTE, DÉSIRÉE
(1777–1860)

The sister of Joseph Bonaparte's wife Julie and Napoleon's former sweetheart, Désirée Clary married Marshal Bernadotte and became Queen of Sweden. The Emperor always remained fond of her but she was ungrateful and eventually hoped for his downfall.

BERNADOTTE, JEAN
(1763–1844)

Marshal Bernadotte, created Prince of Ponte Corvo by Napoleon, was elected Crown Prince of Sweden in 1810 to reign as King Carl XIV Gustav from 1814 to 1844. Napoleon's secret enemy, he plotted to supplant him, ensured the failure of the Russian campaign and betrayed his military strategy to the Allies in 1813.

BONAPARTE, ALEXANDRINE
(1778–1855)

Napoleon's sister-in-law and Lucien Bonaparte's second wife, Alexandrine Bleschamp was the widow of a bankrupt speculator called Jouberthon who had fled the country. The Emperor refused to recognize the marriage, creating a deep rift with Lucien who would not abandon her – they had ten children.

BONAPARTE, CATHERINE
(1773–1800)

Napoleon's sister-in-law, an innkeeper's daughter, was Lucien Bonaparte's first wife.

BONAPARTE, JÉRÔME
(1784–1860)

Napoleon's youngest brother, Girolamo, King of Westphalia 1807–13. He married first Betsy Patterson, second Princess Catherine of Württemberg and third Marchesa Bartolini-Badelli. Known as 'Fifi' because of his love of wine, women and song, he was the clan's rake.

BONAPARTE, JOSEPH
(1768–1844)

Napoleon's eldest brother, Giuseppe, King of Naples 1806–8, and King of Spain 1806–13. He married Julie Clary, sister of Désirée Bernadotte. A greedy speculator and a womanizer, he was no soldier. His defeat in Spain in 1813 made British invasion of France inevitable while his failure to defend Paris in 1814 doomed the Emperor.

BONAPARTE, JULIE
(1771–1845)

Napoleon's sister-in-law and Joseph Bonaparte's wife, Julie Clary, Désirée Bernadotte's sister, was Queen of Naples and then of Spain. Unhappily married, she preferred to keep away from Joseph as much as possible.

BONAPARTE, LETIZIA
(1750–1835)

Napoleon's mother Letizia Ramolino, generally known as 'Madame Mère'. The clan's real leader after the Emperor.

BONAPARTE, LOUIS
(1778–1846)

Napoleon's youngest brother, Luigi, King of Holland 1806–10, married the Emperor's stepdaughter Hortense de Beauharnais. Crippled and half-crazed by arthritis – undoubtedly venereal in origin – he was insanely jealous of his wife, accusing her of imaginary love affairs. His son was the Emperor Napoleon III.

BONAPARTE, LUCIEN
(1775–1840)

Napoleon's younger brother, Luciano, created Prince of Canino by the Pope. He married first Rose Boyer and second Alexandrine Jouberthon. Always jealous of Napoleon, he refused to obey him until the very end.

BORGHESE, CAMILLO
(1775–1832)

Napoleon's brother-in-law Prince Camillo Borghese, a Roman aristocrat, was the ineffectual second husband of Napoleon's sister Pauline Bonaparte.

BORGHESE, PAULINE
(1780–1825)

Napoleon's youngest and favourite sister, Pauline – originally Maria Paola or Paoletta – Bonaparte was created Duchess of Guastalla. She married first General Leclerc and second Prince Borghese. Extremely promiscuous, famed for Canova's nude statues of her, she was also one of the clan's most loyal members.

BUONAPARTE, CARLO
(1746–85)

Napoleon's father Carlo – married Letizia Ramolino.

CATHERINE, QUEEN
(1783–1835)

Napoleon's sister-in-law and Jérôme Bonaparte's second wife, Princess Sophia Dorothea Frederica Catherine was the daughter of King Frederick of Württemberg and the Queen of Westphalia. Fat, intelligent, amiable and loyal, she was the only *ancien régime* royal fully accepted into the clan.

FESCH, JOSEPH
(1763–1839)

Napoleon's uncle and his mother Letizia's half-brother, Giuseppe Fesch was a self-unfrocked priest, financier, money-lender and army contractor but was made Archbishop of Lyons and later a cardinal. The clan's principal financial and spiritual adviser, he was famous for his collection of Renaissance paintings.

JOSÉPHINE, EMPRESS
(1763–1814)

Napoleon's first wife, Joséphine Tascher de la Pagerie married Alexandre Vicomte de Beauharnais – guillotined in 1794, – by whom she had Eugène and Hortense, before marrying Napoleon who divorced her in 1809, when he created her Duchess of Navarre. Never accepted by the clan.

LECLERC, VICTOR-EMMANUEL
(1772–1802)

Napoleon's brother-in-law General Leclerc was Pauline Bonaparte's first husband – she was frequently unfaithful.

MARIE LOUISE, EMPRESS
(1791–1847)

Napoleon's second wife, Archduchess Marie Louise of Habsburg-Lorraine, daughter of the Emperor Franz II and I of Austria, was Duchess of Parma from 1814 to 1847. On the death of Napoleon, by whom she had one son, the King of Rome, Napoleon II, she married her lover Count Adam von Neipperg. A much abler and more intelligent personality than is generally appreciated, she has had a bad press.

MURAT, CAROLINE
(1782–1839)

Napoleon's sister Caroline (originally Maria Annunziata) Bonaparte, married Marshal Murat and became Grand Duchess of Berg and then Queen of Naples. Very hard and ambitious, she forced her husband to betray Napoleon to save their throne.

MURAT, JOACHIM
(1771–1815)

Napoleon's brother-in-law and the husband of Caroline Bonaparte, Marshal Murat, an innkeeper's son, was Grand Duke of Berg 1806–8, and King of Naples 1808–15. Very brave, very stupid and very flashy, deeply mistrustful of his wife – both were unfaithful – he none the less took her advice and betrayed Napoleon in 1814.

NAPOLEON II
(1811–32)

Napoleon's son by Marie Louise, King of Rome from his birth until 1814. He was created Duke of Reichstadt by his Habsburg grandfather in 1818. Although proclaimed Emperor of the French in 1815 he never reigned.

NAPOLEON III
(1808–73)

Napoleon's nephew, the son of Louis Bonaparte by Hortense de Beauharnais, Louis Napoleon Bonaparte was Prince President

203

of France 1848–52, and Emperor of the French 1852–70.

PATTERSON, BETSY
(1785–1879)

Napoleon's unacknowledged sister-in-law and Jérôme Bonaparte's first wife, Elizabeth Patterson was the beautiful and intelligent daughter of William Patterson of Baltimore. She had a son, Jerome – known as 'Bo' – from whom the American Bonapartes descended, but the marriage was quickly dissolved on the Emperor's orders.

Select Bibliography

Contemporary

Abrantès, Duchesse d' (Laure Permon), *Mémoires*, Paris, 1905–13.
   Histoire des Salons de Paris, Paris, 1836–8.
Arnault, Antoine-Vincent, *Souvenirs d'un sexagènaire*, Paris, 1833.
Avrillon, Mlle, *Mémoires de Mlle Avrillon, première femme de chambre de l'Impér-atrice*, Paris, n.d.
Barras, Vicomte Paul-François-Jean-Nicolas de, *Mémoires de Barras, membre du Directoire*, Paris, 1895.
Bausset, Baron Louis-François-Joseph de, *Mémoires anecdotiques. . .* , Paris, 1827–9
Beauharnais, Prince Eugène de, *Mémoires et correspondance politiques et militaires*, Paris, 1958–60.
Beauharnais, Hortense de, *Mémoires de la reine Hortense*, Paris, 1927.
Bertrand, General Count, *Journal du général Bertrand, grand maréchal du palais. Cahiers de Sainte-Hélène*, Paris, 1949.
Beugnot, Count Jacques-Claude, *Mémoires du comte Beugnot*, Paris, 1889.
Blangini, Felice, *Souvenirs*, Paris, 1834.
Bonaparte, Jérôme, *Mémoires et correspondance du roi Jérôme et de la reine Catherine*, Paris, 1861–5.
Bonaparte, Joseph, *Mémoires et correspondance du roi Joseph*, Paris, 1855–8.
Bonaparte, Louis, *Documents historiques et réflexions sur le gouvernement de la Hollande*, Paris, 1820.
Bonaparte, Lucien, *Lucien Bonaparte et ses mémoires* (ed. T. Iung), Paris, 1882.
Boswell, James, *The Journal of a Tour to Corsica; and Memoirs of Pascal Paoli*, Cambridge University Press, 1929
Bourrienne, Louis de, *Mémoires de M. de Bourrienne, ministre d'état, sur Napoléon, le directoire, le consulat, l'empire et la restauration. . .* , Paris, 1831.
Broglie, Duc de, *Souvenirs du feu duc de Broglie*, Paris, 1886.
Caulaincourt, General Louis de, Duc de Vicenze, *Mémoires*, Paris, 1933.
Chaptal, Baron, *Mes Souvenirs sur Napoléon*, Paris, 1893.
Chateaubriand, Vicomte François René de, *Mémoires d'outre-tombe*, Paris 1951–2.
Clary und Aldringen, Prince Karl von, *Souvenirs: Trois mois à Paris lors du mariage de Napoléon et de Marie Louise*, Paris, 1914.
Constant, Benjamin, *Mémoires sur les Cent Jours*, Paris, 1829.
Ducrest, Georgette, *Mémoires sur l'impératrice Joséphine*, Paris, 1828–9.
Fain, Baron Agathon, *Mémoires du Baron Fain*, Paris, 1908.
Fleury de Chaboulon, Baron Pierre-Alexandre-Edouard, *Mémoires pour servir à l'histoire de la vie privée, du retour et du règne de Napoléon en 1815*, London, 1819–20.
Fouché, Joseph, Duc d'Otrante, *Mémoires*, Paris, 1945.
Gourgaud, General Baron Gaspard, *Journal de Sainte-Hélène*, Paris, 1944.
Hautpoul, Alphonse, *Mémoires*, Paris, 1906.
Las Cases, Count Marie-Joseph-Emmanuel-Auguste-Dieudonné de, *Le Mémorial*

de Sainte-Hélène, Paris, 1951.

La Tour du Pin, Marquise de, *Journal d'une femme de cinquante ans*, Paris, 1907–11.

Lockhart, John Gibson, *Life of Napoleon Buonaparte*, London, 1906.

Lombard de Langres, Vincent, *Le Royaume de Westphalie, Jérôme Bonaparte, sa cour, ses ministres*, Paris, 1820.

Macdonald, Marshal Etienne-Jacques-Joseph-Alexandre, Duc de Tarante, *Souvenirs*, Paris, 1892.

Marie Louise, Empress, *Marie Louise et Napoléon, 1813; lettres inédites* (ed. C. F. Palmstierna), Paris, 1955.

Markham, Felix, *Napoleon*, London, 1963.

Marmont, Marshal Auguste-Frédéric-Louis Viesse de, Duc de Raguse, *Mémoires*, Paris, 1857.

Méneval, Baron Claude-François de, *Mémoires pour servir à l'histoire de Napoléon I depuis 1802 jusqu'à 1815*, Paris, 1894.

    Napoléon et Marie Louise, Brussels, 1843.

Mérode-Westerloo, Count de, *Souvenirs*, Paris, 1864.

Metternich-Winneburg, Prince Klemens Lothar Wenzel, *Mémoires, documents et écrits divers*, Paris, 1880–4.

Miot de Melito, Count Jacques-François, *Mémoires*, Paris, 1873.

Mounier, Baron, *Souvenirs intimes et notes du baron Mounier*, Paris, 1896.

Murat, Joachim, *Lettres et documents*, Paris, 1908–14.

Napoleon I, Emperor, *Correspondance*, Paris 1858–69.

    Correspondance militaire, Paris, 1876–7.

    Lettres inédites à Marie Louise, Paris, 1935.

Pelet de la Lozère, Count, Privat-Joseph-Claramond, *Opinions de Napoléon sur divers sujets de politique et d'administration*, Paris, 1833.

Pichon, L. A., *De l'état de la France sous la domination de Napoléon Bonaparte*, Paris 1814.

Potocka, Countess Anna, *Mémoires de la comtesse Potocka*, Paris, 1897.

Rapp, General Count Jean, *Mémoires du général Rapp*, Paris, n.d.

Récamier, Jeanne-Françoise-Julie-Adelaïde, *Souvenirs et Correspondance*, Paris, 1859.

Rémusat, Comtesse Claire-Elisabeth-Jeanne de, *Mémoires, 1802–8*, Paris, 1880.

Rochechouart, Count Louis-Victor-Léon de, *Souvenirs sur la révolution, l'empire et la restauration*, Paris, 1889.

Roederer, Count Pierre-Louis, *Journal du comte Roederer*, Paris, 1909
    Mémoires sur la révolution, le consulat et l'empire, Paris, 1942.

Rocquain, F., *Napoléon et le roi Louis: Correspondance*, Paris, 1875.

Saint-Elme, Ida, *Mémoires d'une contemporaine*, Paris, 1827–9.

Saxe-Coburg-Saalfeld, Duchess of, *In Napoleon's Days (the Diary of Augusta, Duchess of Saxe-Coburg-Saalfeld)*, trans. HRH Princess Beatrice, John Murray, London 1941.

Scott, Sir Walter, *Life of Napoleon*, Edinburgh, 1847.

Ségur, Count Philippe-Paul de, *La Campagne de Russie*, Paris, 1958.

Staël, Germaine de, *Mémoires de Mme de Staël*, Paris, 1818.

Stendhal, *Mémoires sur Napoléon*, Paris, 1930.

    Vie de Napoléon, Paris, 1930.

    Journal, Paris, 1937.

Talleyrand-Périgord, Charles-Maurice de, Prince de Bénévent, *Mémoires du prince de Talleyrand*, Paris, 1891–2.

Talma, *Lettres inédites de Talma à la princesse Pauline Bonaparte*, Paris, 1911.

Thibaudeau, Antoine, *Mémoires de A. C. Thibaudeau*, Paris, 1913.

Thiébault, General Baron Paul-Charles-François-Adrien-Henri-Dieudonné, *Mémoires du général baron Thiébault*, Paris, 1895–6.

Vigée-Lebrun, Marie-Louise-Elisabeth, *Souvenirs*, Paris, 1835.

Later and modern

Bainville, Jacques, *Napoléon*, Paris, 1931.

Bernardy, F. de, *Eugène de Beauharnais*, Paris, 1973.

Bertaut, Jules, *Le Roi Jérôme*, Paris, 1954.
 Le Ménage Murat, Paris, 1958.

Botti, Ferruccio, *Maria Luigia, Duchessa di Parma Piacenza Guastalla*, Parma, 1969.

Casse, Baron A. du, *Les Rois Frères de Napoléon*, Paris, 1883.

Chuquet, Arthur, *La Jeunesse de Napoléon*, Paris, 1897–9.

Cole, Hubert, *The Betrayers: Joachim and Caroline Murat*, Eyre Methuen, London, 1972.

Cronin, Vincent, *Napoleon*, Collins, London, 1971.

Fleuriot de Langle, Paul, *La Paolina, sœur de Napoléon*, Paris, 1944.

Geyl, Pieter, *Napoleon For and Against*, Jonathan Cape, London, 1949. *page* 55

Girod de l'Ain, G., *Joseph Bonaparte, le roi malgré lui*, Paris, 1970.

Gobineau, M., *Pauline Borghese, sœur fidèle*, Paris, 1858.

Hochschild, Baron, *Désiré, reine de Suède et de Norvège*, Paris, 1888.

Larrey, Baron Félix-Hippolyte, *Madame Mère (Napoleonis Mater)*, Paris, 1892.

Lefebvre, Georges, *Napoléon*, Paris, 1936.

Lévy, Arthur, *Napoléon et Eugène de Beauharnais*, Paris, 1926.

Masson, Frédéric, *Napoléon inconnu*, Paris, 1895.
 Napoléon et sa famille, Paris, 1897–1919.
 Le sacre de Napoléon, Paris, 1907.
 Joséphine, Impératrice et Reine, Paris, 1899.
 Marie Louise, Impératrice de France, Paris, 1910.

Melchior-Bonnet, Bernardine, *Jérôme Bonaparte ou l'envers de l'épopée*, Paris, 1979.

Nabonne, Bernard, *Joseph Bonaparte, le roi philosophe*, Paris, 1949.
 La Vénus impériale, Paris, 1963.

Piétri, François, *Lucien Bonaparte*, Paris, 1930.

Rodocanachi, Emmanuel, *Elisa Napoléon Baciocchi en Italie*, Paris, 1900.

Seignobos, Charles, *Histoire sincère de la nation française*, Paris, 1933.

Taine, Hippolyte, *Les Origines de la France contemporaine*, Paris, 1891–4.

Thiers, Adolphe, *Histoire du consulat et de l'empire*, Paris, 1845–62.

Tulard, Jean, *Napoléon*, Paris, 1977. *page* 87

Vandal, Count Albert, *L'avènement de Bonaparte*, Paris, 1903.
 Napoléon et Alexandre Ier, Paris, 1891–6.

Weil, Maurice-Henri, *Joachim Murat, roi de Naples*, Paris, 1909–10.

Index

47
55
59
75 Count Auguste de Forbin
77
91
124 crvy
129 *
167
191
198